MW00461010

Praise for *Taken by*

"Bear attacks are multifaceted, fascinating, and often chilling events. Snow gives carefully researched and detailed first-person accounts of Yellowstone National Park's bear attacks. Her accounts and images inform and let the reader draw their own conclusions. You get involved in tough decisions such as what was done with the sow grizzly with cubs that killed Brian Matayoshi in 2011 in a defensive attack. This bear was judged to have acted normally given the circumstances. Ms. Snow gives accurate advice regarding how to avoid a bear attack. If you want the details of Yellowstone's bear attacks told in vivid detail, Snow's book is the place to go."

—**Stephen Herrero**, Professor Emeritus at the University of Calgary,
author of *Bear Attacks: Their Causes and Avoidance*

"Kathleen Snow's book reads like a series of crime scene reports, only they are not crimes. . . . She uses careful and vivid detail to describe, incident by incident, 146 years of harrowing encounters between grizzly bears and humans in Yellowstone National Park, with a recap of earlier incidents dating back to 1870. These stories, usually told in the words of the people involved, are a nonjudgmental but stark reminder of why we need to respect an animal that rightfully symbolizes the wildness in wilderness."

—**David Knibb**, author of *Grizzly Wars: The Public Fight over the Great Bear*

"Kathleen Snow has done an outstanding job in putting together the details of many Yellowstone bear-human confrontations from numerous sources. She weaves the stories in both a comprehensive and compelling narrative. I have already referenced it during my lectures on bear attacks even while it has been in manuscript form. It is a must-have reference book for anyone interested in human-bear encounters."

—**Steven P. French, MD**, cofounder of the Yellowstone Grizzly
Foundation, author of "Bear Attacks" in *Wilderness Medicine*,

"Kathleen Snow has done an excellent job of chronicling the bear/human conflicts in Yellowstone with this book. She paints a picture of each event with her own prose and includes all the official transcripts detailing the events. This contrast between a writer's view of an incident and the stark forensic details of agency reports allows the reader to imagine each scene from different perspectives. It helps to soften the forensic evidence but also gives a glimpse of the stark reality that rangers and tourists have actually faced every time there is an incident. The bad news is that such incidents will probably always happen as long as

we value wild bears and wilderness. The good news is that they rarely do happen, and bears in general go out of their way to avoid them."
—**Frank Lance Craighead, PhD**, executive director of the Craighead Institute, author of *Bears of the World*

"Valuable for its detailed collection of facts."
—**Lee H. Whittlesey,** Yellowstone Park Historian, author of *Death in Yellowstone* and *Gateway to Yellowstone*

"Kathleen Snow's exhaustive investigation into bear attacks brings home the message that Yellowstone is a wild, predator-rich ecosystem. While the details of these incidents remind us that our safety in bear country is not guaranteed, Snow provides the latest information on precautions to take to avoid a bear attack."
—**Orville E. Bach Jr.,** Yellowstone seasonal ranger of forty-one years, author of four books on Yellowstone

COMPANION BOOKS BY KATHLEEN SNOW:

Taken by Bear in Yellowstone
Searching for Bear Eyes

TAKEN BY BEAR
IN GLACIER NATIONAL PARK

Harrowing Encounters between Grizzlies and Humans

KATHLEEN SNOW

LYONS
PRESS

Guilford, Connecticut

An imprint of The Rowman & Littlefield Publishing Group, Inc.
4501 Forbes Blvd., Ste. 200
Lanham, MD 20706
www.rowman.com

Distributed by NATIONAL BOOK NETWORK

Copyright © 2020 Kathleen Snow

British Library Cataloguing in Publication Information available

Library of Congress Cataloging-in-Publication Data available

ISBN 978-1-4930-4751-2 (paper: alk. paper)
ISBN 978-1-4930-4752-9 (electronic)

∞™ The paper used in this publication meets the minimum requirements of American National Standard for Information Sciences—Permanence of Paper for Printed Library Materials, ANSI/NISO Z39.48-1992.

For my dear friend, Barbara Lewis Spivak

CONTENTS

AUTHOR'S NOTE

One of the points of this book is the importance of that quintessentially human quality called altruism, even in the face of danger. To save a life, someone must find as quickly as possible any bear-attack victim who has been dragged away. The dragging away is itself predictive of predatory behavior, as opposed to a hiker surprising a sow bear who attacks to protect her cubs. In Julie Helgeson's tragedy (chapter 1, "Finding Julie"), four and a half hours elapsed from the time of the attack and finding her alive to when she was pronounced dead, despite the heroic efforts of three doctors and a nurse at Granite Park Chalet. To not go as quickly as possible to try to locate the victim is to sentence that person to the possible fate of being consumed alive.

I wish to thank former Glacier National Park superintendent Chas Cartwright, and current superintendent Jeff Mow, for their generous transparency in releasing the requested Case Incident Records of bear–human encounters that constitute this book. I also thank their Freedom of Information Act (FOIA) officers, Amy Vanderbilt, Denise Germann, and Lauren Alley, and museum curator Jean Tabbert.

Each Glacier Park bear–human encounter within this book has a Case Incident Record identified by number, which includes all relevant information gathered at that time.

For greatest accuracy, I chose to use these original National Park Service archives (and not depend on others' later interpretations). Events of the time, related by those at that time in first-person narratives, are contained in this book. Any errors or omissions are my own.

PART 1

NIGHT OF THE GRIZZLIES, 1967

1

FINDING JULIE

1967: THE GRANITE PARK CAMPGROUND GRIZZLY

Each bear story asks this question: Is it a story about us, or about the bears?

—Douglas H. Chadwick, wildlife biologist
and conservationist (on Montana PBS's *Glacier
Park's Night of the Grizzlies*, September 28, 2010)

Two Fatalities on the Same Night

Fatality Number One: Julie Helgeson
The Granite Park Campground Grizzly: August 12–13, 1967
(Three female bears killed, one cub wounded; no bear proven responsible)

National Park Service–Glacier Park
Case Incident Record Number 679050 (also listed as A7623)
Location: Granite Park Campground near Granite Park Chalet
Date/Time: August 12 to August 13, 1967, 11:45 p.m. to 4:13 a.m.
(four and a half hours)

There was a death before dawn, and then a second death at almost the same time, nine and a half miles to the west. Of course, that is nature.

But at this moment Julie Helgeson was taking in the other side of nature: its beauty. She inhaled deeply atop Glacier Park's Logan Pass,

6,647 feet high, her gaze on a vista of mountains. The time was early afternoon, August 12, 1967. Your young life goes along, she might have thought, as a Midwestern University freshman, and then suddenly you find yourself here—above timberline at Glacier Park. You're working at East Glacier Lodge, so you get to spend the whole summer. And now, having found a boyfriend, you can share all that you see and feel.

What Julie saw here at the Continent's crown, just below Canada, was a vertical park of mountain peaks, named Glacier Park for the glaciers that moved and carved the landscape. High up on either side of a glacier's still-moving path, "hanging" valleys lie, their lakes gem colors from pulverized rock—"glacier flour." Julie had heard Glacier Park called the "Hall of the Mountain King," because its nights are lit by a white moon above black peaks and a star-strewn sky. And what's that sound? You may think wolves from Canada are howling, she'd been told, but it's the wind bringing storms, rain, and hail, even in summer.

And now the choice was made that may have determined Julie's fate: to start off on the Highline Trail, a 7.6-mile eyebrow of a footpath that hugged the cliffs above and below, leading to the historic Granite Park Chalet.

She and her boyfriend Roy Ducat had brought a packsack and two sleeping bags. Perhaps they could sleep on the floor of the Chalet, located deep in the roadless backcountry. But that choice was not possible, as there was no room for them that night.

Mid-August's sun heated the thin air at this altitude, and Julie wore cutoff jeans and a yellow shirt, and Roy, denim pants and a short-sleeved shirt. As Julie felt her well-worn brown leather hiking boots drum across the asphalt of Going-to-the-Sun Road, and then relax into the soft earth of the trailhead, she saw that they were not alone. The comfort of other hikers, their smiles and chatter, filled the same route going to the Chalet and coming back. Roy's black-and-white sneakers left tracks accompanying Julie's on the trail, and now he paused to take out his Kodak Instamatic camera.

"Many first-time hikers stop every ten feet to take photos on this hike that scares severe acrophobes with its exposed thousand-foot drop-offs," writes Becky Lomax in 2009's *Glacier National Park Moon Handbook*.

The trail drops from Logan Pass through a cliff walk above the highway crossing a flowerland that gave the Garden Wall *arête* its name ["a sharp-edged mountain ridge carved by a glacier"]. At three miles, nearly all of the elevation gain packs into one climb: Haystack Saddle appears to be the top, but it is only halfway. After the high point, the trail drops and swings through several large bowls before passing Bear Valley to reach Granite Park Chalet atop a knoll at 6,680 feet.[1]

The term *Park* in the reference to Granite Park above refers not to a separate park within Glacier, but instead to a "large meadow or grassland area surrounded by trees." The Granite Park Chalet is situated in an open area ringed with peaks.

Another man and woman who met Julie and Roy, and slept outside the Chalet near them, were also hiking the Highline Trail. Interviewed at nine a.m. on August 14 by park ranger Riley McClelland, they reported what they had heard on their hike to the Chalet.

"As I sat on the trail when we were eating lunch," the young man said, "we met a family who had told us that up at Granite Park there [were] regularly five bears, grizzly bears, that come in every night and, I don't know whether they said feed on the trash or not."

> But they said there were five bears up there, and when we told them that we were sleeping out, they said we better not sleep out. At this time I really didn't believe it because I didn't think there were that many grizzlys [*sic*] around. . . .
>
> This was the first we had heard of any bears. We continued on and arrived at the Chalet; I figure it was approximately 3:00. The first person we saw was the naturalist up there, and first thing she said to us was, "Did we bring our grizzly bear repellent?" And we said, "No," and laughed. (The naturalist Mr. [redacted] is speaking of is Miss Joan Devereaux, the naturalist stationed at St. Mary [Ranger Station].)

Backcountry chalet users and tent campers had enjoyed Glacier Park for decades, and, until 1967, there was one nighttime terror they did *not* have to worry about: a fatal attack by a bear. In Glacier, as opposed to

Yellowstone National Park, there had been no known bear-caused human fatalities by any bear, grizzly or black, since the Park's establishment in 1910. In fact, compared to Yellowstone, there were few problem bears causing a nuisance, and few bear-caused injuries to people at all. It *was* true that over the years in Glacier, an occasional hiker or backcountry camper disappeared, never to be found, but the cause of those disappearances remains a question mark (see chapter 28, "Still Missing and Presumed Dead").

But Julie and Roy were not thinking about that. As they hiked on toward the Chalet that Saturday, August 12, a light smoke-haze from several forest fires moved through, but not enough to hide the views. They wanted to make their precious free time pay off by seeing every Glacier sight they could. Julie worked in the East Glacier Lodge laundry, where the work was hot and hard. Roy worked as a busboy in the busy dining room at the same lodge.

"Glacier Park Employees Need Ride" (see color photo insert) read the hand-lettered sign Julie and Roy held out to passing motorists, hoping one would stop to pick them up. Park rules for employees in 1967 decreed: "No Beatle-type or hippie haircuts." You even had to phone for permission from your parents to be gone overnight (which Julie had done). Julie and Roy passed muster in that conservative time, and soon, a pickup truck stopped for them, dropping them off here at Logan Pass, where the Highline Trail to the Chalet began.

The adventure they were about to embark upon, which seemed safe enough to them, had already been enjoyed and recommended to them by their fellow East Glacier Lodge employees. So Julie Helgeson, a freshman at the University of Minnesota, and Roy Ducat, a freshman at Bowling Green State University in Ohio, arrived at the Granite Park Chalet, which sat on a broad bench near the timberline. The two-story stone structure topped a rocky and almost bare setting on a rise, with magnificent mountains looming in the distance. Unfortunately, there was no room at the rustic inn, which featured beds and hot meals.

Down in a draw darkened by trees was the Granite Park Campground, 500 feet south of the Chalet, past a locked trail crew cabin beside which three other people would camp. There was no one at the hikers' campground, and Julie and Roy were directed to put down their sleeping bags here, which they did. The campground was only a small cleared area with a few logs to sit on, next to a firepit. You could not even see the Chalet from here.

"I had no qualms and neither did she about sleeping under the stars, no tent. Nothing to be afraid of," Roy told interviewers forty-three years later in the 2010 documentary film, Montana PBS's *Glacier Park's Night of the Grizzlies*. (The title comes from the book of the same name by Jack Olsen, published in 1969.) Julie was the girl at the backpackers' campground, and events would soon involve a second girl asleep under the stars at Trout Lake, nine and a half miles away.

What happened next, over a period of four and a half hours, is recorded in Glacier Park's own bear-attack archives as Case Incident Record Number 679050 (also listed as A7623), which contains accounts told by those involved, including rangers, survivors, and witnesses in the moment, and on the scene. For greatest accuracy, this author chose to go to these original Glacier Park sources rather than depend on others' interpretations. Events related by those at that time are found in this internal Glacier Park investigative file, released to this author under Freedom of Information Act (FOIA) requests honored by Glacier Park personnel.

This is the story these documents tell. Survivor Roy Ducat speaks first, interviewed by an FBI agent and the Park's chief ranger, Ruben O. Hart. The grievously wounded Roy's interview transcript appears below, and also continues later in this chapter. From Roy's bedside in the Kalispell, Montana, General Hospital the following day, August 14 (recorded from 10:30 a.m. to 12:15 p.m.), the interviewers wrote, "He [Roy Ducat] stated that on Saturday afternoon, August 12, he started out on a trip with Julie M. Helgeson from East Glacier Lodge. They were both employees at the Lodge."

> They intended to go to Granite Park and stay overnight. Neither person had been to this location before, but heard about the trip from fellow employees.
>
> The two hitchhiked from East Glacier, starting at 2 p.m. and arriving at Logan Pass at 3:30 p.m. They each had a sleeping bag. Roy had, in

addition, a packsack to carry lunches and a few personal items. Prior to departing they each had a large sack lunch packed for this trip.

Leaving Logan Pass they hiked on the Highline Trail to Granite Park Chalet and arrived there at about 7 p.m. After staying a few minutes, they proceeded to hunt for the hikers' camping area. They left their sleeping bags and packsack at the Chalet.

En route to the camping area they saw three other persons (a married couple and a solo boy) who were camping out in the area near the trail [crew] cabin. The trail [crew] cabin was locked. Roy asked them where the camping area was located. One of the three said that there is a regular camping area and pointed in the direction of the site. Roy and Julie hiked over to the regular camping area. He said he saw a campground sign on the ground. The site had several logs for a fire and a fire pit. They then returned to the Chalet to get their sleeping bags and backpack and remained there until 8 p.m.

Roy noticed fresh garbage in the gully near the Chalet. He stated that he had previous knowledge from fellow employees before making the trip, about bears frequenting the Granite Park Chalet area.

"Five grizzly bears come in there every night," the young married couple—who camped that night beside the locked trail crew cabin above Julie and Roy—told park personnel. They were interviewed the next day, August 13, 1967. Fellow hikers on the Highline Trail had told the young couple about the "bear situation" at Granite Park Chalet, and how grizzlies were there every night, devouring garbage. The young man continued:

But when we, as I said, when we got up there, we did find that garbage was put out every night for the bears to eat and that the bears regularly did come every night. . . . After we ate in the campground, we brought our garbage back up to the Chalet, and at this time, we did see that the garbage was put out for the bears in the small ravine to the west.

(Question: How far from the Chalet?)
It was approximately 250 feet from the Chalet.

Now dark came, and with it the night of the grizzly bear attack. The young ranger-naturalist Joan Devereaux occupied a first-floor room at the Granite Park Chalet, which provided beds and hot food for its guests. On this night, the Chalet was overcrowded with guests. The cost was $12.50 per person, including three meals, so for Julie and Roy, the cost would have been $25, even if all they were doing was sleeping on the already-full floor space. In 1967, not all campers arriving at the Chalet may have been able to afford this amount.

From the trailhead, Devereaux had led a group of twenty-five park visitors, ages eight to sixty-five, to the Granite Park Chalet. There were so many guests at the Chalet that mattresses had to be laid out on the floor. All told, there were seventy people in the area.

"Due to a recent large number of fires," [Devereaux] told her interviewer, ranger-naturalist B. Riley McClelland, at 1:00 p.m. on August 14, "I was sent into Granite Park Chalet as replacement for Fred Goodsell. This was a trip I had made by myself previously, and the first trip I had made with a group of visitors from the Park." She described the trip to the Chalet:

> We started from Logan Pass at 9:00 a.m. on schedule. The whole trip in was one that was quite normal, no incidents, the usual marmots and flowers, etc., eating lunch at about 12:00 and then winding up at the Chalet at about 1:15. The group was about 25 in number. The afternoon at the Chalet was spent rather quietly. People were rather tired and were not interested in going out to the Grinnell Overlook. And so we sat around and watched the smoke from the surrounding fires and sort of relaxed and basked in the sun. The day went quite normal and quiet and when the afternoon and evening came along, and the attraction to the Park—Chalet, rather—came in as usual: the bear appearing in the evening at about 9:30, and the second one perhaps a half an hour later; and after having sung and fed the people, we all settled down and went to bed around 10:30.
>
> A young couple came up to me when they had arrived at the Chalet, [and] asked me where the overnight camping was. I pointed down the hill to the trail crew cabin [which was locked] and jokingly asked

them if they brought their grizzly bear repellent with them. They smiled and said "No." Then I explained that while this was a grizzly bear area, [. . .] they were free to camp there at their own risk. Another young man came up, but I didn't have any conversation with him. I understood he was camping down there. The second couple [Julie Helgeson and Roy Ducat] I had no idea was camping down there; I didn't see them all evening, not until the incident occurred.

The Chalet concession workers had a habit of separating their garbage in order to attract bears to the area; they put this in a place 100 yards from the Chalet in the clearing where the bears could easily be seen when they came in to feed. I was kind of shocked by this; I didn't see them make any attempt to burn this. I understand they do have an incinerator up there.

The bears came in on schedule. It was explained to the [guests] by the people who worked up there that these—that the first one was a black bear, I mean a brown grizzly, a large one, probably 500-plus pounds, and the second one was a silvertip, a little larger than the black-ish one. These were the only two bears we saw in the evening. It was relayed to me by the young man who works up there that there is a third bear that comes in the morning and about midnight. This is a sow with a pair of cubs and she is apparently quite bold and not frightened by much of anything. The evening was brought to a close and the people retired at about 10:30. . . .

The night had been a very beautiful one. There was a half moon, the sky was clear except for the haze created by the smoke, sunset was very, very colorful, very red, again reflecting the smoke in the area.

There were a few small fires that could be seen around the area. Other than that, the air was very calm, and very still; and the night was, again, a very beautiful one.

This, putting us to bed and everyone else to bed, finally everything was quiet until about 12:45, when the screams were heard by people in the Chalet. The daughter of one of the doctors [name redacted] heard this and woke her family and the word was brought downstairs to the Chalet employees and myself. . . .

This photo shows Julie Helgeson's campsite at Granite Park Campground, where in the middle of the night a bear attacked Julie and her friend, knocking them out of their sleeping bags and then dragging Julie away.
PHOTO FROM CASE INCIDENT RECORD NUMBERS 679050 AND A7623

What was happening to Julie and Roy down in the draw at the Granite Park Campground, where they had been sleeping alone?

"We had not seen any bears," the severely injured Roy Ducat told his interviewers at his bedside at the Kalispell General Hospital. The FBI agent and the chief park ranger wrote in their report that "At approximately 8:00 p.m. they [Julie and Roy] left the Chalet area for the camping area with the sleeping bags and packsack."

Upon returning to the camping site they ate part of their sack lunches, finishing about 9 p.m. They had a couple of sandwiches left over which [Roy] cached under a log about 200 yards from their camping site. Roy said that he had a candy bar in his packsack. The two remained in the camping site and prepared for the overnight stay. The old thin bag was laid down on the ground while the other was placed on the top for a cover. At dark they got into bed with their clothes on except for hiking boots. He was wearing blue denim pants and a short-sleeved shirt. She was wearing cutoff jeans and a blouse. The packsack was placed within reach of the bed.

After talking for awhile, they fell asleep. Roy remembered being awakened once by a small animal which he described as a squirrel. It was running around in the immediate area of the bed. After being awakened by the squirrel, Roy got up and went over to the nearby stream to get a drink of water. He then retired again.

Roy stated that he had not seen any bears either during the day or on this evening before retiring. I asked Roy if he knew the difference between a black bear and a grizzly and whether he had seen them before in his lifetime. He said he had seen black bears in Yellowstone National Park and one black bear in the Lake McDonald area, Glacier National Park. To his knowledge, he had never seen a grizzly. . . .

Roy stated that he again fell asleep. While in a sound sleep he remembers being awakened by Julie, who was on his right.

She told him to pretend he was dead.

Suddenly he and Julie were knocked about five feet outside of the sleeping bags by a blow. He was on his stomach facing down. Julie was about two feet away. The bear "gnawed" into his right shoulder. He made every effort to remain still and kept his eyes closed. The bear went to Julie and chewed on her but then returned and chewed on his left arm and on the back of both legs near his buttocks, but he did not once utter a sound.

The bear returned to Julie, at which time he could hear bones crunching when the bear chewed on her. He recalled he had heard her say, "It hurts," on two occasions. She yelled "Someone help us." She started to scream. Roy heard the bear dragging her away rapidly down the hill. All the time she continued to scream. Her voice faded away as though the bear were dragging her rapidly for a considerable distance.

Roy jumped up and ran over to the area where the other three campers were staying. He recalled stumbling over objects en route.

I [interviewer] asked him at this time how he knew it was a bear. He said that he kept his eyes closed at all times except once, when he distinguished a faint outline of a bear in the darkness.

This animal also had a distinct bear odor. At no time did he hear any other animal in the area where this animal was attacking. It was obviously one bear.

The one glimpse he got of the bear revealed it was on all fours. Roy recalled that the bear braced his feet on [Roy's] back once when it was chewing on him.

After reaching the area where the other campers were located, [Roy] awakened the person sleeping in a blue sleeping bag. He did not recall whether the other two persons were awake at this time.

"Help me, help me," someone was screaming. The husband of the couple camping near the locked trail crew cabin described this to his interviewers:

Mr. [redacted]: That night, it was a very clear night, no wind, very calm and [not] overcast; it was completely clear. The moon was very bright that night, being as it was so clear. We did not see the couple return to their campsite; however, we saw [the other boy] come down, and this was probably around 10:00 or 10:30. This is all; we must have fallen asleep at that time and didn't wake up until we heard the screaming. . . . I heard words clearly, and the main words I heard were just "Help me, help me." Someone was yelling this over and over again. I told the ranger that night that I thought I heard [the victim] say "Mommy, help me," over and over. People in the Chalet said they heard her yelling "He's stabbing me." [. . .]

The screaming, I thought that somebody had come into [the] campsite after dark and we hadn't seen them, because it sounded to me like a very young girl screaming, and I thought that some little girl in the campsite was having a nightmare, and this is maybe where I got the "Mommy," I don't know. But then, this screaming went on, it seemed like for a long time, it was probably about a minute and a half or two minutes, and it seemed to get farther and farther away and die down

An armed ranger points out the location west of Granite Park Campground where searchers found bear attack victim Julie Helgeson. She was still alive.
PHOTO FROM CASE INCIDENT RECORD NUMBERS 679050 AND A7623

and finally it reached a crescendo and went down from there and finally was stopped. . . .

We didn't know what to do, we were just sitting up in our sleeping bags, perfectly still and just looking at each other, and then we heard some rustling, and the boy [Roy] who had been camped down below came up to [redacted] campsite and heard them saying something, and I didn't know what they were saying; I couldn't hear them.

Mrs. [redacted]: He kept saying "A bear, a bear."

[The husband]: I guess we heard him say a bear. We didn't know what had happened, and then [he] said that the boy asked him if we were still in the campsite and if we were, he wanted to come up and tell us. And so they both came up to our campsite and told us. We immediately, apparently grabbed our boots and our clothes, as much as we could, and then I grabbed a flashlight, and before we had gone to bed, I forgot to mention this, [she] had said "What happens if we see a bear?" I said, "The only place around here to go is to climb up to the top of the trail cabin."

As soon as they came up and told us, the boy told us that the bear had grabbed the girl and taken her away. . . . On our way to the trail cabin [to get on top], I think the boy [Roy] said he was cold, or something, and [redacted] said, "Run get our sleeping bags." I said [redacted], get your sleeping bag around him; so he got his sleeping bag around him, and the boy lay down on the sleeping bag. [Name redacted] and I climbed up to the top of the trail cabin and shined our flashlight around the immediate area to see if the bear was still around. I didn't know anything about what would happen, or anything. [The other boy] stayed down. Let's see, we shined the flashlight around the area to make sure the bear was gone, or if we could see the bear or see what was happening.

And then, I think by this time, the [people at the] Chalet had also heard the screams, and we saw a light at the Chalet from the top of the cabin. The campground is down in another draw; it is down in a low area that contains both of these streams, and you can't see the Chalet from the campground area. But we saw it from the top of the cabin; and as soon as we saw that light, we started signaling to them, signals of three flashes over and over again.

"Fourteen people went down to the area," naturalist Joan Devereaux continued in her interview with park officials, adding:

After quickly getting dressed, I called for the radio and I turned it on and waited for it to warm up and then a party of about 14, mostly men and two or three girl employees and myself, went down to the area. We were being signaled by loud cries from three of the people who were camping down there, and by flashlights. It was very obvious that there was some difficulty down there, so we headed down. We moved quite rapidly. We reached the scene at about 1:05 [a.m.] and discovered immediately the young boy laying there.

He had been placed in a sleeping bag by one of the young men back up there with him. We were informed then that there might be another person and he started mumbling and moaning about the girl having been dragged off.

I immediately began talking over the radio to the west side and the fire cache area over there. After several attempts the word came through and they began to understand what we were talking about, and I radioed in that we had an emergency—that there was some bear damage and it was very critical. [I] informed them that there were two doctors at the place, and all we needed at the present was a helicopter to get these people out because this person I had seen [. . .] it was serious, and that the doctors felt that this was more important than bringing any surgical equipment up. They did ask, though, for a transfusion apparatus, plasma, if not, preferably whole blood; and also for some morphine or some pain killer and perhaps some more gauze, etc., since there was no first-aid equipment at all up at the Chalet [as stated in report], and what I had was definitely not adequate to take care of this type of a wound.

"Find Julie, find Julie!" the badly injured Roy Ducat kept pleading to his rescuers. He was clearly in shock. Park officials continue their account of Roy's interview after the attack:

[Roy] remembered asking these people to find "her," meaning Julie, and to scare the bear away. One of the campers had him lay down on the sleeping bag. These people yelled toward the Chalet: "Bear—bring lights and [a] gun." Several people came from the Chalet. They placed a sleeping bag on a bedspring and hauled [Roy] to the Chalet. One of the men from the Chalet said he was a doctor; another said he was a surgeon.

Roy was placed on a table in the Chalet and first aid was rendered by the surgeon. Roy remembered being conscious throughout the entire ordeal. He also emphasized that he remained silent all the time during the attack.

Throughout the interview we directed the questions and Roy answered to each. He appeared to be very stable emotionally, and was cooperative in relaying details in the incident. We thanked him for the information and wished him a speedy recovery.

—Ruben O. Hart, chief park ranger

"The young man was quite damaged," ranger-naturalist Devereaux continued in her interview. She described some of his injuries:

He himself had . . . two compound fractures of the left arm, multiple deep lacerations of his back, both legs, sparingly on the chest, abdomen, and head. He was in initial shock; his condition was generally fair. We returned to the Chalet, the remainder of the party, and all of us, having placed the young man on one of the bedsprings that was found down there to use as a stretcher in order to get him back up. This was near the trail crew cabin. We were fortunate that there were some old beds there that we could use for a stretcher. We returned to the Chalet, still not quite sure about the young girl, whether she was really there, or anything about it. After returning, the boy mumbled more and we were definitely positive. We talked to the young couple, and a boy was down there, and it became clear there was another person involved, and I began to try to get people organized to go look for her.

At this time it came over the radio that a helicopter would be in in about 20 minutes, so we had to delay the search for her in order to go out there and build enough light in the form of fires to bring the helicopter in. The layout for the landing was behind the second housing facility on toward Logan [Pass]. There is a clearing out there where the helicopter pilot had previously brought in some refrigerators. We set four fires in a cross-type position in order to give him some direction. Everybody with all available flashlights formed a circle in between all of these, and particularly, we used two Coleman lanterns to light up two stakes we couldn't get out of the ground for fear he would run into them. The 'copter came promptly [to] the area.

The doctors were working with the young boy, doing what they could, not doing much really of anything, because they didn't have the proper equipment and felt that he was better off just being left alone. The 'copter landed after having been given directions with the aid of a young man up there. One of the visitors who had worked with 'copters before helped me bring the helicopter in. We were giving him wind direction and everything, had things all set up. . . .

The landing was quite difficult and the area without the lights was exceedingly black since the moon had gone down by this time, and all the light that was coming out was starlight, and definitely not enough to land anything in this type of situation. . . .

Mr. Bunney [a Glacier Park Law Enforcement Ranger] arrived and I was quite relieved to see he had brought, as I had requested, a gun with him. This added to the moral[e] of the people who were with me. After he came down and we got the boy back into the 'copter in order to send him out right away, communications and requests were made to West Glacier that they call the Flathead Airport [where] the 'copter was to land, and request a doctor and an ambulance meet the 'copter.

"Find Julie! Find Julie!" Roy Ducat had said to the first person he aroused from sleep, and again and again to his rescuers. Later, there would be controversy surrounding not only the practice of feeding garbage to grizzly bears, but also whether search parties should have been sent out more quickly to help find Julie—especially given the large number of people present in the nearby Granite Park Chalet, and the total of seventy people in the area. (Although none of these people were armed, it could be argued that such a large number of potential searchers would have been helpful in locating Julie sooner, and possibly saving her life.)

Ranger-naturalist Devereaux continued her account:

Mr. Bunney took my party of men down with him and his rifle, which I said encouraged them more, to look for the young girl. Some women had been listening over the hill and had been hearing cries, faint cries of "help." And so they [. . .] had some definite direction to go, at least to go downhill from the camping area. They left for this and headed on down the hill and I remained up topside to do what I could up there. Two of the doctors stayed with me; the third went down with the ranger. . . .

The party was gone, I'm really not at all sure how long; under pressure, time is quite deceiving. Perhaps 20 minutes. As hearsay, I understand they searched for her for a while. Finally she came out again with a cry of "help," and they immediately rushed to her and found her there. Again, hearsay; I understand that she was found in very bad shape, wearing nothing but her cutoff jeans, and had been dragged perhaps 150 feet or so, not much more than that.

They returned back up to the Chalet again and [used] a bedspring for a litter to bring her back up. . . . The men came up with the girl and I had been able to get the women out and back up to their rooms, out of the way. . . .

They brought her in and I was told she had a puncture of her left thorax, going through to her lung from the rear. On seeing the girl myself, her—one of her arms, right now I don't know which one, I believe it was her right arm—was very, very badly mauled, and again I was told it would [have] had to have been amputated. There was nothing they could have done to save it. The wounds on her were from the back side of her, and again they discovered that there was a second wound in the chest cavity area, and perhaps this, too, had gone through to her lungs. I'm not sure. . . .

According to Devereaux, the bear had consumed "large chunks of flesh" (see below), although this was contradicted later in the Board of Inquiry report, which indicated that the bear had not consumed any part of her body.

Devereaux went on to say:

Her legs were in very bad shape. Large chunks of flesh had been removed and there was definitely a great deal of blood lost. There was not much damage . . . done to her face—some scratches on her neck and so forth; perhaps these were gained by being dragged so far by the bear. I'm not really sure at all what he dragged her by; perhaps it was by the arm, in this case, since it was so badly mauled. There were marks on the rest of her body, [which was] badly abraised [*sic*], but I guessed this was [probably] by being dragged by the bear.

She was conscious when they brought her in, mumbling quite coherently, complaining about hurting, but she moved her right arm which was so badly torn, and so it was obvious she was not quite, really feeling any pain in this arm at all.

There was a young priest there who took the obligation of consoling her and stayed at her head and talked to her while the doctors worked and looked at the rest of her wounds. They injected some of the plasma, and, I understand, gave her some morphine.

At this time the second helicopter began to arrive. Doctors worked for some time with her. Some of the men were holding lights and everything; there wasn't much light in the Chalet at all. One of the wives, the wife of one of the doctors, was a nurse, so we had three doctors and a nurse, again making it a little more comfortable for the rest of us. Again, as the 'copter began to come into the area, I went out to set up my landing apparatus again. . . .

The young girl expired just shortly before the helicopter arrived there; I believe it was some time after 3:30–3:35 [a.m.], or somewhere near there. [In actuality, death was pronounced at 4:13 a.m.]

I was not on the scene when she died, but I was informed shortly thereafter. The 'copter came and they put her on a litter, fastened her to the right outside of the helicopter, and Mr. Bunney and the pilot then departed. . . .

"We were on top of the cabin," the couple camping nearby continued in their interview, relating what happened that night and the next morning.

At this time, it seemed a lot longer, but a group from the Chalet came down [at] approximately, they said they got there about—at this time, when we were on top of the cabin, we looked at our watch and it was 12:55 [a.m.]. The group from the Chalet said that they reached our point at five after one. I think it was a little later than that. But that's what they say. It may be true. Joan [Devereaux, the ranger] brought the group down with the radio; they had a big fire pot [a large, two-handled tin basin with a lit fire within, for illumination and, hopefully, to repel the bear] and they came down.

At this time there was a doctor with them, and he immediately started administering what first aid he could to the boy. This is probably what I should have done to start with, but I didn't think of it. We had our small first-aid kit there; I believe that was the only first-aid kit that was available. Joan then immediately got on the radio and called for help and called for a helicopter.

In the meantime, the doctor had decided to get the boy immediately up to the Chalet as fast as we could, and there were old bedsprings nailed to the trail [crew] cabin around the windows [to keep bears out], and these were taken down and the boy was placed on a bedspring and I think there was approximately six or seven of us who started carrying the boy back to the Chalet. Joan and a number of people stayed down to keep radioing. . . . We got the boy up to the Chalet. . . .

Meanwhile, the other group had come back and they said that they had radioed for a helicopter and that it was on its way. Then, I think, everybody kind of milled around for a few minutes and then somebody started telling us that we needed wood to start fires in a large circle around in an area where the helicopter could land. And this occupied everybody's time for a while . . . they carried a lot of kindling wood in a store room and everybody carried kindling wood out; I think we started four or five fires around in a circle. Then, we started the fires and we all got in a large circle and pointed our flashlights down so the helicopter could see where to land; and he came right in and made a perfect landing right in the center of the circle, and immediately the pilot and the ranger with the gun got out. They then went and got the boy and carried him to the helicopter and, I don't remember too much of this; we were around the ranger and they were starting to organize a party to go out and get the girl.

(About what time was this?)
That, I really don't have any idea. I didn't even look. It must have been some time between, probably around 2:00 [a.m.] then, this happened. A number of us, we got the fire pot again and we got a lot of flashlights and we started back down the trail [to find Julie].

(This was with the ranger [with the gun]?)
This was with the ranger. He was leading it. So we started walking back down the trail toward our camp and we found fresh grizzly bear

droppings right on the trail **so** *the bear must have followed the first group right back up the path* [emphasis added].

But we were yelling and shining our flashlights around and we saw no sign of the bear. We then went down to the trail [crew] cabin and from there went more or less south to the campground, to try to find the camp where the two people [Julie and Roy] [had] camped. We found this fairly readily; it was, the trail goes down and bends toward the east, away from the creek, and the campgrounds are off the trail close to the creek, so we got off the trail and went down and we found their camp very quickly, let's say 200 feet out from the camp—not that far, excuse me—it was closer to 50 feet.

It wasn't very far until we lost all the blood spots and we then, everybody slowed down, stopped, and we tried to find where the brush was torn down, and where the grizzly possibly could have gone. We were more or less walking in a random direction from here.

We didn't know what to do. We were just walking around when we heard the girl, we were still yelling and I imagine she heard us yelling, and she gave out a scream. Then we knew right where she was. We started walking toward her. We found her then. We think approximately 100 to 150 yards away from the camp. . . . Dr. [redacted], one of the doctors, came with us, and he immediately started administering first aid.

She, the girl, was laying on her back [probably her front], and she, her back wasn't lacerated at all, except for just one hole that had gone in and punctured her lung. You could see her breathing through this hole. I guess she could hardly breathe. Her lung was punctured. Like I said, [the doctor] started administering first aid with what he had, and he covered up this hole as best he could. As soon as we found her, a group of about, probably four or five, went immediately back to the trail [crew] cabin to get another bedspring off the side of the trail [crew] cabin so we could carry her back. . . . In the meantime, the doctor was doing everything he could, and he covered her with coats and shirts and everything else. He made bandages out of shirts.

(Did you have a radio with you?)

No, we didn't. No. We tried to make her as comfortable as possible; the doctor laid her on her back and she wanted to go back on her stomach. The doctor wouldn't let her, for some reason or other. He said it was better for her to be on her back. Meanwhile, the group who went to get the bedspring went back by route of their camp and picked up both of their sleeping bags and brought those down, and we laid one sleeping bag on the bedspring and, I think, five or six men very carefully picked her up and put her on the sleeping bag [. . .] and then we put his sleeping bag over her. Then we started back and we carried her back to the Chalet as fast as we could.

She was conscious the whole time, talking . . .

"Would you hold my hand, please? I'm scared," Julie said to one of her rescuers, who had also been camping outside near the locked trail crew cabin. He took her hand. The couple who had camped near the locked trail crew cabin concluded their interview, describing the attempt to save Julie's life:

They said there were three doctors. I only knew about two, the surgeon and the doctor that had come with us. They immediately started working on her. . . . And just as the helicopter [returned for the second time], the [pilot] made one circle, and just as he was coming in for the landing, the doctor came out and told us that the girl had died.

The investigation began that afternoon, August 13, at 1:10 p.m. "There is blood on the false hellebores," dictated chief park naturalist Francis H. Elmore into a recorder as he followed the path searchers had made to find Julie.

We are now following the trail of the sleeping bag down through the brush, and some of the trees—some of the shrubs, I should say—are a little mashed down. And there's blood on some of the false hellebores, and there is quite a lot of blood drippings along the way here. There's a lot of mashed-down Glacier lilies and others. Twenty yards from the campground a purse was found. We are now proceeding along the line of mashed grass to the site.

[A second searcher, name redacted]: We had reached this point and we couldn't find the trail, so the ranger-naturalist had everybody be quiet, and at this time we heard the girl yell for help again, and then we all just ran down in the direction we had heard the sound.

Francis H. Elmore: This is the chief naturalist again. We are now at the site where the girl was dragged, which is a considerable distance from where they were camping. There are steripads and a couple pieces of clothing with blood on them. A couple of lifesaver packs laying on the ground, and there's a wrapper from a Hershey bar, and quite a bit of blood on the ground. This is actually where the girl was found and given first aid.

[Redacted]: We came down, we found the girl laying on her face, and she was crying at the time and quite bloody, and the doctor started to give her attention. Part of the crew ran up and got [a] bedspring from the trail [crew] cabin to use as a stretcher.

Francis Elmore: The girl had a mark on her wrist indicating she was probably wearing a wristwatch, which was not found at the scene, and we are slowly going back over the trail now, looking for it.

[Redacted]: Well, all she had on was a pair of cutoffs, the rest had [been] torn off her, and she had some [clothing] under her face, so we supplied our coats and shirts and sweaters to keep her warm until they could get back with the bedspring and the sleeping bags in which the party was originally sleeping when they were attacked by the bear.

Francis Elmore: Talking to people involved here, [it] sounds like the attack was an unprovoked attack; we do not know at this moment. It is said that they were awake and saw the bear sniffing around and the girl said, "Let's play dead," and at that time the bear supposedly attacked.

[Redacted]: Well, approximately 12:45 or 12:50 [a.m.], some of the guests in the Chalet, particularly one doctor's wife, was awakened by the sounds of the girl screaming coming down from the campground area, screaming, "My God, he is stabbing me," and she continued screaming for some time.

Francis Elmore: Evidently, they did play dead for awhile, while the bear was attacking. Up by the trail [crew] cabin, however, the girl did not start screaming until she was being dragged off. We are now at the site, which is perhaps 100 yards down from the trail [crew] cabin to where the bear dragged the girl.

The girl was evidently very rational when she was first seen by these people; they started to bandage her; she said that her chest hurt, and when they turned her over to do some more bandaging, she said that her back hurt. We have just retraced the steps that the bear took, bringing the girl down here, and it paces out [at] 140 yards. We found no evidence of the wristwatch on the way up or back.

We are back again at the site where the girl was first given first aid by the doctors. The girl evidently was put on the bedspring and carried back to the Chalet, and about halfway up the hill she supposedly lost conscious[ness]. The doctors thought then she probably was dead. However, she was taken up to the Chalet and two doctors remained there. There happened to be at the Chalet three doctors and a trained nurse. Fortunately, they did all they could for the girl. After the girl was taken into the Chalet, the doctors started working on her. . . . About the time of the helicopter's arrival, more or less, the doctors had reported that the girl had died at 4:13 a.m.

[Redacted]: Well, after we had heard the screams and proceeded down to the trail [crew] cabin, we found the boy laying in a sleeping bag, which of course was quite bloody, and one of his arms was severely chewed up. Later we found he had a compound fracture, or several fractures in his arm, in both upper arm and lower arm; anyway, half the party carried the boy up to the Chalet on the bedspring.

The rest of us remained at the trail [crew] cabin and debated some five or ten minutes [. . .] about looking for the girl. We couldn't hear any screams at this time, or any noises. We were without any weapons at all, and we didn't have too many flashlights, so we proceeded on back to the Chalet, and helped them to bring the helicopter in and helped them load the boy. We sent him on his way, and when the helicopter arrived, it brought in Ranger Bunney, I believe his name is. He was armed with a gun, and we proceeded back down the hill to look for the girl as soon as he arrived, and then we found her way down here. . . .

After we had taken the boy to the Chalet and came back down the trail again, to look for the girl the second time, there was *a time lapse of probably an hour* [emphasis added]. During this time lapse we returned and there were fresh bear droppings on the trail, indicating that possibly the bear had followed us up to the Chalet. [S]ome of the people in the party [also] reported heavy breathing in the bushes near us, several times.

Actions to protect other Park visitors, as well as the hunt for the responsible bear (or bears), came next. At 6:25 a.m. on August 13, Assistant Superintendent Jack B. Dodd wrote in his notes:

I notified Superintendent [Keith] Neilson at Many Glacier Hotel of the tragedy. Trails to Granite Park will be closed, and we are to hunt for the bears and eliminate them. [By 8:00 a.m.], Wildlife Ranger C. R. Wasem, Research Biologist Clifford Martinka, Seasonal Park Ranger Kerel Hagen, and Chief Park Naturalist Francis H. Elmore were dispatched to Granite Park armed with three rifles and one pistol, with instructions to search for adult grizzly bears in the immediate vicinity of Granite Park, and if found, to exterminate them.

At 10:30 a.m. the Associated Press remarked to a Park spokesperson that "the bear tragedy was the only story of significance in the Nation so far today."

The Park Service tasked six highly qualified individuals to pursue the responsible bear, or bears, and kill them—not necessarily a task that any of these professionals would choose to do.

The "weather during the operation was hot and dry with little cloud cover and calm to light breeze wind conditions," wrote research biologist C. Robert Wasem, who with five others participated in the hunt. He had been called at 1:00 a.m. the morning of the attack, was up at 4:45 a.m., and reported to the chief ranger's office at 5:50 a.m. By 8:45 a.m. the first party of Wasem, research biologist Clifford Martinka, chief park naturalist Francis Elmore, and seasonal park ranger Kerel Hagen had arrived by car at the Granite Park trailhead, leaving on foot for the Chalet and searching for bears on the way. "Forest fire smoke created hazy conditions, making sighting with binoculars and [spotting] scope a bit more difficult," Wasem wrote.

Wasem's "Log of Granite Park Grizzly Attack Hunt, August, 1967" continues below:

Sunday, August 13

Arrived at Granite Park Chalet at 11:05 a.m. No bears along trail. Met party of 55 or so en route from Chalet to Going-to-the-Sun Road [the visitors, beating a hasty retreat from the Chalet]. . . .

Spent most of afternoon investigating attack and attack area and glassing [looking through binoculars at] areas around Chalet for bears. Elmore made tape recordings of conversations with Chalet employees and took 35mm color photos. . . .

One dark silvertip sow grizzly with one cub located with binoculars one mile SE, and below Chalet at location of small lake on topo map. These two watched for 2 [and ½] hours, 4:00 to 6:30 p.m., before they disappeared from view.

Garbage placed at usual spot at 7:15 p.m. as bait to attract bears for possible destruction. At about 8:30 p.m., crew organized at shooting stations to wait for bears to come to bait station. All shooting done from rear Chalet balcony. At 10:08 p.m. a large dark silvertip grizzly without cubs was shot and killed. Estimated weight of female—350 pounds.

At 10:20 p.m. a smaller brown-black semi-silvertip grizzly came to bait station and was shot and killed. A female with estimated weight of 250 pounds.

During the bear hunt, the nights were "cool and clear, with temperatures in the forties and low fifties," wrote Wasem. The crew went to bed at 11:00 p.m.

At 6:15 a.m. the "remaining garbage was gone in [the] morning, indicating some other animal came in to feed during the night after 11:00 p.m. Carcasses of destroyed bears, [Wasem noted, were] not bothered."

Spent 2 hours between 7:00 and 9:00 a.m. looking for bears. Hiked 2 miles toward Fifty Mountain, glassing countryside. No bears seen.... 1½ hours were spent between 10:00 and 11:30 a.m. making 35mm photos and body measurements of 2 bears. Stomach and intestinal contents examined—only berries and leaves of *Vaccinium membranaceum* (Giant Whortleberry) and other bits of natural vegetative foods were found. Heads and front feet were removed, salted and placed in plastic bags....

Talked to Chief Ranger Hart and Assistant Superintendent Dodd on radio at 8:15 p.m. re: hunt, trail closure, and visit tomorrow of *Life* magazine reporter.

Shooting crew went on watch at 9:00 p.m. No fresh garbage was put out—what little existed was incinerated.

At about 10:30 p.m. approaching grunting sounds alerted crew to possible action. Bear shied away, however, not coming to bait station.

Tuesday, August 15

At 12:00 midnight, 3 of crew went to bed with 2 staying up on watch. All-night watch schedule set up. At 12:30 [a.m.] bear again approached but drifted away again. Hagen sprained ankle coming down rear balcony steps in dark. Back to bed.

At 12:45 bear again approached and finally was shot and killed at 12:50 a.m. Shea's eyebrow cut on rifle scope from recoil. Two cubs with sow ran uphill to tree-rock cover. No attempt was made to shoot them. Estimated weight of sow was 275 pounds. Watch maintained remainder of night.... Two cubs stayed in vicinity until about 5:00 a.m. or so but did not approach mother's carcass or bait station....

At 8:00 a.m. Shea and Wasem, while on way to trail [crew] cabin to obtain rope with which to drag bear carcasses, spotted 2 cubs below and S. of Chalet, and with Martinka gave chase south and down steep drainage for 1½ miles. Martinka shot 5 times and wounded 1 cub, which left blood trail. Cubs lost in dense shrubs and cliff area....

Wednesday, August 16

Shea and Wasem left Chalet at 10:15 a.m. While hiking Highline Trail spotted 2 cubs far below in lake basin SE of Chalet. One appeared to have a jaw wound and kept dipping its head in small stream. Otherwise both appeared healthy and active. . . .

Summary of Grizzly Bears in Granite Park Chalet Area in August, 1967

- Dark silvertip female—killed.
- Brown-black silvertip female—killed.
- Dark silvertip with cubs—last seen 1 mile SE of Chalet at 6:30 p.m. on Sunday, August 13.
- Dark gray female with two 8-month[-old] cubs—killed. Two cubs still in area, with one wounded around mouth. Cubs last seen at 10:45 a.m. [on] Wednesday, August 16, in basin, SE of Chalet.
- Buckskin-colored yearling or two-year-old. Not seen by hunting party. Last seen at Chalet area about ten days prior to August 13.

So what bear (or bears) were responsible for killing Julie Helgeson? Was that bear (or bears) caught and killed? In the final Glacier National Park Report, "Grizzly Bear Attacks at Granite Park and Trout Lake, August 13, 1967," the following speculation is provided:

Was the Killer Bear [at Granite Park] Destroyed?

The third bear (the sow with cubs, thought to be the offender) was destroyed at Granite Park at 12:50 a.m., August 15, 1967. This was exactly 48 hours and 5 minutes after the fatal attack. There was no blood on the animal's muzzle or on feet or claws; however, the 48-hour lapse would allow blood remains to wear or rub off the animal. Several small dark stains were noted on several front claws and the pad of one front foot. These were sent to the FBI Laboratory in Washington, DC, along with several hairs taken from the animal's mouth. Neither the stains nor the hair were of human origin.

See additional details from this report at the conclusion of "Finding Michele" (chapter 2, page 54). It should also be noted that the above dark

After Julie Helgeson's fatality, rangers shot this adult female grizzly and dragged the carcass on a wooden sled from Granite Park to a helicopter, for transport to West Glacier Park Headquarters.
PHOTO FROM CASE INCIDENT RECORD NUMBERS 679050 AND A7623

gray female bear's digestive system did *not* contain evidence of human consumption. It is likely that two more deaths resulted from this bear's extermination, as her eight-month-old cubs would probably not have been able to survive without their mother.

What caused the attack and death of Julie Helgeson? Seasonal biologist David S. Shea, in his paper titled "Theories," written on August 18, 1967, suggested the following possibilities for the fatality near Granite Park Chalet.

- Excessive heat making bears cranky.
- Lightning exciting the bears.

- Lack of huckleberries and other natural food.
- Stored food of the victims.
- The fact that [Helgeson] was menstruating, or nearly so, thus inciting female bears to attack a "rival," or some other reason.
- Possibly perfume or other cosmetics attracted the animals.
- The fact that most recorded attacks are by females may be significant, even if no cubs are present.

An inventory of Julie Helgeson's property was taken at Park headquarters by chief park ranger Ruben O. Hart on September 5, 1967. "Property found near scene (114 yards from campsite) where Miss Helgeson was found on August 13, 1967," included the items listed below:

- Female sweatshirt, torn in many places and extremely bloody.
- Brassiere, which was also bloody.
- One portion of bra strap was found about 15 feet along path above final resting place.

Julie's property found at Granite Park Chalet, removed by the attending doctor, included the following:

- One yellow blouse. It was torn in many places and apparently cut with scissors by the doctor, who removed the article. It was covered with blood over approximately one-half of the material.
- Cutoff jeans. This article contained numerous tears and holes. It was also cut by scissors, apparently by the doctor who removed the article. This article was covered with blood.

The following items belonging to Julie M. Helgeson were in a packsack, along with Roy Ducat's personal items:

1. 1 Blue Jacket
2. 1 Pillow Case
3. 1 pair Wrangler Jeans

4. 1 pair Brown Hiking Boots
5. 1 Pink Sweater
6. 1 coin purse containing $2
7. Hair Cover (White)
8. Tooth Brush and Tooth Paste
9. 2 Tampax
10. Mirror and Comb
11. Lipstick
12. 1 Hair Clip

What did the official inquiry report say?

The Glacier Park Board of Inquiry Report analyzed the attacks on both Julie Helgeson, at Granite Park Campground, and on Michele Koons, at Trout Lake (see Glacier National Park Report, "Grizzly Bear Attacks at Granite Park and Trout Lake, August 13, 1967," at conclusion of chapter 2, "Finding Michele," page 54).

Writing to Julie's parents must have been one of the most difficult notifications any National Park Service director has ever made. Director George B. Hartzog Jr. wrote: "I know there is nothing we can do to alleviate the grief of your daughter's death in Glacier National Park. I do want you to know we are deeply shocked by this unfortunate accident, and I extend to you on behalf of the National Park Service our most sincere sympathy and condolences."

Julie Helgeson's parents, who had visited their daughter at Glacier less than two weeks before her death, requested the return of her remains and her belongings, which were sent.

Julie and Roy "were just a wonderful couple. Sweet," the young man camping near them outside the trail crew cabin later told interviewers. This man was also the person who held her hand. A dying person's sense of touch, some nurses believe, is the final sense to depart before death.

Two additional points can be made here. First, as stated earlier in the author's note, the quintessentially human quality of altruism (even in the face of danger) is important. In order to save any bear-attack victim who has been dragged away, someone must find that person as quickly as possible. The dragging away is itself predictive of predatory behavior, as opposed to a hiker surprising a sow bear who attacks to protect her cubs. To not go as quickly as one can to find the victim is to sentence that person to the fate of possibly being consumed alive.

Second, is it possible to learn more about the issue of persons attacked while in their sleeping bags?

It turns out that, yes, this had happened before. Julie Helgeson was not the first person to be attacked while in a sleeping bag. In fact, her death might accurately be called "The Sleeping Bag Grizzly #3."

In early August 1956, "The Sleeping Bag Grizzly #1" event occurred. According to the Glacier Park report "Human Injuries Before 'Night of the Grizzlies,' 1945–1966," "Toby Johnson received minor bites while in his sleeping bag at Stoney Indian Pass. The lone bear was believed to be a grizzly." This attack is thought to have been predatory in nature (see chapter 23, "Finding Toby").

On July 8, 1962, "The Sleeping Bag Grizzly #2" occurred near the Granite Park Chalet. "Bear Injures Man in Sleeping Bag," reported *Hungry Horse News* on July 13. "Anthony G. Netting, Pittsburgh, Pa., a graduate student at Columbia University, was injured by a bear in Glacier National Park." The report continues below:

> Netting was sleeping out by himself in a sleeping bag near Granite Park Chalet July 8 about 11 p.m. A bear cuffed the bag, inflicting seven puncture wounds and claw marks in his shoulder and right arm.
>
> Netting slept the rest of the night at Granite Park Chalet, having been given first aid by Ranger-Naturalist Robert J. Reimler, Marshall, Minn.
>
> He hiked down the next morning with the naturalist party.

The "Human Injuries Before 'Night of the Grizzlies,' 1945–1966" report also mentions the Netting attack, above. "The next incident involved [redacted] at Granite Park Chalet on July 8, 1962. Mr. [redacted] received minor lacerations when a grizzly, believed to be a sow with young, took a swipe at him after he attempted to chase her off as she was sniffing at his sleeping bag."

Now, in 1967, officials wondered if the same mother bear who attacked Mr. Netting could be the offender in Julie Helgeson's death. Five years before, she may have investigated the person of Anthony G. Netting in his sleeping bag near Granite Park Chalet, with an earlier set of cubs. It should be noted that Netting did not "play dead," and immediately fought back.

In "Finding Julie" ("The Sleeping Bag Grizzly #3"), the tragedy of this first-known fatal grizzly attack was unimaginably compounded by yet another fatal predatory grizzly attack in Glacier Park on that same night of August 13, 1967. The two attacks were nine and a half air miles from each other, separated by the 9,000-foot summit called Heaven's Peak.

Ironically, Roy and Julie, as Park employees, had been invited to join fellow employees Michele Koons and her four friends that night, who were camping outdoors at Glacier's Trout Lake. See the next chapter.

2

FINDING MICHELE

1967: THE TROUT LAKE CAMPSITE GRIZZLY

We had intended to go to Arrow Lake and use the cabin. But we met some people who said it was already full.

—Young woman of second couple (of four
persons camping with Michele Koons)

Fatality Number Two: Michele Koons
The Trout Lake Campsite Grizzly: August 13, 1967
(One female bear killed, proved responsible)

National Park Service–Glacier Park
Case Incident Record Number A7623 (as Granite Park Campground
incident is secondarily listed)
Location: Trout Lake Campsite (lower end of lake)
Date/Time: August 13, 1967, approximately 8:00 p.m. to 4:30 a.m.

Michele Koons and the young man were not alone. They were camping out in the Glacier Park backcountry, together, along with three other people.

A grizzly bear attack couldn't happen again, and not that same Saturday night into early Sunday morning of August 12–13, 1967. But it did. Again, the safest sleeping space (inside a chalet's stone walls, or in a shelter cabin made of wood) was full of other campers/backpackers.

Michele Koons and her friends' backcountry camp at Trout Lake. The log in the background is the area where Michele was sleeping in her sleeping bag, without a tent. PHOTO FROM CASE INCIDENT RECORD NUMBER A7623

This could be called "The Sleeping Bag Grizzly #4."

Michele was not in charge of their party of five, but she belonged. The companionship and safety found within a group are some of the pleasures of hiking and camping with others, under the vast bowl of stars. The experience perhaps reflects a comforting feeling of tribal-human origin. While a bear forages alone, people share safety in numbers. Michele and her four friends surely made enough noise, by their very passing, their conversation, their campsite organizing and laying out of sleeping bags, to warn off any grizzly bears.

During the four-and-a-half-hour period from the beginning of the Granite Park Campground grizzly attack to the time it took Julie Helgeson to die, Michele Koons and her group of friends were also attacked by a predatory grizzly bear. The bear had begun its investigation and food taking at Michele's and her friends' campsite around 8:00 p.m. *Predatory* here means that the probable motivation of the attack was to treat the human being as food—in other words, prey.

Michele, like Julie Helgeson (chapter 1), was also a nineteen-year-old college student, and also an employee of Glacier Park, Inc., the Park's concessioner. She worked as a general clerk in the gift shop at Lake McDonald Lodge, and this was her first year of employment. Michele, from San Diego, died in Glacier Park, as stated in her death certificate, "due to severe hemorrhage and shock due to mauling and partial devouring by bear."

The Trout Lake area had had frequent warnings of serious bear trouble. Nine days before, a grizzly already noted for aggressive actions toward people had caused trouble once again at Trout Lake. "Encounter Bear at Trout Lake" reads a newspaper clipping from *Hungry Horse News* of Friday, August 4, 1967, included in the Glacier Park Case Incident Record Number A7623. "John Cook and Steve Ashlock, 14-year-old Columbia Falls youths, were [the] latest to have an encounter with a bear at Trout Lake."

> The boys were out on the logjam, and returned to their camp about 8:30 p.m. to see what they believe was a grizzly bear—a big one—going toward their packs.
>
> Steve remarked: "We threw rocks and yelled, but he got madder, and reared up, and continued toward our packs."
>
> The boys returned to the logjam, and heard him ripping up the packs.
>
> Next the bear went to the lake for a drink and then toward the boys. A dead fish distracted him. The bear ate the fish and returned to the packs.
>
> The frightened youths left for the Lake McDonald Ranger Station 5½ miles away, and reported the mishap to Seasonal Ranger Leonard Landa.
>
> Next door, the Clacks put them up overnight and gave them a good breakfast.
>
> Steve and John returned to Trout Lake the next morning. Packs were damaged, food tins punctured and the pup tent slightly damaged.
>
> Incidentally, they caught 14 cutthroat trout.[2]

Eight days later, on August 12, Michele, accompanied by a young man, another couple with a leashed dog, and a third young man set out for their overnight adventure at the backcountry campsite, carrying packs, fishing gear, food, and sleeping bags. Michele wore a sweatshirt which read "Calif. W. College," blue jeans, a cotton flower-print shirt, a pink scarf, and a brown [later indicated as green] belted suede jacket.

Michele had accomplished her goal: to hike the steep trail to Trout Lake at an altitude of 3,980 feet. She looked around: The campsite was in a bowl circled by mountains. Howell Ridge above was densely forested with pine, fir, and spruce. Serviceberries and huckleberries (bear favorites) grew there, and rainbow trout swam in the lake, which could be crossed by a logjam at this lower end.

Then, "A bear is coming!" Michele told one of her fellow hikers, a young man.

During his later interview, this young survivor provided a handwritten statement (also transcribed into typewritten form), both of which are included in the Glacier Park Case Incident Record Number A7623. This and the subsequent survivor statements were given to park ranger Laurel W. Dale that same day, August 13. The young man describes their hiking group meeting up and starting out for their adventure to Trout Lake.

"[Names redacted] came over to Lake McDonald Lodge on 8/12/67 at 11:00 [a.m.] approx. Approx. 12:00 p.m. the five of us hitchhiked to base to Trout Trail, and started the trail about 2:00 p.m. After setting up camp at the end of Trout Lake," he continued, "and putting food in trees, we went fishing until 8:00 p.m."

> After fishing we started supper and from the same direction that the wind was blowing Michele noticed a bear. She said, "A bear is coming." We left the camp and started a new setup with firewood while the bear ate our food (½ hour). Then [we] went up to the old camp and got sleeping bags, blankets and a few cookies. We decided to stay because it was too dark and the flashlight would not suffice to go back home; because at that time it appeared the bear had left across a logjam.

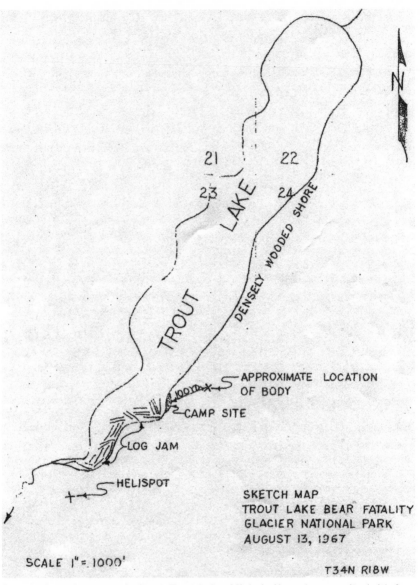

SKETCH MAP
TROUT LAKE BEAR FATALITY
GLACIER NATIONAL PARK
AUGUST 13, 1967

SCALE 1"=1000'

T34N R18W

Sketch shows bear attack site at Trout Lake. Michele Koons's campsite (with four other persons) is indicated above the logjam at the bottom of the lake. From the campsite the solid line in the middle indicates the 100-yard distance to where she was found (center of sketch).

ILLUSTRATION FROM CASE INCIDENT RECORD NUMBER A7623

The bear or bears (?) wandered through the campsite all night. [Redacted] was asleep and the bear ripped through his bag and his shirt and he ran to a tree. [Redacted] did likewise after they were bothered.

Michele and myself were also shortly after confronted by the bear; after sniffing me, he started tearing into Michele's bag and there was no way she could get out. After a couple of minutes I also ran up a tree (4:30 in morning). We remained in the tree until it was light enough and could hear the bear carrying off the bag and Michele. Just after we left the site at daybreak (6:00 a.m.), [redacted] later told us she had spotted the bear. Arrived at the ranger station about 8:00 a.m.

(Signed August 13, 1967)

[Name redacted]

Describing the moment just before Michele first saw the bear, the young man of the second couple told his interviewers that "We fished till about 8:00 and [redacted] started cooking a hot dog, and a trout that he had caught."

Michele was sitting on a stump when a bear appeared no more than 10 feet from her. At this time we left the camp (8:15 p.m.) and observed the bear go through and eat the food. Within 15–20 min. the bear left the area for the woods. We moved the camp area to the edge of the lake hoping that the large fire we built would keep any bear away.

We got to sleep about 11:00–11:30 [p.m.] and [were] awakened about 2:30 a.m. by a bear looking around the camp. We stayed still and didn't move, with the sleeping bags over our heads. He went away soon. The same incident occurred somewhat later, and we could hear the bear going through the bushes and water in the near and far distance.

About 4:15 a.m. the bear came back—sniffed [redacted] and me, then went to [redacted] and took a swing at his sleeping bag, tearing the sweatshirt on his back. Immediately he climbed a tree—at this point I saw our chance ([redacted] and I) to get out of the camp to a tree. [Name redacted] thought we would be safer to stay still in the sleeping bag. Refusing to go, I pulled her out of the bag, ran down the beach, and helped her up a tree, then I got into a tree myself.

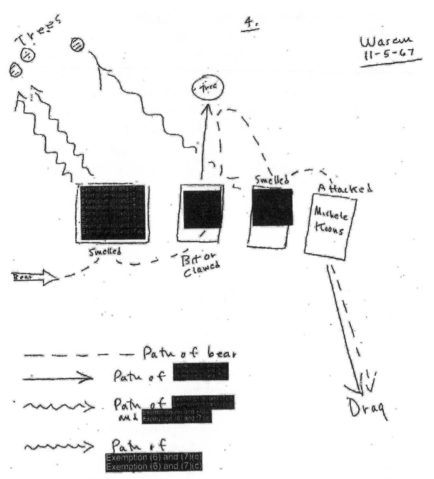

Sketch shows Michele Koons's campsite with four sleeping bags in a row. The bear smelled the first one, bit or clawed the second, smelled the third. At the fourth sleeping bag (shown to far right), the bear attacked Michele and dragged her away. ILLUSTRATION FROM CASE INCIDENT RECORD NUMBER A7623

As I was doing these things I could hear [redacted] yelling to Michele and [redacted] to get out of their sleeping bags. As I could tell, [redacted] came out of his unzipped sleeping bag, running, and within a few seconds I heard Michele yell out "My arm is gone," and then soon again she yelled out "Oh my God—I'm dead."

[Name redacted] stayed in the tree a while longer, which was right in the camp area, but soon got down and came to a tree where we were (approx. 4:30 a.m.). We stayed in the trees till 5:50 a.m., when it became light enough to see the trail. We could still hear the bear rustling in the brush, so we did not go to check if Michele was dead or alive. I thought I could hear the bear crushing her bones, so we decided negatively on looking for her.

We hiked back to the McDonald road and got a ride with a man getting ready to hike in to Trout Lake. He and his wife took all of us to the ranger station, where we told the story to the ranger. [Name redacted], the ranger, and I went to Trout Lake again with a first-aid kit and a gun to check on Michele's condition.

(Signed August 13, 1967)

[Name redacted]

In another statement from a second young man, he estimated the time Michele first saw the grizzly as an hour later that evening.

At 9:00 p.m. Michele spotted a grizzly and we took off. We stopped 50 yds or so down the beach. He proceeded to eat all our food. He left and we went back and gathered packs, wood, and took it down the beach. We saw the bear cross the ford of logs. We built a big fire and sat and talked. I dozed off after a while (11:30 or so), and when I awoke they told me a grizzly had been sniffing around the camp.

It was somewhere around 3:00 [a.m.]. We built up the fire and they went to sleep. I was awake for a long time. Then I heard splashes in the water and all kinds of noises. He came [bear] from the shore and smelled [names redacted]. Then he came at me. I lay perfectly still and hoped he would go. Instead he bit into the bag and I lit out. I must have scared him like he did me. Ray said he jumped back. But I was almost to the tree by then, and I climbed a good 35–40 ft.

The bear followed lazily to the trunk of the tree and stood up. Then [names redacted] took off. The bear retreated for 6 steps or so and went to [redacted] and Michele. He sniffed [redacted] and then went to Michele. [Name redacted] then lit out and ran to [redacted].

Michele couldn't get out of her zipped bag. The bear started to pull and drag the bag over the logs. I was right above him since I had no chance of running to [redacted]. Michele screamed something like "He's got my arm off." Then I yelled for her to unzip and she said the bear had the zipper in his mouth or something. Then she screamed— "Oh God, I'm dead."

I heard no more sounds from her. The bear just dragged the bag up the hill and I heard bones crunching.

As soon as he was 50 yds away I went down and put some clothes on, having been in my underwear. I joined [names redacted] and we stayed treed till 6:00 (1 and ½ hours). Then we took off. It was then that I noticed how badly ripped my sweatshirt was, from the bear. He just missed. I saw it was ripped at 4:30 [a.m.], but didn't know how serious it was. We couldn't be sure if it was 1 or 2 bears.

(Signed August 13, 1967)

[Name redacted]

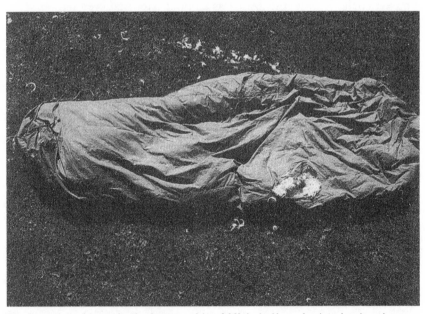

The bear ripped tears in the bottom side of Michele Koons's sleeping bag (opposite the zipper side), in which she was sleeping at Trout Lake on August 13, 1967. PHOTO FROM CASE INCIDENT RECORD NUMBER A7623

In another statement to interviewers, the young woman of the second couple described being somewhat bear-aware, and that the group had tried to keep their food out of reach of any hungry bears.

Michele and [redacted] joined us on this hike at Lake McD. Arrived at Trout Lake about 5:00 p.m. Set up camp at the fireplace site. Put all food in one knapsack and hoisted it up in a tree. Then all 5 of us went fishing. We fished in and near the camp until about 8:00 p.m.

Hot dogs were being cooked [when] Michele said, "Here comes a bear." It came right into camp. All of us ran to the beach. The bear rummaged through camp, eating the food, as it was all out. It took one of the packs, or something anyway, up the hill and began tearing it up. Then it came back to the camp. It was in camp about 20 min. We started to build another fire by the beach.

Suddenly the bear just left camp and went across the logs at the foot of the lake. We moved all of our sleeping equipment down to the beach. We left all of our other food at the old camp, other than a bag of cookies and some Cheez-Its. We built the fire up to a good size, brought in more wood for the fire and [to use] kind of as a barricade. We stayed because we only had one small flashlight.

We had intended to go to Arrow Lake and use the cabin, but we met some people who said it was already full [emphasis added].

[Name redacted] crawled into his bag, but couldn't get the zipper up, so it was partially open. I and Ron laid on one sleeping bag and opened another and used [it] as a blanket. Michele and [redacted] were in their respective sleeping bags. We were all in a semicircle around the fire. [Names redacted] and I fell asleep, eventually. I think the other two were also.

After I had been asleep for about 2 hrs., I heard something. I looked out and I thought I saw the bear. I told everyone to duck into their bags. The bear seemed to walk at the edge of the water and went up to the original camp. The campfire had died to coals by now. [Names redacted] tried to build up the fire again, and they also set the cookies that were left out on a log. The fire was beginning to burn well and all got into our sleeping bags again. The bear then came back and I heard the bear snatch the cookie bag and take it away. He walked over and around the camp. It got real quiet and seemed like the bear was gone. We kept building the fire up. [Name redacted] finally awoke then. We all laid there and waited for daylight.

The bear could be heard in and around the camp all night long. Once we heard the bear in the water and also immediately in the brush above us; this is when we thought there were more than one.

Suddenly, I saw the bear come loping toward me because of the campfire. I could see its face and hear it breathing. I crawled into my bag. I could hear the ripping of a pack or bag as I lay inside my bag. The bear seemed to move around the back of the camp.

Suddenly, [redacted] jumped up and said, "The goddamn bear tore my shirt," and he was up in a tree immediately. (This is what I heard.) I peeked out once and saw [redacted] standing up. I heard the bear coming toward us and [redacted] said that [we've] got to go, and make a run for the trees. [Name redacted] stood up and shouted and yelled and this must have startled the bear. We ran and made the trees near the original camp. [Name redacted] helped me up a tree and then he climbed up next to me.

I could hear [redacted] shouting and telling Michele and [redacted] to run, and we started yelling to them also to run. I couldn't see any of this, as we were too far from the campfire.

I heard Michele screaming. Paul could see what the bear was doing and kept us informed. The next thing I saw and heard was [redacted] running toward us and shouting for me. He seemed to be in shock. [Name redacted] yelled, "He's pulling her up the hill." [Michele] screamed; we kept yelling to her, but we heard no more from her.

[Name redacted] was yelling, "She's dead, she's dead!"

We stayed in the trees until daylight. [Names redacted] climbed down, got jackets and shoes, got us down, and we ran for the trail. I thought I saw the bear as we went up the trail but I didn't say anything to [names redacted]. I was not sure it was the bear. We got to the Lake McDonald Ranger Station about 8:00 a.m. and reported to the ranger.

This is approximately the story as recorded by Larry Dale.

(Signed August 13, 1967)

[Name redacted]

When their second turn to be interviewed by the investigating rangers arrived, the couple who had brought a leashed dog along, a young man and woman, further explained, "We did not know the rule that a dog was not allowed on the trail. The dog's name was Squirt and belongs to [redacted]. He was on a leash at all times and sometimes was carried by [names redacted]. The dog did not bark at all, not once as the party walked along the trail to the lake. As camp was being set up, the dog stayed near the camp with [redacted] and Michele Koons."

The couple continued their account:

When four of the party went fishing, Michele had the dog, as she did not fish. When the bear was first noticed, the dog did not whimper or bark. [Name redacted] untied the rope and carried the dog to the lakeshore. All the time the bear was raiding the camp, [redacted] held the dog in her arms. He did not bark. [Name redacted] held the dog as wood was gathered for the campfire. A log was laid near the fire and the dog's leash was looped over the log and the rest of the leash was coiled right next to Denise and her sleeping bag. The dog was at this time in between the log and [redacted]. She had her arm and hands on the dog at all times. This was where the dog lay during the night.

Approximately at 2:00 a.m. the bear was heard over at the original campsite. [Name redacted] woke up, then. The dog put its front paws [words missing] and looked over at the area where the noise was coming from. It made a low growl in its throat. [Name redacted] put the dog under the sleeping bag and the dog laid there until [names redacted] ran for the trees at approximately 4:30 a.m.

The dog did not whimper at all when [redacted] yelled out at the time the bear tore his shirt and he jumped out of his sleeping bag. [Name redacted] and the dog just lay cuddled in their bag, she holding it in her arms. When [names redacted] ran for the trees, they left the dog. But before they ran, [redacted] had untied the collar from the dog's neck. [Names redacted] were momentarily discussing whether to run or not. As [names redacted] hesitated partway up the slight incline to where they climbed the trees, the dog came bounding over to them. Apparently it fled the sleeping bag at about the time [redacted] did, although she did not know this. [Name redacted] picked up the dog, helped Denise up the tree, and threw the dog up to [redacted].

The dog did not make any sound at all, all the time the two of them were in the tree together. The two boys were close enough to [redacted] and the dog to hear any noise from the dog, but heard none. As daylight came, [redacted] went into the camp and got some personal items and the collar and leash for the dog. They all then proceeded to the Lake McDonald Ranger Station.

Comment: We did not know the rule that a dog was not allowed on the trail, but we did know a dog must be kept on a leash while in the Park—as he was.

(Signed August 14, 1967)

[Names redacted]

The dog was not mentioned in the initial statement because we felt that its presence [was] not at all significant in the case.

(Signed August 14, 1967)

[Names redacted]

Looking for causative factors for the fatality, if there were any, park ranger R. Wasem noted among other items the presence of Michele Koons's cosmetics bag. In his report, a reconstructed account titled "Individual Bear Damage or Injury Report" for the Subdistrict McDonald [Lake], Wasem noted that "Party of five arrived and set up camp at Lower Trout Lake Campsite. Put all food up in tree in knapsack (was cosmetics bag in knapsack?) Fished."

His report continues:

8:00 [p.m.] [Party] stopped fishing. All but ultimate victim fished (how many fish caught, and how many handled the fish that were caught?).

8:10–8:15. Started cooking hot dogs.

8:15–9:00. Grizzly came into camp from direction wind was blowing (evidently smelled odors of cooking food and could not have been far away, as bear appeared within a few minutes after cooking began—bear very probably would have appeared eventually and would have done so if nothing had been cooked).

Bear came right into camp (bold, unafraid). All 5 ran down beach about 150 ft. as bear ate all food, tearing into packsack(s), which had been lowered to ground. (*Bear apparently interested only in food at this point. Cosmetics case may have been hauled away at this point* [emphasis added in original report].) Group set up new camp No. 2 alongside beach as bear continued to eat food.

8:30–9:20. Bear left camp by walking across logjam. Bear in camp about 20 min.

Group retrieved sleeping bags, blankets, etc. and 1 bag cookies and 1 box cheese crackers. Set up new camp and built large fire.

11:00–11:30. Group talked until then, then most dozed off.

1:00–2:30 a.m. Bear returned and wandered through Camp No. 2. Took cookies (*and may have made off with cosmetics bag at this point* [emphasis added in original report].)

2:30–4:15 a.m. Bear in and out of camp several times, could be heard in water and in bushes. (*May have taken cosmetics bag during this period* [emphasis added in original report].)

4:15 a.m. Bear came loping into camp—could be seen by campfire (*campfire burning according to one survivor*). (*Bear very bold—unafraid* [emphasis added in original report].) Group sleeping in semicircle next to fire.

A. Bear smelled [name redacted] with dog and [name redacted]—no follow-up.

B. Bear went to [redacted] and bit into bag or took a foot swipe at it, tearing shirt on his back. He leaped up and yelled a few words, then ran to a nearby tree and climbed 35–40 ft. into tree. Bear jumped back, apparently startled, then slowly followed to base of tree and stood up.

C. [Names redacted] then got out of bag and with dog ran to near[by] Camp No. 1 and he helped her into a tree and threw dog up, then he climbed up another tree. He had to argue a bit with her to get her to go, finally pulling her from sleeping bag. Bear retreated a bit while all this was going on—after it had come back from tree [redacted] had climbed.

D. The [three others] began shouting to [name redacted] and Michele Koons to leave bags and run (*noise and excitement may have excited bear further* [emphasis added in original report]).

E. Bear went to [redacted] and sniffed bag—no follow-up. [Name redacted] then climbed out of bag and ran to tree near [others] immediately after bear [undecipherable].

F. After sniffing momentarily at [redacted], the bear went to Michele and immediately began tearing into bag. (*She may not have been able to get zipper undone and/or bear had mouth on zipper part of time. Girl had no opportunity to get out* [of] *bag* [emphasis added in original report].)

G. [Name redacted] climbed tree at approx. 4:15 a.m.—only a few minutes after attack began.

H. [Name redacted] came out of his tree and ran to other 3 and climbed a tree in their vicinity.

4:15–6:00 a.m. [The others] stayed in trees remainder of night, until daylight.

6:00 a.m. 4 survivors climbed down from trees and immediately hiked away from area to McDonald R. S. [Ranger Station]. Two of party believed they saw bear in trees as they departed. Also heard it rustling in brush.

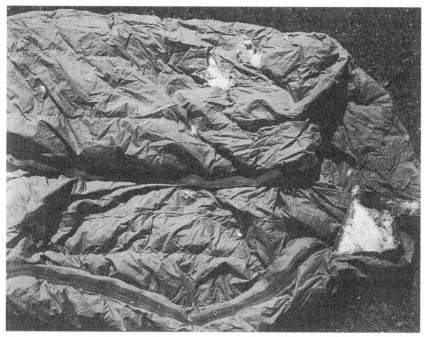

Close-up view of front side, upper portion of Michele Koons's sleeping bag, showing multiple rips and tears. PHOTO FROM CASE INCIDENT RECORD NUMBER A7623

So then, where was Michele, and what had happened to her? Finding Michele became the subject of park ranger Leonard I. Landa's August 22 report to the chief park ranger. "At 8:30 a.m. I left from the Ranger Station for Trout Lake. [Names redacted, two from the party of five, both men] went with me to point out the area of the incident. [At the time of the incident], they were afraid to look for Michele, as they were afraid the bear was still in the area. They thought they heard it still in the woods."

Landa's report continues:

We took my pickup and drove to the trailhead and started up the Trout Creek Trail. About ¼ mile up the trail I sent the boys back for a first-aid kit. About ½ mile up the trail the visitor [who had volunteered to come] tired, and I left him. The boys soon caught up with me and we went on together.

The boys and I arrived at Trout Lake about 10:00 a.m. We entered the camping area and called for Michele. We proceeded to the scene of the camp and began tracing for signs of Michele. We followed feathers from Michele's sleeping bag and found it about 20 feet above the camp. It was bloody and torn. We followed a blood trail for about another 52 feet and found a coat and blouse Michele had been wearing. They were badly torn and very bloody. Going up into the woods about 35 feet the boys and I found Michele's body. Because of the extensive mauling to the body, it was evident the girl was dead.

Just as we found the body, Max Edgar arrived by 'copter. Bert Gildart arrived by foot just after the 'copter.

Initially, Park engineer Max Edgar had volunteered his services that morning to help with the ongoing fire emergency in the park. Instead, he "volunteered to accompany the helicopter pilot on the search and rescue mission [for Michele]. After a quick look for a younger man and finding none available, my offer was accepted."

In his "Report on Bear Incident at Trout Lake," Edgar continued:

With the assistance of Chief Park Ranger Hart, a rescue kit consisting of blankets, Stokes litter, body bag, first-aid kit, morphine and hypodermic syringe, and a borrowed .30-06 rifle was assembled and packed on the helicopter. The helicopter lifted off at approximately 10:00 a.m. and arrived at Trout Lake about 10:30 a.m. We scanned the easterly shore of the lake without sighting the campsite. As we returned down the lake, the campsite was spotted and we swung around for a better look.

A young man rushed out on the lakeshore and waved us in. At the same time we noticed a man and his black horse close to the lakeshore. The pilot made several circles while he studied the situation and then came in for a hover landing on huge floating logs near the shore. I jumped from the helicopter, rifle in hand, and made my way ashore. The helicopter took off to make a normal landing on a hillside clearing at the foot of the lake.

The horseman, (Mr. [redacted] of Columbia Falls, Montana), informed me that an armed ranger and two young men were already in the area searching for the girl. He said they had found an ear near the campsite. I started up the hill and met Seasonal Ranger Leonard Landa. He informed me that he had found the girl and that she was dead.... I estimated the body, where found, was approximately one hundred yards from the campsite....

The upper portion of the body was nude. The lower portion of the body was clothed in the remnant of a blue stretch denim skirt, and there was a sanitary belt around the waist. There was a silver or white gold ring on the third finger of the right hand. The ring was about ⅜ [of an inch] wide with a raised ridge in the center of the band.

Both rangers, the horseman, and the pilot assisted me in placing the body in the body bag. I noticed that the body was still limp; rigor mortis had not yet set in. The bag was placed in the litter and the ranger, pilot, and I carried it to the helicopter. As we started out for the 'copter, a blood-drenched piece of cloth and a bloodstained belted suede leather jacket were picked up from the ground and placed on the litter. I do not recall how close these objects were to the point where the body was found. The cloth was a cotton print white with pink and blue flowers.

Leaving the .30-06 rifle with Ranger Gildart, we took off with the helicopter and returned to Headquarters with the body. During the return flight, radio contact was made with Headquarters to inform the Superintendent that the girl was dead. I also learned at this time that her name was Michele Koons.

Upon arrival at Headquarters the body was transferred to a patrol vehicle and delivered to [name redacted] at the Waggener & Campbell Funeral Home. I assisted [him] in removing the body from the bag and escorted it to the mortuary.

While there I saw the body of the Granite Park bear victim. I noticed puncture wounds in the legs and asked what caused the girl's death. Mr. [redacted] explained that the bear had bitten through the back chest wall exposing the lung and that the girl had bled to death....

Earlier that morning, at 8:30, assistant superintendent Jack B. Dodd was still considering the possibility (and hoping) that Michele had survived.

At that hour, in his notes, typewritten later as a report, Dodd wrote that "Chief Ranger Hart informed me while I was at the Park Administration Building that a bear incident had been reported to him involving a troublesome bear at Trout Lake by Seasonal Ranger Leonard I. Landa. He had instructed Ranger Landa to go to Trout Lake with a rifle and to eliminate the bear."

Dodd's report continues:

At 8:45 a.m., Dodd wrote that he was informed "Miss Koons was still at Trout Lake and was injured."

At 9:00 a.m., Dodd added, "The last thing heard from Miss Koons was her screaming and saying that the bear was tearing her arm off. Also that she was dying. . . . Seasonal Ranger R. C. Gildart was dispatched with a rifle . . . to Trout Lake in order to assist Ranger Landa, who had taken two of the three young men back to Trout Lake with him."

At 9:20 a.m., after another helicopter and pilot could not be located, the sleeping pilot who had previously flown first the injured young man, and then the body of Julie Helgeson out of the backcountry at Granite Park Chalet, was awakened. Also, "It was immediately decided by [Chief Ranger] Hart and myself to close the two trails to Trout Lake, such as had been done at Granite Park."

At 10:00 a.m., the helicopter took off for Trout Lake, carrying Park Engineer Max Edgar, first-aid supplies, and a rifle.

At 11:30 a.m., "Helicopter with pilot and Max Edgar returned to Park Headquarters with body of girl. Edgar took body on to Kalispell [Montana] in a station wagon."

At 12:25 p.m., Assistant Superintendent Dodd wrote that he called the coroner in Kalispell to verify the identification. "He described the wearing apparel of the girl. Said she had on remains of blue denim shorts, and remains of a white blouse with printed design, a green suede leather jacket and a broad band ring on her right hand and a ring with a setting for an emerald-shaped stone on the third finger of the left hand; however, the stone was missing. He advised that fingerprints would be taken and photographs of the body."

At 12:55 p.m., a reporter from the *Great Falls Tribune* called, "but the name of the girl was withheld." Next to call were reporters from CBS News in New York City and CJHG Television in Lethbridge, Alberta, Canada.

At 1:40 p.m., Glacier Park Superintendent Neilson was able to reach the father of Michele Koons, and had the very difficult task of informing him of the death of his daughter.

Decades later, Michele's parents spoke of receiving that telephone call and the sorrow of their loss to interviewers for the documentary film, Montana PBS's *Glacier Park's Night of the Grizzlies*. "She was always thinking of other people," Mr. Koons said of his daughter, Michele. And he also added, "I think about what civilization has done to bears."

A last task remained to be done on August 13, 1967. An unidentified member of Park personnel handwrote a "Grizzly Bear Disposal Report," which followed the search for the bear (or bears) responsible:

Bert Gildart and I left for Trout Lake at about 2:00 p.m. 8/14/67 [the day after the attack] from Lake McDonald Ranger Station. Going on in we saw no fresh bear sign or bear in the Trout Lake area.

We arrived at Trout Lake at 5:00 p.m. We put out salmon for bait and stayed at the Lower Trout Lake Campground until 8:45 p.m. We saw no sign of the bear to this time.

We left for the Arrow Lake shelter cabin at 8:45. On the way up the trail we saw fresh grizzly tracks and droppings but did not see the bear.

On 8/15/67 we planned to leave the shelter cabin at 4:00 a.m., but because of poor shooting light we stayed around the cabin. At about 5:40 a.m. Bert said he saw a bear outside. We both got our rifles ready and waited for more sign of the bear. About five min. after first sighting the bear, it appeared again directly in front of us, coming up the bank from the creek in front of the Arrow Lake cabin. The bear seemed to have little fear of us. We were talking at the time it came over the bank, and upon seeing us the bear made no attempt to run or hide.

The bear looked at us and after starting up over the bank a couple times it stopped and studied us carefully. At this point Bert and I shot the animal. One shot from each of our rifles immediately killed the bear at 5:45 a.m.

Behavior of the bear exhibited little fear of man. I am sure the bear must have been aware of our presence in the area before coming around the cabin. We had been talking both outside and inside the cabin so it should have heard us. We were also talking after the bear was first sighted. Instead of leaving when first sighted, the bear went down the bank to the creek and then came up the bank again, closer to us. The bear made no attempt to lunge or run toward us, nor did it show any fear by making an attempt to run.

Although Julie Helgeson and Michele Koons were finally found, questions are still asked to this day about what happened to them, and why. The official Glacier Park report on the two grizzly-caused deaths included detailed explanations according to what was known at that time. A portion of the "Grizzly Bear Attacks at Granite Park and Trout Lake, August 13, 1967" report is reproduced here.

In analyzing the two incidents, a number of details common to both are evident. These are:

1. Both occurred to group campers—five in the party at Trout Lake and two at Granite Park. In addition, three other campers were nearby at Granite Park.
2. All three persons injured or killed in the attack were young people in their late teens.
3. Both incidents occurred on August 13, 1967.
4. Both occurred in the early morning darkness about 4½ hours apart.
5. The camping sites were both in the backcountry, reached only by trail. Both were over 4 miles from the nearest road by trail.
6. Weather conditions were identical—cool (temperature in the upper forties), clear, dry, and very calm, with light smoke haze from several forest fires.
7. There was no evidence of provocation, teasing, or molestation of the bears by any of the campers.

8. There was no evidence that the campers had any drugs or that the bears could have eaten any.

9. No drugs or rodent control poisons are used at these camping sites.

10. Both attacks were directed to people lying on the ground in the open and in sleeping bags.

11. Both victims killed were Caucasian females.

12. The Trout Lake girl [Michele Koons] was in her monthly menstrual period, while the Granite Park victim [Julie Helgeson] evidently expected her period to begin at any time.

13. Both suspect bears were old adult females of about average size (225 and 265 pounds).

14. Both attacks occurred within 28 to 32 hours after a severe, dry lightning storm.

15. Neither victim made an attempt to escape until attack had begun.

16. These two deaths by grizzly bears were the first known in the recorded history of the Park.

Major differences between the two attacks were:

1. One grizzly (Granite Park) had two cubs. The Trout Lake grizzly had none.

2. There was some first-quarter moonlight remaining at the Granite Park attack. There was no moonlight at Trout Lake at 4 a.m.

3. The campers at Granite Park had no campfire, while those at Trout Lake kept one blazing most of the night.

4. Little food was in possession of the Granite Park campers. Those at Trout Lake had been unwillingly feeding the bear periodically for eight hours.

5. The Trout Lake bear did consume some human flesh. There was no evidence that this was the case involving the Granite Park bear [despite statement by ranger-naturalist Joan Devereaux that "large chunks of (Julie Helgeson's) flesh were gone"; see chapter 1].

6. The attack at Trout Lake was the culmination of 8 hours of intermittent harassment on the part of the bear. At Granite Park the attack was sudden and unexpected.

7. The Trout Lake site was near a lake at 3,890 feet elevation in a heavily forested spruce-fir zone. That of Granite Park was on mountain

terrain at approximately 6,300 feet near the Continental Divide in the very upper limits of the spruce-fir zone.

8. The sow grizzly at Granite Park had a deep laceration in the pad of one hind foot. The Trout Lake grizzly had no apparent physical defects or injuries.

Was the Killer Bear [at Granite Park] Destroyed?

The third bear (the sow with cubs, thought to be the offender) was destroyed at Granite Park at 12:50 a.m., August 15, 1967. This was exactly 48 hours and 5 minutes after the fatal attack. There was no blood on the animal's muzzle or on feet or claws; however, the 48-hour lapse would allow blood remains to wear or rub off the animal. Several small dark stains were noted on several front claws and the pad of one front foot. These were sent to the FBI Laboratory in Washington, DC, along with several hairs taken from the animal's mouth. Neither the stains nor the hair were of human origin.

Was the Killer Bear [at Trout Lake] Destroyed?

Specimens of the bear's stomach contents were sent to the FBI Laboratory in Washington, DC. Examination of the specimens at the FBI Laboratory revealed that the stomach contents had human hair, thus leaving little doubt that this was the attacking bear.

(**Note:** One other possibility is that this bear was an opportunistic feeder that came across the body after the attacking bear left, and consumed human hair at that time.)

The official report concerning the Trout Lake grizzly concluded:

In Summation

From the statements, interviews, and other investigations, it appears that an aggressive hungry old grizzly sow ignoring a burning fire came into a campsite occupied by five people at Trout Lake. The bear had obtained food several times earlier at the same location. It caused four people to run and climb trees. Resultant confusion and noise probably excited the animal, which, upon encountering the only member of the party remaining within reach, proceeded to vigorously attack and drag the victim away. The victim, a girl, was a regular user of several cosmetics, and in addition was experiencing her menstrual period. Body odors from either or both possibly caused the bear to press its attack upon this particular person. Physiological stress resulting from extensive lightning storms and old age with corresponding physical ailments of the bear, and unknown reasons, might have been factors in the attack.

Questions were raised in the Glacier Park investigators' minds about the fact that Julie Helgeson carried two tampons in her pack, and that Michele Koons was wearing a sanitary belt.

Are bears attracted to menstrual odors?

In his 2002 information paper, "Bears and Menstruating Women," Yellowstone bear management specialist Kerry A. Gunther stated that a study by Cushing (1983) suggested that "polar bears are attracted to odors associated with menstrual blood." Gunther added, "Herrero (1985) analyzed the circumstances of hundreds of grizzly bear attacks on humans, including the attacks on the two women in GNP [Glacier National Park], and concluded that there was no evidence linking menstruation to any of the attacks. The responses of grizzly bears to menstrual odors have not been studied experimentally." As for black bears, Gunther cited Rogers et al. (1991): "Menstrual odors were essentially ignored by black bears of all sex and age classes."

Gunther reported that

[t]he question [of] whether menstruating women attract bears has not been completely answered (Byrd 1988). There is no evidence that grizzlies are overly attracted to menstrual odors more than any other odor, and there is no statistical evidence that known bear attacks have been related to menstruation (Byrd 1988). However, park visitors have been injured and killed by bears (Gunther and Hoekstra 1996). If you are uncomfortable hiking and camping in bear country for any reason, you should probably choose another area for your recreational activities.[3]

Could the outcome for Julie, Roy, and Michele possibly have been changed? While there are many things you can do to improve your chances of enjoying a safer outdoor experience, there is no guarantee (see chapter 30, "Safer Travel in Glacier Park Bear Country").

Nine years after 1967's "Night of the Grizzlies," an eerily similar grizzly-caused death occurred, in 1976. Once again, a young woman was dragged from her sleeping bag by a grizzly, but this time it didn't happen near the remote, roadless Granite Park Chalet, or the forested wilderness of Trout Lake. Instead, it took place at the Many Glacier car campground, near the Park's famous Many Glacier Hotel. This could be called "The Sleeping Bag Grizzly #5." See the next chapter.

PART 2

FATAL SUMMER OF THE GRIZZLIES, 1976

3

FINDING MARY PAT

1976: THE MANY-GLACIER TWIN GRIZZLIES (PLUS MOTHER BEAR?)

I woke up to the sounds of a bear and buried myself in my sleeping bag and remained very still but was continually being pulled toward the opposite end of the tent, where my friend was being attacked. She was emitting low screams and my sister, in the middle, was telling her to lie still—play dead.
    —STATEMENT OF WITNESS [NAME REDACTED], EXHIBIT #19

Fatality: Mary Patricia Mahoney
(Two male sub-adult bears killed, none proven responsible)

National Park Service–Glacier Park
Case Incident Record Number 761630
Location: Many Glacier Campground, Site #74
Date/Time: Thursday, September 23, 1976, approximately 7:00 a.m.

In the dark, in Glacier Park, we humans like to think that we are safe where we sleep. There we lie sprawled, helpless as babies, consciousness clouded, until the waking self arrives to pick us up again. If we don't feel safe, we would have trouble falling asleep.

Mary Pat Mahoney, age twenty-one, was sleeping in her red sleeping bag in her tent, with two friends, in the Many Glacier Campground near

Mary Pat Mahoney's tent, in which she was asleep with two friends, was extensively torn and then entered by the attacking grizzly, which dragged her away.
PHOTO FROM CASE INCIDENT RECORD NUMBER 761630

the famous Many Glacier Hotel. Two more friends slept in a second tent close by. The friends' vehicle was parked near their tents at Campsite #74. Fourteen other persons slept in the auto campground that night, and a ranger was on duty at the trailer that was functioning as the Many Glacier Ranger Station. The night was cool and clear, with only the sound of a light wind. The time was just before dawn.

G. George Ostrom's 1976 article for *Hungry Horse News* (Kalispell, Montana) was headlined "Where the Girl Died." In it he described the scene as it was the night Mary Pat slept there:

> Many Glacier Campground sits in the jack pines just west of Swiftcurrent Lake. The campground itself is one of the most popular in Glacier Park, not because of its immediate facilities, but because it is surrounded . . . and almost overwhelmed by the magnificence of its setting. To this writer, Many Glacier is one of the most beautiful spots on the face of the earth, towering peaks, glaciers, rich forests, and abundant wildlife ranging from beavers and chickadees to bighorn rams and eagles. It is a paradise on earth, but last Thursday morning it was turned into a hell by rampaging grizzly bears.[4]

The grizzly bears he referred to were the so-called Twin Grizzlies, young adults between two and three years old, both males, brownish-black with silver-tipped hairs. Their mother had been seen with them several times earlier that summer. Grizzly mothers are known for their fierce protection of their young, risking their own lives at times to save their cubs. They give birth, suckle their cubs, and accompany them while teaching them what they will need to know when the mothers are no longer with them.

But at some point, fertility intervenes, and the female grizzly drives off her young, forcing them to survive on their own. She then mates with a male grizzly. This had been observed to occur in this case, meaning the orphaned Twin Grizzlies faced an uncertain future, alone. Without their mother, they chose to stay together for a while.

—⁓—

Mary Pat was also a young adult, a University of Montana (Missoula) student. She and her four friends were eager to see the sights at Many Glacier, and to enjoy each other's company. They drove their car, as directed, to the far-east side of Many Glacier Campground, two hundred feet from park ranger Fred Reese's trailer, and nosed the vehicle into Campsite #74.

They set up two tents next to the car, shaking out their down sleeping bags and laying them inside. In the first, a two-man tent, Mary Pat chose to sleep on the right side, next to the thin tent wall. The second young woman chose the middle, and the third (the second one's sister) stretched out on the left. The two other friends crawled into sleeping bags in their own tent. And so to sleep.

Before dawn arrived (which would not occur until 7:13 a.m.), the temperature grew slightly cooler, with a forecast of showers and thunderstorms to come. Light was slowly growing brighter around Mary Pat's tent, which was an A-frame made of red, purple, and yellow nylon. The time was approximately 7:00 a.m.

Then a Glacier Park horror occurred.

A grizzly bear penetrated through the right side of Mary Pat's and her two friends' tent at Campsite #74. It was after something—but what? There was no food in the tent.

—◦—

What Mary Pat and her friends did not know was that a culvert-type bear trap had been baited and set up at the opposite end of the Many Glacier Campground. Rope barriers, streamers, and barricades divided it from the rest of the campground. Its purpose was to capture a grizzly, hopefully one of the Twin Grizzlies, which had threatened a number of people late that summer. At the Many Glacier Campground itself, the bear pair had already gotten food from the top of a bear-proof garbage can. The Twins were easy to identify, because they were the same size (210 and 220 pounds) and the same silver-tipped dark color, and they traveled together.

As ranger Robert R. Frauson explained later to the Glacier Park Board of Inquiry, the bear trap was set in response to the Twin Grizzlies' activities just days before Mary Pat's mauling. Four days before, the Twin Grizzlies had visited Fishercap Lake (located just two-tenths of a mile from the Many Glacier Campground), threatening people in broad daylight. This "incident that occurred recently, [without] food orientation, was at Fishercap Lake this past Sunday, [with] two fishermen and a girl, local Montanans."

Frauson continued:

The girl was sunbathing on the east shore on the sand and two bears approached and went up and sniffed her feet.

This girl played dead and the bears continued around the south end of the lake to the west end inlet where these two fellows were fishing with waders. They saw bears coming and departed the area, and they moved out and probably ran along the north end of the lake, and [the] bears pursued, running also after them. One man elected to go into the lake and a bear followed him out into the lake. He layed [*sic*] into the lake and tried to make himself as inconspicuous as possible; [it's a] very shallow lake. Bear went out and grabbed him by one foot and shook him by the wader foot. He screamed and hollered, left, and the other man had gone to a tree, climbed a tree. The same bear went over to the tree, climbed the tree from the opposite side of the tree. The man fell out of the tree, departed for the lake, shed his waders, and waded out to the other man in the lake. The other man shed his waders, and they beat their way or swam or treaded down the middle of the lake. It's fairly shallow and muddy to the other end, and the girl came out to the area here.

And there was a man who observed this, [the] smelling of the girl's feet. He came in and alerted the rangers, and Ranger Reese responded, called Ranger Kortge at St. Mary, went up the valley, and in the meantime, the people had come east through the brush and into the area here. The rangers went up and cleared the area, closed the trail. They closed also the trail to Iceberg Lake and Ptarmigan for these two bears. The ranger stayed in the valley, went on up as far as Redrock Falls, Redrock Lake, and cleared people out of the valleys. . . .

Next, Ranger Frauson told the Board of Inquiry about another Twin Grizzlies encounter where the bears had obtained food, which occurred one day before Mary Pat's mauling.

The next incident [involving the two bears] would be two illegal campers, man and wife, from . . . Dearborn, Michigan, who hiked to Redrock

Lake, set up a camp, and had a camp there. The area was closed to hikers.
. . . These people were ticketed for illegal camping. . . . They gave a ranger
a rather rough time in a conversation. The people came back after this
time to their camp at Redrock to remove it. This is after the ticketing.
While they were at the camp, two bears came in and proceeded to [. . .]
get into their food at Redrock Lake. They departed on the other side of
the stream, just very close to them, and watch[ed] them dismantle their
food. They stayed there quite a while and then they decided that they
couldn't recover anything and departed for the ranger station here.

On moving to the ranger station the two bear[s] came close to
them and tended to follow them. They hollered at the bears and clapped
their hands, and the bears [desisted] and took off. They came in and
reported to Ranger Reese again that the bear[s] was up at their camp
and had taken the food. And this was at dusk when they arrived in
there, and it was at [that] time that Ranger Reese called me [about]
this incident.

And this is the prelude to the next day when the mauling, the fatality occurred. . . .

After the incident at Redrock Lake we set a trap in the west end
of the [Many Glacier] campground in case these bears came this way.

It was reported on this incident also that it was after dark or dusk
when this came about. Also in management our bulletin boards around
throughout the campground area here were geared toward being alert
to bears, protection of your food source, and the closures of trails, trail
junctions, and the like.

Also within the campground, the campground was barricaded with
rope barriers and streamers and barricades to concentrate the campers
toward the east end or near the ranger station.

—◦—

Mary Pat and her four friends were sleeping in their two tents, two hundred feet from the ranger station. The four survivors, interviewed at the
scene by ranger Fred W. Reese, described what happened next in their
written statements (Witness Exhibits #12, 19, 16, and 17):

Witness 1: I was in our tent when I was awakened by pawing. Mary Pat, the victim, was to my immediate right. She started screaming because the bear was pawing her. I told her to play dead, but evidently she was unable to because of shock. The bear, whose silhouette I saw, did not behave in any rational manner but was [unclear] tearing away when 2 of the party beeped the horn. . . . Sleeping bag torn up, and tent also.

Witness 2: I woke up to the sounds of a bear and buried myself in my sleeping bag and remained very still, but was continually being pulled toward the opposite end of the tent where my friend was being attacked. She was emitting low screams and my sister, in the middle, was telling her to lie still—play dead. The tent had fallen down. Our friends in another tent escaped and ran for the car and honked it, which scared the bear, and two of us ran for the car and told some campers nearby to tell the ranger.

Witness 3: I heard Mary Pat screaming and [saw] a bear around her. . . . I got out of the tent and ran to the car, where I started sounding the horn. I didn't see Mary Pat run away. I saw the bear—[a] young bear— run with a sleeping bag in his mouth.

Witness 4: We were sleeping in a tent next to the one in which the woman involved was sleeping. We heard heavy panting [from the bear], and our friend screaming. I was able to get out of my sleeping bag and run [with] my tentmate to the car, where we began blowing the horn. We saw the bear run off after blowing the horn for 1–2 mins. I saw him drag off a sleeping bag—don't know if Mary Pat was in it.

Where was Mary Pat? Now the desperate task was to find her, immediately.

"Where is your missing friend?" Ranger Reese asked the surviving young women. They were still huddled inside their vehicle, seeking refuge. In his handwritten note (page 68), the ranger (referring to himself as "Reese") details what the women said.

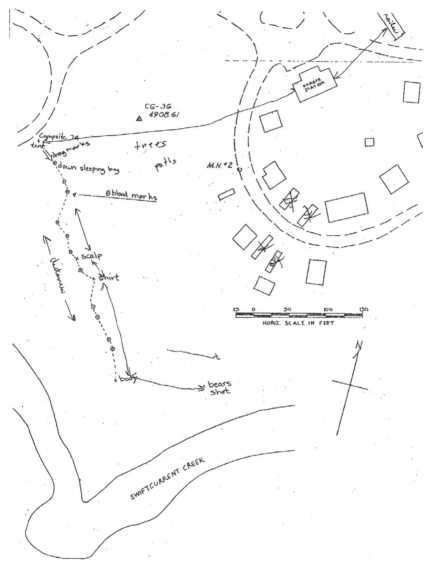

Sketch of Many Glacier Campground showing ranger station (top right) and Mary Pat Mahoney's Campsite #74 (top left, near road). Dotted line indicates the direction in which the bear dragged her (toward Swiftcurrent Creek). Circles indicate where fragments of sleeping bag and clothing were found. The line ends where the two bears were shot.

ILLUSTRATION FROM CASE INCIDENT RECORD NUMBER 761630

The girls stated, "Mary Pat Mahoney is missing. She may have run away. There was a bear in our tent." Reese asked what direction, and they were not sure of the direction. Reese proceeded to look for Mary Pat Mahoney, walking in a southerly direction from the campsite, into the woods. . . . At about 25 feet from the tent (which was collapsed), the sleeping bag was found, quite torn apart at one end and with a small amount of blood. In proceeding toward the south behind the campsite, a trail was found which included blood, parts of flesh, and a bloody pullover cotton T-shirt. This trail continued from the campsite to approximately 300 yards into the woods in a southerly direction, toward Swiftcurrent Creek. At this point the body of Mary Patricia Mahoney was found, facedown. A determination was made that she had no pulse or respiration. She had been partially eaten, particularly her left arm (almost completely gone from the shoulder blade to the wrist) and her middle back area.

Help arrived soon. Here is what Ranger Robert M. Frauson saw (handwritten in his "Supplementary Case/Incident Report") when he responded to the urgent call to help Ranger Reese.

When I pulled into the campground there was a group of vehicles to the left with people running around. Two girls were embracing each other and were hysterical. Fred Reese said a girl was dead (Mary Patricia Mahoney), in the brush toward the creek. There was a man (California State Park Ranger) with Fred. I asked if he could use a pistol, [and] he said yes. I gave him my .357 (loaded with hollow points). Told he and Fred to guard the body and help the other campers vacate the campground, which Fred had closed. (It was thought there was one bear.) The four girls were packing their camps. All other campers were notified earlier to pack up and move out. I got the girls' names and addresses from Fred and went to the ranger station at 7:45 and tried to radio Chief Ranger Sigler. The phone was also tried; neither would work. Found phone that would work but had trouble with the operator (they would say Wait a minute, and leave me hanging). Finally talked with Sigler about incident. . . .

I started to return to Campsite #74 in my vehicle when I received an URGENT radio call from Fred Reese that the bear was coming back to Mary's body. There was great confusion and hollering when I arrived at Site #74. Kortge radioed he was close near [name redacted] house. Fred Reese was shouting from the Fire Cache area, and there was still shouting from the direction of the creek. It was difficult to know which direction to go; then I heard [redacted] call that the bear was at the body and he was up a tree over the body, so I went that way just as Kortge and Altemus arrived. We (Frauson and Kortge) [ran] through the heavy lodgepoles and brush.

I sighted a bear off to my left a fair distance and shot it in the shoulder. It spun around toward me. Then I saw a second bear to the left of the one that I had shot. I lost sight of both bears. I called to Kortge that I had hit one, but there was a second bear. . . . We pressed forward to the creek; could find no bears, thought they had crossed Swiftcurrent Creek. Kortge did not see any bears. [Name redacted] joined us and we checked the gravel bars.

We started a sweep back through the lodgepoles with [name redacted] between Kortge and I. [Name redacted] saw a bear. I could not see it; Kortge shot it, and I came around besides Kortge and also shot the same bear. The bear that I had shot first was laying beside the other bear. I put another shot into the first bear I had shot and Kortge put a coup de grace into the head of each bear.

The bears were both dark-colored silvertips. We checked to make sure they were dead. I put the two shotguns back in my car and picked up some yellow engineer tape, felt pencil, and clipboard, so Kortge and Altemus could flag and map the route Mary had been dragged. (I called for a veterinarian to check the bears.)

We started at the body and walked back to Campsite #74. I photographed in black-and-white and color 35mm [film]. . . . Kortge, Altemus, and Frauson put Mary's body in a pouch at the site where she lay. . . . The body pouch with Mary's body in it was carried back along the route she had been dragged. Body parts were picked up by Frauson and placed in the pouch as we moved along. ([Pieces of] yellow engineer tape mark[ing] the spots were placed by Kortge and Altemus; [they]

also noted [locations] on their sketch map and photographed [them].)
[. . .]

I photographed the grizzlies as they examined [them]. We denoted
the bear that I had shot first by notching the right ear for identification.
We called it Bear #1. The one Kortge shot would be Bear #2. Both bears
had signs of blood on their front claws. Bear #2 had signs of blood on a
rear pad. Mouths were fairly clean ([they] may [have drunk] water from
stream after eating on girl). Old blood on nose of [Bear] #2. Mtn ash
berries [found] in intestinal tract.

Note: Neither bear had human remains in its intestinal tract. So then,
what bear (or bears) was responsible?

Mary's condition when I first saw her, she was laying facedown
[redacted].

At approximately 0725 hours [7:25 a.m.], [redacted] and Reese
returned to the campground and immediately notified all the campers of the death and to get up and evacuate the campgrounds. Everyone complied, and the campground was completely evacuated by 0745
hours [7:45 a.m.].

Mr. [redacted] was questioned by District Ranger Bob Frauson
about whether or not he was qualified to use a pistol. [Name redacted]
said, "Yes, I am." He was assigned to guard the body while Frauson
and Reese were making the necessary phone calls and interviewing the
victim's camp mates. [Name redacted] returned to the body at approximately 0740 hours [7:40 a.m.].

Reese took the four remaining girls from Campsite #74 to the
ranger station residence where Mary Ann Penttilla [a ranger's wife]
provided some coffee and assisted in trying to calm down the girls.
Statement-of-witness forms were given to each girl, and they were
allowed to fill these out at their leisure (exhibits #16, 17, 18, and 19).

[Name redacted] made out a statement-of-witness form (exhibit
#20).

Reese returned to the body site at about 0815 hours [8:15 a.m.].

At approx. 0823 hours [8:23 a.m.], a grizzly bear(s) came very aggressively toward the body from the west. Reese's weapon did not function.

[Name redacted] climbed up a tree in the immediate (40 feet) vicinity. Frauson and Lloyd Kortge, St. Mary sub-district ranger, came forward very quickly, to the body site. Frauson fired his shotgun and hit a bear. At this moment, a second bear was seen in the close vicinity of the other bear. Both bears disappeared. Frauson and Kortge went forward. Kortge suddenly saw a bear stand up on its back legs, 20 feet away. Kortge fired his shotgun and killed the second bear, which fell dead beside the other bear.

The bears were covered with some plastic and cardboard boxes to prevent a rapid deterioration and to aid in future examination.

The county coroner [name redacted] arrived and examined Mary Pat Mahoney, [and] removed the body to the coroner's office in Browning, Montana.

—pages one and two of three pages

What would you call a fatal bear attack in 1976?

Ranger Reese uses the terminology "Offense/incident code 420200—Death due to bear molestation." In his Supplementary Case/Incident Record, exhibit #7 consists of a student enrollment paper, and identification for Mary Pat Mahoney. Other exhibits include "Medal believed to belong to Mahoney which was found near the sleeping bag. This item is in storage at Park Headquarters." Also, "Eyeglasses belonging to Mahoney which were found at mauling scene. This item is in storage at Park Headquarters."

The kind woman who helped comfort the four survivors was Mary Ann Penttilla, whose husband was a ranger from the St. Mary Ranger Station in Browning, Montana. In her Supplementary Case/Incident Record, which is exhibit #22, she described the four friends' states of mind:

The girls were all in a state of confusion. [Name redacted] (sleeping in the middle of the three girls) awoke first and said "What's going on" as she felt a paw on her. She looked over to the side, by Mary Pat Mahoney

—U.S. DEPARTMENT OF THE INTERIOR —
NATIONAL PARK SERVICE
SUPPLEMENTARY CASE/INCIDENT RECORD

ORGANIZATION (PARK) NAME

Glacier National Park

CASE/INCIDENT NUMBER

7 6 1 6 3 0

LOCATION OF INCIDENT

Many Glacier Campground Site #74

DATE OF INCIDENT
MO 0 9 DA 2 3 YR 7 6

NATURE OF INCIDENT

Death Due to Bear Molestation

COMPLAINANT'S NAME

Mary Patricia Mahoney

COMPLAINANT'S ADDRESS

Exemption (6) and (7)(C) Highwood, ILL.

RESULTS OF INVESTIGATION

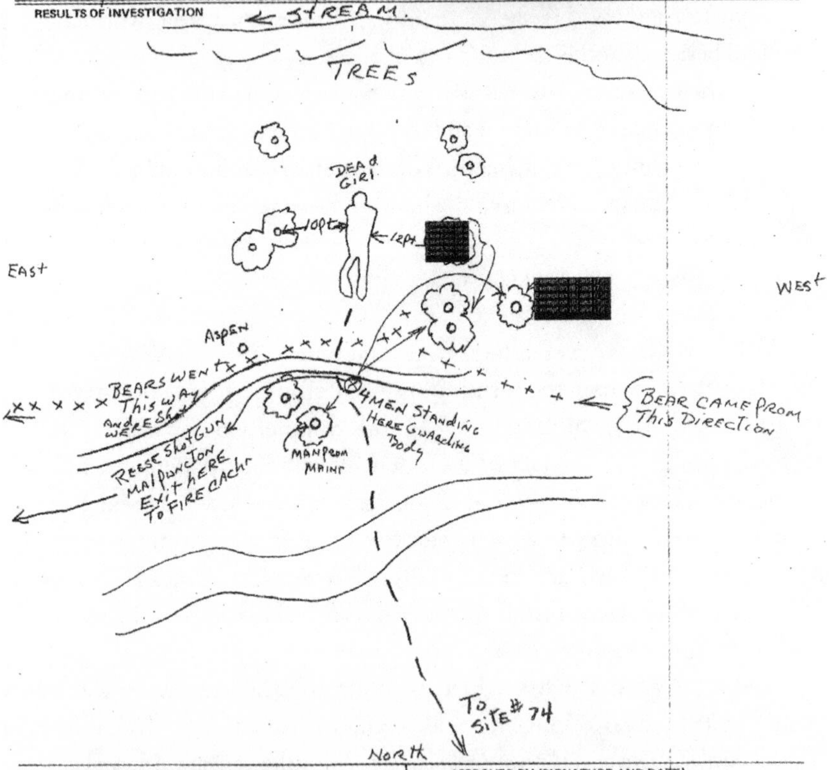

SUBMITTED BY (SIGNATURE AND DATE)

D.S. + M F... 9/29/76

APPROVED BY (SIGNATURE AND DATE)

Phil R. J.L. 10/7/76

Sketch shows Mary Pat Mahoney (figure at top center) when found. Dotted line from Campsite #74 (bottom of page) is direction from which a bear dragged her. A second bear appeared from the west (right side of page). Circled X at center indicates where four men stood guarding her body.

ILLUSTRATION FROM CASE INCIDENT RECORD NUMBER 761630

(deceased), and saw the silhouette of a bear in the darkened tent. She said, "Lie still; don't move." The sisters slipped down deep in their bags and were still. Mary Pat was groaning a low guttural sound and was not lying still. . . .

I asked the girls about their menstrual periods. None of them was having one. I asked if they were wearing perfume [or] deodorant, [and about] the clothes that they had cooked dinner in. They said they weren't [wearing perfume or deodorant], and that they had eaten only vegetables and cheese on the night of the 22nd of Sept. They said they had discussed what they would do if a bear came into their camp right before they went to sleep. They decided that they would play dead. They kept a fire going very late. . . .

[Name redacted] . . . was the most rational of the four girls, and convinced the two sisters not to go back into the woods and look at Mary Pat's body. They said they wanted to pay their last respects. [Ranger] Reese tried to convince them not to, and I told them that her body had already been placed in a body bag and that they probably could not see her anyway. [Name redacted] had been the best friend of Mary Pat Mahoney.

[Name redacted] was most unwilling to accept the death and became very pale. I had her lie down several times. She did not want to discuss the incident at all, and said that she knew no more than [redacted], and if anyone had any questions, [they should] ask [redacted]. She did not want to return to Missoula via Logan Pass.

The [names redacted] sisters were furious and scared. [Name redacted] was extremely bitter and taking [the] names of everyone. She wanted to know if these two bears that were shot had been seen before in the area.

—◦—

Would any one of us want to be ranger Bob Frauson, to whom fell the task of informing Mary Pat's family of her death? Frauson took witness statements from the four surviving women in the ranger station, and later wrote that he had "talked to them about Mary's religion and [the] best way to contact [her] family."

They thought it would be best to talk direct to the family and not through a priest or friend. One girl said she would talk with the family, but none really knew the phone number. I had trouble with [my] phone again, but finally got an operator who would stay with me. I contacted Mrs. [name redacted]. She said her husband was at work. I told her that I had very bad news.

I told her that her daughter had been camping with four other girls and was dead from a bear mauling. [I] tried to help her out. I told her I had contacted a priest [name redacted]) to administer last rites. . . .

I had each girl call their home immediately and talk with their family and what their plans were.

——◆——

It is now 2019, forty-three years later. Mary Pat's loss is grieved by her family and friends to this day. She was buried in Illinois at 9:15 a.m. four days after her death, the funeral attended by her parents, two brothers, and two sisters.

Those who only read about what happened to Mary Pat join her family in wanting answers. The Board of Inquiry findings are summarized in the Park news release of November 3, 1976, reproduced in part below.

A National Park Service Board of Inquiry which investigated the death of a 21-year-old Illinois girl in a grizzly bear attack in Glacier National Park reported her death was the first such incident to occur in a major park campground and lacked any apparent explanation or motive, Lynn Thompson, Director of the National Park Service's Rocky Mountain Region said today.

"The evidence is that there were more people–bear encounters within the park this year, and in the Many Glacier area in particular, than in any previous year," the board said in its final report. "With increasing visitation in the park . . . this trend can be expected to continue, with the possible result of more management problems and more incidents."

The Board of Inquiry said Mary Patricia Mahoney of Highwood, Illinois, and her four companions had followed or exceeded all recommended safety precautions prior to the fatal attack in the campsite they shared in the Many Glacier Campground the morning of September 23. Some 14 other persons occupied other campsites in the immediate area. The girls' campsite was clean, with neither food nor other odorous materials that might have attracted the bear, or bears. The board said it is questionable whether the fatal attack on Miss Mahoney could have been avoided. . . .

"Based on this experience," the board's report concludes, "it is apparent that guidelines should be developed for bear-related closure and management of developed areas, including campgrounds. Further, there may be a need for quicker analysis and interpretation of field observations and data so that they might be used in bear management actions."

Two bears were killed following this incident (the Twin Grizzlies, sub-adult bears). Considering the lack of forensic evidence involving the Twins (whose intestinal tracts showed no human remains), speculation in and outside of the Park Service centered on the theory that perhaps the female bear—their mother—might have attacked Mary Pat by herself. Her two sub-adult young, the Twins, once driven away, might have rejoined her afterward for a short time. According to this hypothesis, the Twins then approached the body and were the ones who chased the rangers up into trees. The Twins were the ones shot and killed, perhaps driving the female bear away, into cover. She was never found.

A number of Park Service personnel stated that an unknown adult grizzly bear appeared the next night at the Many Glacier Hotel area, rooting up earth, tossing rocks, and ripping down a snow fence. Was this the female bear returning to the scene? The Board of Inquiry considered this possibility, and its official report stated that "The [redacted] is inconclusive as to which bear did the mauling of Ms. Mahoney, or, indeed, whether the two bears destroyed were involved."

One Board of Inquiry member spoke up about the dangers of this possibility. "These two bears that are dead, they certainly didn't hesitate to hit people in the daytime. There is no reason to believe that there isn't another bear involved, who is actually a killer bear, and may decide to take somebody else in the daytime" (name redacted, "Board of Inquiry Transcript of Proceedings," exhibit 32, page 62).

— ◆ —

G. George Ostrom provided a requiem. In his September 29, 1976, *Hungry Horse News* article, subtitled "After the Girl Died," he concluded with this:

> I drove around the Lake and up onto the hill above the beautiful old hotel [Many Glacier Hotel] where I could gaze up both of the awesomely beautiful valleys that twist down from the Continental Divide into Swiftcurrent Lake. I thought about the dead girl and about the grizzly bears. I thought about my oldest son who had slept out in that same campground a few nights before, and for the first time in over 40 years of loving Glacier Park, my second home, I felt fear.[5]

— ◆ —

This tragedy, once again involving predation on a person in a sleeping bag, might be termed "The Sleeping Bag Grizzly #5." On July 24, 1980, four years later, Ms. Jane Ammerman and Mr. Kim Eberly would be sleeping peacefully in the far east of Glacier Park under the stars, on the sandy shore of an oxbow in Divide Creek, when the Divide Creek Grizzly awakened and dragged them from their sleeping bags. See the next chapter.

PART 3

FATAL SUMMER–AUTUMN OF THE GRIZZLIES, 1980

4

FINDING JANE AND KIM

1980: THE DIVIDE CREEK CAMPSITE GRIZZLY

60 percent of the scat [bear droppings] included onion, watermelon seeds, potato skin, carrot skin, glass: brown & clear, fibers? String? Cellophane, paper, gum wrapper, hairs (human).

—WILDLIFE LABORATORY SUPERVISOR, MONTANA FISH, WILDLIFE AND PARKS, SEPTEMBER 3, 1980

Fatalities: Ms. Jane Ammerman and Mr. Kim Eberly
(One male bear killed, proven responsible)

National Park Service–Glacier Park
Case Incident Record Number 801073
Location: Eastern Glacier Park: Divide Creek / St. Mary River Bridge
Date/Time: Thursday, July 24, 1980, approximately 4:00 a.m.

Theirs was a Midwestern friendship set in the West's "Crown of the Continent," Glacier Park. Two young people—Minnesota's Jane Ammerman and Ohio's Mr. Kim Eberly—met on June 1, 1980, as summer employees at Lake McDonald Lodge. Lake McDonald itself is on Glacier's far west side, its long, tranquil waters reflecting the Lodge set among glaciated peaks, knife-edge ridges, and forests.

For that year, 1980, the Park's bear management plan points out that "Wildlife species in the park include black bears and grizzly bears, the latter a threatened species protected by the Endangered Species Act of 1973. Populations of both species appear to be relatively stable and self-regulating. A population of 200 is estimated for grizzly bears (Martinka 1971, 1972, 1974), and 500 for black bears."

Thirteen years had elapsed since 1967's "Night of the Grizzlies," the first recorded bear-caused fatalities in Glacier Park history. All Glacier Park dumps had long since been closed, and feeding bears was strictly prohibited.

Jane Ammerman, who worked as a waitress in the dining room, and Kim Eberly, in his second year as a bellman, attended the now-mandatory employee orientation, which included a twenty-five-minute film titled *Bears and Man*.

In hindsight we can look back and reflect on events that may have foreshadowed what lay ahead. The fact that Jane and Kim watched this film might be said to be the first such event.

A second sign appeared in exhibit #13 in Case Incident Record Number 801073, titled "Orientation Session for Concession Employees—June 5, 1980." Before showing the film, West Lakes District naturalist Reed Detring "briefly explained our concerns about the interaction of bears and humans in Glacier National Park, and how this could affect the employees; both as park visitors themselves, or in their role as employees in passing along information to the park visitors they are here to serve."

Specific subjects later covered in detail included:

1. Overnight camping permits required of everyone, and reasons for this. . . .

15. Toward the end of this session, the 1979 incident involving Bill Eberly and [name redacted] Tesar, both NPS employees, and a grizzly sow with two cubs was used as an example of what can happen. (*It was not known at the time, incidentally, that Eberly's brother Kim Eberly was in the session* [emphasis added].) The point was made that despite all precautions being taken by Eberly and Tesar, they were attacked and Eberly was repeatedly mauled by the sow grizzly.

Kim and Jane were probably shocked when officials used the example of his brother's mauling the previous year, while Bill Eberly was working on a fishery survey for the Park.

A third event may have been the fact that Black's Dump (outside the park), near Jane and Kim's camping place (which was *inside* the park), had been closed, but was still being used illegally by people who were dumping garbage. "Onions, watermelons, potato skins, [and] carrot skins" were later found in the responsible bear's intestine. Even a bear-killed pig carcass was later discovered to be "scattered all over the dump," which was then foraged by grizzly bears. The route from Glacier Park to Black's Dump lay along the sandbar of Divide Creek, near where Jane and Kim had decided to camp Tuesday and Wednesday nights.

A fourth sign appeared in the later-discovered presence "70 feet away from their campsite of fairly fresh grizzly scat [droppings] . . . and several day beds [where bears sleep during the day]," according to ranger Gerald Ryder's testimony at the later Board of Inquiry. This possibly indicated recent and continuous bear use, perhaps coming and going to Black's Dump ("Board of Inquiry Transcript of Proceedings," page 32).

Fifth, Park statistics given in the Case Incident Record indicate that there were "25,000 backcountry 'user days' in 1980," on seven hundred miles of trails, while at the same time there was "one grizzly for every eight square miles," often on those same trails (the energy-saving path of least resistance for bears).

A sixth sign of potential trouble came from Dr. Chuck Jonkel (University of Montana, Missoula) who informed the later Park Board of Inquiry that 1980 was "the second poor food year [for bears] in a row." The bears were thus "stressed and more aggressive."

Of course, most of these "signs" were unknown to Jane and Kim, and they had already been on two overnight backpacking trips together. One of these was on July 2, 1980, when officer Sue Bradford issued a backcountry permit to Kim Eberly, a copy of which was included in the Case Incident Record. The "number of people" is written as "2," and the target campsite as "Camas Lake." Among the warnings written on the permit is "Extra Bear Warning."

Almost all Park employees use their scarce free time to explore the Park, enraptured as any visitor. Now, on Jane and Kim's third trip on Tuesday, July 22, 1980, they checked out of work, sharing their plans to hitchhike to Waterton Lakes National Park (crossing the border into Canada), and finally hitchhiking back to Lake McDonald Lodge. They were due to sign in for work on July 24 at 3:00 p.m.

But this they did not do. Friends and colleagues noticed, and were worried. Where were Jane and Kim?

The last to see them alive were a Park bus driver, steering the famous red bus (an open-top bus for visitors driven by a "gear-jammer," so called because they need to "jam gears" to get up and down the Going-to-the-Sun Road), and a married couple who saw them later that same evening as they left to set up their camp at Divide Creek.

The Glacier Park, Inc., bus driver picked the two hitchhikers up at Avalanche Creek. He recalled their appearance: a happy couple, she with red hair and he with black, wearing their hiking boots and backpacks. Her hair color was striking enough that she was affectionately called "Red" by friends and colleagues back at the west-side Lodge. He drove them in the open-top bus, dropping them off at the St. Mary Village on the Park's far-east side. They had planned to stay at the commercial KOA Campground (for cars and recreational vehicles as well as tents) outside the Park. But as ranger Gregory Kerwin (St. Mary Ranger Station) wrote in his Supplementary Case/Incident Record, dated August 5, 1980, they changed their minds.

> Mr. and Mrs. [redacted] observed a male and female hiker matching the description of Kim Eberly and Jane Ammerman walking with packs in a westerly direction over the St. Mary River toward Divide Creek between 1900 and 2000 hours [7:00 to 8:00 p.m.] the evening of Tuesday, July 22, 1980.

At the time of the attack early Thursday morning (approximately 4:00 a.m.), the Case Incident Record noted "the temperature was 65–67 degrees Fahrenheit, overcast and cloudy because of a weather change at approximately 0300 hours [3:00 a.m.]. There had been some rainfall during this time, but only slightly more than a trace."

Now the sun shone. Later that morning of July 24, Robert Shanahan was enjoying fishing at Divide Creek, near the St. Mary River bridge. He spotted colorful objects caught on the six-foot-high Glacier Park steel boundary stake driven into the middle of the streambed. Curious, he was moved to investigate, pulling out an orange two-man tent, jeans, and a blue stuff sack. The jeans were still belted, and in the pocket Robert found a soaked wallet with identification for Kim Ray Eberly. This he found very disturbing. Meanwhile, his son-in-law, Scott Brewster, had moved upstream to try fishing there, only to spot a nude body partly in the water.

Upon receiving the emergency call, "Rangers with the fishermen traveled to the bridge which crosses the St. Mary River near the KOA Campground," wrote ranger Gerald Ryder in his Supplementary Case/Incident Record, dated July 28, 1980. They were joined by two tribal policemen (Divide Creek separates Glacier Park and the Blackfeet Indian Reservation), and personnel from the Glacier County sheriff's office. This is what they found:

Mr. [redacted] pointed out the human foot he had first sighted which was partially submerged upstream. [The two men] returned to the bridge and the rest of the group crossed the stream and continued up the west stream bank to where the nude body of Jane Ammerman was found lying facedown, head downstream. Ms. Ammerman's right foot and right hand were in the water. [Redacted] A part of Ms. Ammerman's scalp was missing. A light blue, fiber-filled sleeping bag was strewn beneath the body. Tufts of the fiber fill were scattered around the body.

Continuing the search upstream, an illegal camp and the nude body of Mr. Eberly were found. Mr. Eberly's body was lying facedown, head downstream, on the rocky east shore across from the camp. Mr. Eberly had multiple bite and claw wounds and his left arm appeared to have been bitten several times. The calf of Mr. Eberly's left leg [redacted]. . . .

I decided the group should vacate and preserve the incident scene. All personnel were removed from the immediate area and stringent security began. . . . Mr. Arnie Anderson, FBI agent from Cut Bank,

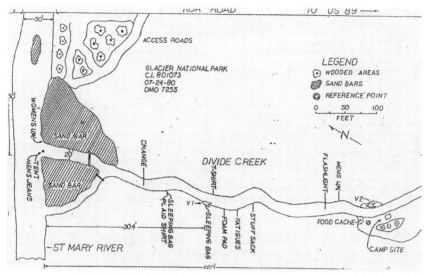

Overview of terrain where the victims were recovered. Victim 1 (Jane Ammerman, "V1") found beside Divide Creek next to sleeping bag, and Victim 2 (Kim Eberly, "V2") found on opposite side of Divide Creek from their campsite.
ILLUSTRATION FROM CASE INCIDENT RECORD NUMBER 801073

Montana, arrived at 1455 [2:55 p.m.]. Agent Anderson along with a Tribal and NPS Photographer departed for inspection and photography of the scene. [Law Enforcement Specialist] Robert Burns arrived at 1525 hours [3:25 p.m.] and with this ranger went to the incident scene. During this time Riddles Funeral Home from Browning, Montana, arrived, and the bodies were removed at approximately 1630 hours [4:30 p.m.]. . . .

While setting the [aluminum culvert bear] trap in [St. Mary Campground] loop "A," three loud rifle shots were heard coming from the general direction of the incident scene, followed by a series of other shots. Approximately 10 shots altogether were fired. This ranger and Greg Kerwin, park ranger trained in bear management, traveled to the scene and found a large group of people surrounding a dead grizzly bear. [Redacted] fired the first three shots which apparently had killed the bear. With the authorization of Tribal authorities, the bear was removed by [redacted] to the St. Mary fire cache, where it was photographed, some measurements taken and weighed (258 pounds). The bear was secured and made ready for transport to Bozeman tomorrow [Wildlife Laboratory at Montana Department of Fish, Wildlife, and Parks]. At 0150 hours [1:50 a.m.], all personnel secured for the evening.

Who shot the bear? Ranger Ryder interviewed that person, writing his report, dated July 28, 1980:

At 1020 hours [10:20 a.m.] I met with [redacted], [the] individual who shot the grizzly bear. . . . He had just arrived at the northwest side of the bridge over the St. Mary River, shut off his headlights, adjusted his rearview mirror, and then saw the bear in the middle of the St. Mary River about halfway between Mr. [redacted] and the culvert trap set on reservation land. Mr. [redacted] indicated he pulled on the vehicle lights and the bear bolted to the SW shoreline. Mr. [redacted] who was shooting a 7mm rifle, shouted and the bear partially raised on hind legs and turned to the left. Mr. [redacted] fired and the bear spun to the left and Mr. [redacted] fired again and the bear traveled a short distance and fell. Mr. [redacted] fired again and missed. Several Tribal members were at the scene, including [redacted], Tribal Policeman, and [redacted], Glacier County Sheriff's office. Both officials fired rounds at the bear from close range, six .38 rounds and one 12-gauge shotgun slug respectively. My arrival at the scene and subsequent removal of the bear are covered [earlier] in this report.

At 1150 hours [11:50 a.m.], Chief Ranger Sigler arrived at St. Mary Ranger Station and toured the incident scene. Investigation activities for the day involved extensive photography and examination of the immediate incident scene. Security of the area late into the evening preserved the integrity of the scene.

July 26, 1980, at 0630 hours [6:30 a.m.], all the culvert [bear] traps are again checked, [and] they are empty. . . .

July 27, 1980, at 0715 [7:15 a.m.], a check of all bear traps reveal no bear or sign of bear near the traps.

A heartbreaking item in the Case Incident Record is the "Inventory of Personal Items." On July 30, 1980, ranger David M. Ortley listed some of these.

Evidence Taken from Incident Scene
(1) Eureka "Sunshine Mountain" Alpine Tent—Orange/Tan
(1) "Snow Lion" sleeping bag, polyester filling—Royal Blue
(1) unknown make sleeping bag—Navy Blue

[some of Kim's belongings]:
(1) Red plaid shirt
(1) Yellow T-shirt, "Go Climb a Glacier"
(1) Men's blue jeans with leather belt

[some of Jane's belongings]:
(1) Roll Kodacolor print Film 110, exposed to #5—Confiscated by NPS
(1) Timex ladies' watch, plastic band—Stopped [at] 8:50 [a.m. or p.m., not known]
(1) 3 x 5 Diary

[their jointly owned] food container:
NPS plastic food bag [found untouched by bear, hoisted up in willows]
(1) Clear Baggie
(2) Freeze-dried coffees, Hills Brothers
(1) Brown Paper Bag: Jane A. printed on front
(1) Hard-Boiled Egg (intact)

Park Service investigations continued, and the following relevant pieces of information emerged. The Glacier Park, Inc., red bus driver provided his handwritten report on the last time he saw Jane and Kim. Information within may help to explain why Jane and Kim did not stay at the KOA Campground (as they had said they would). This Supplementary Case/Incident Record is dated 7/30/80, and the driver's name is redacted.

I picked up Kim and Jane approx. 6 p.m. on Tuesday at the Avalanche Creek Turn-Off. I knew Kim fairly well, and he introduced me to Jane. I was on my way to Many Glacier to pick up a girl to go to dinner at Johnson's Café. I dropped Kim and Jane off at the entrance to the KOA Campground at approximately 7:30 p.m. after we had stopped briefly at St. Mary's Lodge, so Jane could look up a friend from school. . . . I proceeded to Many Glacier and then to Johnson's. At Johnson's, a friend of my date suggested that we go to the St. Mary's [Lodge] Lounge to see the Mission Mt. Band. We did, and saw Kim [and] Jane and sat with them. . . . To be honest, I can't recall what we talked about through the course of the night; it was just general talk. They left St. Mary's at approx. 11 p.m., and that was the last I saw them. . . .

They asked me about campgrounds along the way and I said that there were several along the lower St. Mary Lake. As we got into St. Mary Village, I suggested the KOA as it was the closest to our area. They said they were going to stay there and then "go hiking," they didn't know where to.

This report of the sighting of Jane and Kim is thought to be the final time they were seen alive.

Another relevant piece of information: Ranger Reed Detring referenced Kim Eberly when he led the employee orientation film, *Bears and Man*. In his Supplementary Case/Incident Record, dated July 30, 1980, Detring wrote, "I led a short discussion with a question-and-answer motif on camping in bear country. *One of the individuals who asked a question after the film was identified to me as a brother of* [grizzly mauling victim] *Bill Eberly, named Kim Eberly* [emphasis added]. This identification resulted from the discussion posed by other members of the orientation team in which they used the Bill Eberly incident from the previous autumn."

Ranger Greg J. Kerwin detailed "the results of searches by NPS personnel of the area around the site where Eberly and Ammerman were killed." His report is dated July 30, 1980, included below.

I examined every track, scat, game trail, and day bed [where bears sleep during the day] during the searches. I photographed and measured

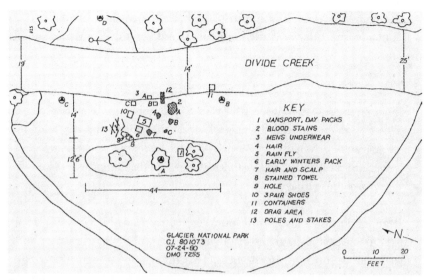

Campsite and strewn belongings of Jane Ammerman and Kim Eberly, with location of Kim Eberly's body (stick figure) shown on opposite side of Divide Creek.
ILLUSTRATION FROM CASE INCIDENT RECORD NUMBER 801073

each track. I collected three relatively fresh scats which were sent to the Wildlife Lab at Bozeman. The game trails were flagged. Representative bear hairs found along these trails were collected and sent to Bozeman. I photographed several of the day beds where bear hairs were found.

As far as I can tell, the tracks indicate that two different bears have been in the area within two weeks of the accident. Bear #1 has a front track which measures about 4⅞ inches wide at the pad and about 5 inches from back of pad to front of toe. This print matches the 3-year-old [later found to be 5½ years old], 258-lb., dark brown grizzly bear shot near the scene of the accident. It also matches the mud print taken from Eberly's navy blue Early Winter pack. This bear appears to have been using the area for some time. One old track from this bear had a small sprig of green growing in it.

Another print had spiderwebs in the toes and claws marks.

Bear #2 has prints on the north shore of the St. Mary River. . . . I suspect it is a black bear.

Ranger Robert N. Frauson inspected the Black's Dump area (which was outside the Glacier Park boundary), and on July 28 wrote up his findings.

Sunday 7/27/80

Frauson drove over to inspect Black's / St. Mary Dump. There is a "pit closed" sign on the road. There is a locked cable gate with a very loose cable (can be driven over by veh[icle]). There is a lot of garbage dumped outside of the gate and fresh garbage dumped in the dump. Seagulls are feeding on the garbage.

Ranger Frauson also wrote on Wednesday morning, July 30, 1980, that the necropsy (animal autopsy) yielded the following information: "8 bullet holes were found in the bear, Two broken hairs from the tongue [which would prove to be human], Thirty hair and fibers were removed from the intestinal tract (25 were bear hair, 4 or 5 were questionable fiber or human), Twenty roundworms, 100 hookworms."

As to which bear might be responsible, Ranger Kerwin noted in a separate report, titled "Listing of Bear Sightings in St. Mary Area for 1980," dated August 9, 1980, that *thirty-four bears* (emphasis added), both grizzly and black, were counted "from [a] computer printout and personal communications."

The Certificates of Death for both Jane and Kim listed "shock and hemorrhage as a consequence of attack by bear, with multiple puncture wounds and tissue removal."

Now it was up to Glacier Park's Board of Inquiry to examine the investigative evidence (only a portion of which is presented below), and write up its report of findings and recommendations.

[At 8:30 a.m.] the Board of Inquiry convened in public on July 31, 1980, in the lobby at the National Park Service employees' dormitory at the district headquarters of the Hudson Bay District near St. Mary, Montana.

The Board members first visited the scene of the maulings and were given a résumé of the investigation by Park Ranger Jerry Ryder. The

Board also, at that time, visited the open pit dump hereinafter referred to as Black's Dump. . . .

Prior to the mauling deaths of Mr. Eberly and Ms. Ammerman, bears caused only one reported incident of property damage in the St. Mary area within Glacier National Park. On July 6, 1980, a medium-sized brown adult grizzly with panda markings damaged a tent and sleeping bag and broke into a food cache at a backcountry campsite at Red Eagle Lake some nine miles via foot trail from St. Mary.

What initially caught the attention of the second reporting fisherman at Divide Creek, which led to his discovery of Jane Ammerman? The "Transcript of Proceedings" includes the following report from Ranger Ryder:

> At that point Mr. [redacted] indicated to me that he fished on up the stream to a point about this—about this point here, where the brush is thick, and it makes it almost impossible to get through there unless you get into the water. He began to step into the water; he noticed a blue bag or something, a blue color lodged under an overhanging willow bush, which was partially submerged in the water. Looking beyond that on the shoreline up to a point about here, he thought he saw a human foot in the water and extending out of the water. [p. 26]

What did the investigating rangers do and see at the scene?

> Ranger Ryder: "There was a pair of jeans, fatigue-type army pants found in the stream and in that pant there was in one of the pockets a small little purse, a leather coin purse that had a driver's license in it of Miss Ammerman. That's the way we identified her, and then the fact that she had red hair and the license was that of a red-haired person." [pp. 36–37]
>
> Ranger Ryder: "There were no fire rings. That was a very secluded spot. It's 480 feet upstream from the confluence of the Divide Creek with St. Mary's River and it's surrounded by heavy brush and there was no evidence that people had been frequenting that area really at all." [p. 40] [Note: Jane and Kim camped near the sandbar.]

Mr. [redacted]: "They didn't check into the Lodge, either, or one of the other cabins?"

Ranger Ryder: "No. They didn't have a great deal of money with them. I think Miss Ammerman had $20.00 and Mr. Eberly had something like $32.00, $36.00 with him. So they had been traveling light. You know, to save money, I would imagine that maybe they camped in this area. I can't put any other logic to it." [p. 49]

Was Black's Dump, just outside the Park, a possible contributing factor to the events of July 24, 1980? The "Transcript of Proceedings" continues, below.

Mr. [redacted]: "Yes, by Tribal Resolution 1080, all the dumping sites on the reservation have been closed . . . for years. . . . This [Black's] particular dumping ground is on private, non-Indian-owned land. Not owned by any member of the tribe." [p. 53]

Ranger Ryder: "For instance, just six miles down the road is Chewing Black Bone Campground, and that garbage is handled by a large truck that comes with a big dumpster and they take the garbage to Browning and dump it there." [p. 59]

Mr. [redacted], Public Health Service, Division of Indian Health: "The problem that we do have is you can recommend that the dump be closed and everybody will agree on that fact except for the money problem. Who will close the dump and who will bury it?" [p. 68]

Superintendent Iversen: "We will take every action we can to get that dump cleaned up, buried, the horse gone [a dead horse someone had left at the dump], and if it's okay, obstruct access to the dump." [p. 73]

What did the investigators find out about the grizzly bear which was shot and killed?

Ranger Ryder: "Bob Frauson preserved the claws by wrapping a paper bag around the claws and taping them to preserve any evidence that might be there. We did measure the bear's—some of the canine measurements; that is, the teeth measurements." [p. 32]

Ranger Frauson: "The measurements are fairly critical on a bear, and the first measurements we took of the day were the canine index or the index of the teeth. The upper teeth or canine teeth were 62 millimeters, point to point. The lower corresponding teeth incisors, I believe they are called, were 55 millimeters." [p. 74]

Frauson continued: "I stood in on the autopsy at the morgue of the two people in question. Here again, there were many, many wounds on the bodies; bites of the same size. We measured with a metric ruler and with scales; photographs were taken of all these different wounds. You could tell what direction the bite came from by the way his teeth were angled and their size. They came out very, very close to 62 millimeters. [p. 75] There was a stomach ulcer in the bear that measured 2 square centimeters." [p. 78]

Frauson continued: [In the intestine] they found 20 bear hairs and 4 reddish hairs, 1 to 3 inches long, a few up to 5 inches long. And this again is the Wildlife Laboratory. By comparison, these were identical to the hair sample of the girl, the reddish hair. . . . All right, from the bear's tongue there were two short hairs; one of the short hairs on the tongue of the bear was there, one of the hairs was from the male victim, and black." [p. 79]

Frauson continued: "The scat sample which was right—I don't know, maybe . . . a little more than 60 feet away—the scat sample which was fresh had hair of both humans and it had a piece of shirt and a green material. . . ."

Mr. Ryder: "There were green fatigue-type pants found at the scene." [p. 83]

Mr. Shellenberger: "Reed Detring, who showed a movie on bears, titled *Bears and Man* . . . and then the question-and-answer session began to flow from the concession employees. They became very, very enthusiastic and it got quite detailed, into conduct and their theories of bears and bear attacks. The [Bill Eberly] mauling of last fall was used as one of the examples by Ranger Trulock to illustrate one time. That is the confrontation—surprise confrontation on the trail. That was the case with the sow and cubs." [p. 97]

Ranger Frauson: "Between here and there it's just like the Panama Canal for animals to migrate from one place to another; they have to run the gauntlet through St. Mary's here. We have seen grizzl[ies] swim St. Mary's Lake by Two Dog Flat and they do readily swim it, but I think many of them would probably go this way [indicating]. You see, what a gauntlet they have going from forested mountain area to make migration back and forth. It is, when you're talking about habitat, it is migration out for wildlife except when there is ice on the lake." [p. 105]

The overall conclusions of the Board of Inquiry are included below.

Facts of the Incident

Bloodstains on the ground and on some of the camp gear indicated the attack had initially taken place at the campsite and that the victims either were dragged or, possibly, managed to move to where they were found.

A food supply consisting mainly of items still in sealed containers, except for two apples, was hung 7 to 8 feet off the ground in a willow approximately 50 feet from the campsite. This food was contained in a Glacier National Park plastic sack. These sacks have printed on them complete information concerning proper behavior in bear country. There was no evidence that there had been a fire at the campsite or that any meals had been prepared. There was no garbage or trash in the vicinity that could be associated with the camp. . . .

The location of Mr. Eberly's and Ms. Ammerman's campsite in what amounts to an isthmus between Upper and Lower St. Mary's Lakes would indicate it was on the most logical route for bears moving between the park and garbage sources outside the park. The campsite was in heavy brush with restricted visibility. There were few tall trees available in which they could have sought refuge from a bear. A permit would not have been issued by the park rangers for the place they camped.

The tent, which was found snagged on a stake where Divide Creek joins St. Mary's River, had one side torn open. The tent was zipped closed. . . . The warmth of the night (probably in range of 60 to 65 degrees F) and the fact that the tent was zipped closed indicates that Mr. Eberly and Ms. Ammerman likely were sleeping on the tent fly, Ensolite pad, and the sleeping bags outside the tent. . . .

Autopsies of the victims, necropsy of the bear, and laboratory testing of specimens indicate the following:

1. The cause of death for each of the victims was shock and loss of blood.
2. The scat contents of the bear contained cellophane, Styrofoam, and cantaloupe rind, among other things, indicating it was feeding on garbage somewhere.
3. Evidence of sexual activity between the victims is inconclusive.
4. Ms. Ammerman was not in the menstrual period.
5. Bite marks on the victims' bodies matched the dentition of the bear that was shot.
6. There were no ear tags, lip tattoos, or tag or snare scars on the bear which would indicate that it had been captured or handled previously. The health and condition of the bear was considered normal, with no disease or abnormal level of parasites. . . .

The dump previously referred to as Black's Dump is located a half-mile north of the town of St. Mary's on the eastside of US 89. It is fee patented land owned by [redacted] and is within the boundaries of the Blackfeet Reservation, but it is not subject to regulation by the Tribe. Although posted with a prominent, though crude "Pit Closed" sign, it showed signs of considerable recent use when inspected by the Board. In fact, sometime during the night of July 30, a dead horse was deposited at the dump. The situation at this dump reflects the desperate need for the formation of a cooperative refuse district involving all jurisdictions within Glacier County.

Conclusion

While the victims were camped in a nondesignated area, their camping practice (etiquette) was such that it did not appear to be a major attractant for the bear. . . .

Of the five persons fatally mauled by bears in Glacier National Park, four have been employees of Glacier Park, Inc. . . . . Mr. Eberly and Ms. Ammerman were present at the Lake McDonald orientation on June 5, 1980.

Recommendation

With the increased frequency of fatal injuries, including the recent Canadian fatal maulings involving both black and grizzly bears, the Board feels the time has come to clearly state in our literature that the potential for death from bears, even though slight, does exist.

— ⌣ —

Giving his opinions on the danger of bears, Glacier Park, Inc.'s, president (responsible for all concessions, including those at Lake McDonald Lodge, where Jane and Kim worked) wrote to the Board of Review chairman on November 25, 1980:

I believe the problem is far greater than camping in a nondesignated area. I have often expressed my disagreement with your bear policy, and if continued, I predict that it will result in more tragedies.

Bears have lost their fear of man; not only because they are exposed to man's food supply, but they are not made to respect those areas set aside for man's use. . . .

I have heard the explanation that the maulings are the result of greater use of the backcountry. This last isn't true. The Great Northern Railway Company operated thirteen backcountry chalets [in 1915] which were served by some twelve hundred horses taking visitors to those locations. The backcountry use was greater then than it is now, without injury to Park visitors.

Why did you not have maulings then? Why do you not have maulings reported in the Forest Service? The answer is that the bears are conditioned to avoid man. How? Simply by shooting near them so they know they are not welcome. You don't have to kill them or even wound them to get the message across.

In 1915, what did visitors on all of those 1,200 horses see? "It was the next day that I made my first close acquaintance with bears," Mary Roberts Rinehart wrote in her memoir, *Through Glacier Park in 1915*. "Firearms are forbidden, of course, and the rangers kill them only in case of trouble. Naturally, so protected, they are increasing rapidly. They find good forage where horses would starve. Mr. Ralston, the park supervisor, saw a she bear with three cubs last spring. There are no tame bears, as in the Yellowstone."

> Then: "Here's a grizzly," [the guide] said. "You might want to stand near the horses."
> We did. The grizzly looked the exact size of a seven-passenger automobile with a limousine top, and he had the same gift of speed. The black bears looked at him and ran. I looked at him and wanted to.

And where did Mary Roberts Rinehart finally see the black bears, and then the grizzly? It was "where the hotel dumps its garbage. That was rather a blow, at first. There was a considerable stench."[6]

⚊⚊

What follows demonstrates the tragic aftermath of the loss of Kim Eberly and Jane Ammerman. "The wallet of Mr. Eberly was returned to the family via registered mail #3021" on July 29, Ranger Ryder wrote on August 9, 1980. The address was Kim's hometown in Ohio. The three photographs developed from Jane's camera were sent to Jane's parents on August 18, 1980, by Charles R. Sigler, chief park ranger, who added, "If we can be of further assistance, please feel free to contact us."

Jane's mother, Margaret, told Michael Robbins (*Rocky Mountain Magazine*) that Jane had specifically picked Glacier as the national park where she wanted to work. "Glacier was her favorite. She wrote us that she was having a great time, that everybody was unbelievably friendly, and that the scenery in the park was beautiful. Every chance she got, on her time off, she'd go hiking."[7]

Jane Ammerman and Kim Eberly were both nineteen years old. At the University of Minnesota–Duluth, Jane was majoring in parks and recreation management. Kim studied at the University of Montana (Missoula), and fought dangerous wildfires as a professional crew chief. We may honor them by pausing to remember what it's like to be young and just starting out in the world.

———

In the next chapter, rangers find a torn-up camp with evidence of grizzly bear activity. But where is the camper?

5

FINDING LARRY

1980: THE ELIZABETH LAKE CAMPGROUND GRIZZLY

After walking about 100 yards, we found the torn-up camp of Mr. Gordon. In about a 50-foot radius, we found a torn and flattened nylon tent, a torn yellow foam pad, a sleeping bag, a backpack, and a torn stuff sack near shredded food wrappers. Down the trail 50 yards was a red down jacket in the trail, with a bear paw print on it. We were appalled.
—William F. Conrod, resource management ranger,
Supplementary Case/Incident Record,
October 3, 1980

Fatality: Laurence B. Gordon
(One male bear killed, none proven responsible)

National Park Service–GlacierPark
Case Incident Record Number 801998
Location: Belly River drainage, Elizabeth Lake Foot Campground (lower end)
Date/Time: Friday, September 26 or Saturday, September 27, 1980, time unknown
Remains found October 3, 1980

"You're going to be eaten by a rogue bear," Larry Gordon's mother kidded him. Of course, that seemed inconceivable. So Larry sent her a postcard showing three bears, one circled, with the words "rogue bear" written underneath.

After visiting his father in Oregon, Larry traveled through the bear country of the Canadian Rocky Mountains and then south to the United States and Montana, registering at the Pioneer Hotel in Cutbank. Preparing to enter Glacier Park, he wrote that in an emergency, officials should contact friends at the Pioneer. Then, shouldering his frame pack and grasping his wooden walking staff, this commercial airline pilot vanished into the magnificent vistas of Glacier Park.

At this point in the year—September 25, 1980—the largest crowds of Park visitors were gone. Significant snowfall could be expected at any time. As the Park Service requires, Laurence B. Gordon registered for and received a Backcountry Use Permit #10506, which he then had to cancel with the reissue of a revised permit.

Ranger William Penttilla explains: "A Mr. Lawrence [*sic*] Gordon came to the Many Glacier Ranger Station on the morning of September 25 at about 0900 hrs [9:00 a.m.] because the route he had planned on taking to Elizabeth Lake was closed." In Penttilla's Supplementary Case/Incident Record, dated October 6, 1980, he noted:

> That was the trail going thru the Ptarmigan Tunnel to Elizabeth Lake. *It was closed due to a bear problem on the day previous* [emphasis added].
>
> Since the only two rangers in the area were on the trail to Ptarmigan Lake and Tunnel on that day, I was the only person at the station to help Mr. Gordon with his problem.
>
> When he explained his problem and produced his permit, I called the St. Mary Visitor Center to discuss possible alternatives. . . . I gave the telephone to Mr. Gordon and he discussed possible alternate backpacking routes. Since he still wanted to camp at Elizabeth Lake, the route around by Poia Lake and Red Gap Pass was agreed on [a much longer hike].
>
> We discussed the bear problem on the Ptarmigan Trail as well as all of the recommended safety precautions to take while camping. He

didn't appear to be overly concerned or worried about running into bears. He impressed me as being a very capable person and one who would not take unnecessary risks.

Mr. Gordon did not have a vehicle, and the Entrance Station, where the Poia Lake Trail starts, is some distance from the Many Glacier Ranger Station. I offered to give him a lift to the trailhead. I needed to go partway, anyhow, to feed the Park Service horse.

On the ride to the trailhead, Mr. Gordon stated that he was anxious to hike in the Glacier area and that this was his first trip to the area. . . .

We discussed the problems with bears that backpackers may encounter, and again, mentioned the precautions.

He said that his plan was to camp at Elizabeth and make day hikes out of there. He mentioned that some of his time would be spent in camp since he was an avid reader. . . .

Our conversation on the way to the trailhead was mostly about the beauty of Glacier and what gorgeous scenery he would see on his trip.

I dropped him off at the Entrance Station at about 1030 hrs [10:30 a.m.] and bade him farewell.

The last to see Larry alive was probably ranger William Penttilla.

Hindsight reveals the probable importance of the "bear problem the day before" (September 24). Due to that incident, the trail Larry had intended to take, through the Ptarmigan Tunnel to Elizabeth Lake, was closed. Ranger Reed E. Detring explains: "September 24, 1980: Three hikers in the Many Glacier Valley were confronted by a grizzly bear at Ptarmigan Lake," he wrote in his Supplementary Case/Incident Record dated October 12. "They discarded their packs and went to the Many Glacier Ranger Station. The bear tore into the packs and received food. The result of the incident was the closure of the Ptarmigan Trail."

After this bear incident of September 24, rangers immediately acted to protect backcountry hikers. Trails and campsites were closed, and in his report, Ranger Detring noted that on "September 25, 1980, Rangers Bob Baker and Chris Metzger performed campground evaluations at Helen Lake, Elizabeth Lake at the head and Elizabeth Lake at the foot [both along the Belly River]. They removed the bridge at Elizabeth Lake at the foot. They returned to the Belly River Ranger Station at 1900 hours [7:00 p.m.]."

These rangers did not report spotting Larry's campsite at the time. Presumably he was still hiking in to Elizabeth Lake.

Ranger Penttilla had informed Larry about the "bear problem," but Larry still wanted to go to Elizabeth Lake, nestled deep in the roadless backcountry. In the vertical world of mountainous Glacier Park, the lakes in the valleys are a respite. From the summit of Ahern Peak you can look down at the gemlike Elizabeth Lake and Helen Lake, almost 4,000 feet below. "On the great Continental Divide, America's wilderness spine," writes Bob Sihler in *Climbing Glacier National Park*, "Ahern Peak is surrounded by some of the park's most spectacular mountains, and several of the park's remaining (and shrinking) glaciers are visible from its summit."[8] Perhaps this was an ascent Larry wanted to try. The book adds this warning: "It is a *long* way to medical care. It literally could take all day to get medical help from here."

But Larry had things to accomplish, according to his friends at the Pioneer Hotel, who wrote later to Park personnel. "I'm very sorry you didn't know Larry personally, as he was a remarkable young man. The reason for his trip to the mountains was to be by himself for a time before coming to stay here with us. We got to know him quite well, and our children hung on his every word."

So it was that, alone by choice, Larry arrived at his Elizabeth Lake Campsite beside dry meadow grass, now golden, several climbable trees, and a large willow thicket. An experienced backpacker, Larry set up a comfortable camp, stretching a protective rain fly over the buff sides and green bottom of his tent. He snapped photographs that were later found and sent to his mother.

Then, beside the pebbled lakeshore, Larry sat reading, cradled by Natoas Peak and Seward Mountain. His books included a pocket Bible and daily reading material that he marked as he read. For September 26, his marked-with-pen page reads "The Unblameable Attitude: '*If . . . thou rememberest that thy brother hath ought against thee . . .*' Matthew v. 23." For September 27, his marked page reads "The 'Go' of Renunciation: '*Lord, I will follow Thee whithersoever Thou goest,*' Luke ix, 57."

Larry was due to return to Glacier's front country on September 29.

Like the creatures surrounding him, Larry was able to take care of his practical needs and traverse the vicinity, perhaps viewing Dawn Mist Falls. The Blackfeet name for Elizabeth Lake is "'Otter Lake': *Amonisi-omahxikimi*," author Jack Holterman notes.[9]

But after a day's travel Larry could return to the human comforts of a good sleep on his Therm-a-Rest yellow air mattress, in his own blue down bag.

It was true that he was camping alone, which is not recommended. But hiking companionably with others is an entirely different experience than to do so by yourself. At its best, experiencing nature when you are alone can be a spiritual, even transcendent, experience, perhaps one that Larry was hoping to have.

The facts appear to show that at some point, after a day hike, Larry returned to his campsite to a shocking discovery: A grizzly bear had torn it apart. The bear was no longer there, but it had chewed two of his books, which Larry placed in the bottom of his pack. (The bear could not have made the punctures while the books were in the pack.) The last frame on his camera's film captures his torn-apart campsite. Perhaps Larry had decided to break camp and return to the safety of a ranger station to report the bear-caused damage. Evidence seems to show he was wearing two T-shirts, a long-underwear shirt, white cutoff pants, and leather hiking boots.

Then the grizzly returned.

—◦—

Days later, on September 30, another bear incident occurred. In the chronicle of finding Larry, this incident determined what happened next. It should be noted that if the three hikers referenced in Ranger Detring's report below had continued on to their Elizabeth Lake Foot campsite (for which they had registered, and where Larry died), they would have discovered his remains. Ranger Detring's record, dated October 12, continues:

September 30, 1980: At approximately 0900 hours [9:00 a.m.], three hikers were treed by a grizzly bear about one-third of the way down Glenn's Lake from the Campground at the Lake's head. The bear was reported to be a large brown grizzly bear with tips of hair along the back a lighter color. There was also a band of lighter-colored hair from [the] midpoint on front legs over shoulder to midpoint of the other leg. The bear also was reported to have had a tag in the left ear.

The three hikers were held up the tree for approximately three hours. The bear made a couple of unsuccessful attempts to climb the tree, but did reach approximately fifteen feet up the tree. The three hikers departed the incident scene at approximately 1200 hours [12:00 p.m.] and went to the Belly River Ranger Station. They found no one at the station and hiked on to Chief Mountain Customs to spend the night.

October 1, 1980: The above three hikers reported the incident of 9/30/80 to Ranger Terry Penttilla. . . .

October 2, 1980: Rangers Detring and Conrod . . . patrolled the Belly River area to investigate the treeing incident at Glenn's Lake and to retrieve items left by the hikers. At approximately 1100 hours [11:00 a.m.] it was discovered that the Belly River Ranger Station had been broken into by a bear with window damage at the station and door and window damage at the Fire Guard cabin. Significant items found included two cans of boot dressing with teeth marks found outside of the station and one medium-sized grizzly track outside of the Fire Guard cabin. . . . At approximately 1800 hours [6:00 p.m.] a portable bear trap was installed at the Belly River Ranger Station.

At approximately 1900 hours [7:00 p.m.], Dan O'Brien, flying out of Belly River in the helicopter, *reported a camp set up at Elizabeth Lake Foot Campground* [emphasis added]. Ranger Detring asked Ranger Conrod to go there the next morning and ask the campers to leave the area, since Belly River drainage would be closed because of the trap.

So it was that William F. Conrod, resource management ranger, began searching for the registered camping party (Larry Gordon) at Elizabeth Lake Foot Campground. It's clear that some ranger duties take an emotional toll, as captured in Ranger Conrod's Supplementary Case/Incident Record, pages 2–3, dated October 3, 1980.

FORM NO. 10-344
(Rev. 3-73)

U.S. DEPARTMENT OF THE INTERIOR
NATIONAL PARK SERVICE
SUPPLEMENTARY CASE/INCIDENT RECORD

ORGANIZATION (PARK) NAME	CASE/INCIDENT NUMBER
Glacier National Park	8 0 1 9 9 8

LOCATION OF INCIDENT	DATE OF INCIDENT MO DA YR
Elizabeth Lake Foot Campground	1 0 0 3 8 0

NATURE OF INCIDENT

Bear Mauling Fatality

COMPLAINANT'S NAME	COMPLAINANT'S ADDRESS

RESULTS OF INVESTIGATION

Sketch of Area Including Campsite and Body Site.

Trail

Scale 1" = 50'

23'7"   Tent
              16'2"

Tree A   Tree B

239 feet

Lakeshore

Elth

Elizabeth Lake

Body Site

Wi

Willow Thicket

SUBMITTED BY (SIGNATURE AND DATE)

Rood F Weston   10/12/80

APPROVED BY (SIGNATURE AND DATE)

Charles B. Sigler   10/24/80

Sketch of Larry Gordon fatality site, including campsite with tent (to the right) and body site within the round willow thicket (bottom left).

ILLUSTRATION FROM CASE INCIDENT RECORD NUMBER 801998

I arrived at the foot of Elizabeth Lake at about 10:30 a.m., 10/03/80, with my wife. We inspected the campsites around the outlet of the lake, without finding any persons, or equipment. There were no fresh tracks in the trail. After checking the campsites, we spent about 30 minutes eating a snack, and bandaging feet at the lakeshore beach. We puzzled [at] the absence of campers. At about 11:30, we decided to hike up the lake, just to look around for any tracks, or sign of activity. We thought we had visited all the campsites, but were mistaken. We had been there only one time before.

After walking about 100 yards, we found the torn-up camp of Mr. Gordon. In about a 50-foot radius, we found a torn and flattened nylon tent, a torn yellow foam pad, a sleeping bag, a backpack, and a torn stuff sack near shredded food wrappers. Down the trail 50 yards was a red down jacket in the trail, with a bear paw print on it. We were appalled.

Mr. Gordon's camping permit was attached to his pack frame, and gave his name and address, and indicated he was alone, and due out on 9/29/80. At this stage, we had not found any blood, or evidence of injury. We hoped Mr. Gordon had walked out, as we had not found his boots.

We made a cursory search of the vicinity, including the rest of the meadow, and the edge of the nearby willow patch. Numerous game trails went into the willows. However, we did not feel it was prudent to follow them at this time.

At 12:00 we began hiking out to Belly River Ranger Station, to call out on the base radio set. Handheld portable radios cannot reach the park repeaters from here, so communication is limited to the line-of-sight radio channel. At about 12:05, District Ranger Frauson called me on the line-of-sight radio channel.

I made the first report of the situation, and confirmed his suggestion of need for the helicopter and more personnel.

We stayed put and continued a cursory search. I located Gordon's wallet and identification in his backpack. A note in his wallet gave a person's name in Cutbank, Montana, to call in case of emergency.

A shirt was found down the beach about 100 feet from the pack. It was wet, but was un-torn. Of particular interest were what appeared to be a drag mark in the beach pebbles, and regular spaced depressions, [which] could have been bear tracks.

Where the pebbles gave way to meadow grass, a drag mark in the dry meadow grass pointed to the willow patch. . . . The only suitable climbing trees were at the campsite. An outhouse about 150 yards away was found tipped over, with bear tracks on the wall.

But not found was the camper. Where was Larry Gordon? Ranger Conrod's report continues.

The first helicopter trip arrived at around 1400 [2:00 p.m.], with Dan O'Brien and John Benjamin. Jerry Ryder and Reed Detring flew in later. The willow patch was checked from the air for sign of a body, and for bears. Negative results . . .

With O'Brien and Benjamin, I walked into the willow patch along the trajectory of the drag marks in the grass. No blood or debris was found along the drag mark. A game trail continued into the willows from the drag mark.

We followed this to a bloody shirt, and nearby found the body remains partially covered with dirt and vegetation. The two hiking boots, skull, several bones, and a pair of shorts, were all that remained. There were no soft parts left, nor skin.

The rest of the afternoon was spent mapping and photographing the area. The human remains and camp gear were gathered up and flown out, and all personnel were flown out by about 1730 [5:30 p.m.].

Ranger Detring's record dated October 12 adds more facts about what rangers found:

The skeletal remains of Mr. Gordon included a skull with no mandible [jaw], the brain intact, a piece of pelvic bone, and two pieces of leg bones, probably femurs. A pair of hiking boots [was] also found at the body site. They were peeled down and contained no skeletal parts. A pair of white cutoff pants were found containing a Bible and a comb. . . . Close to the body site two T-shirts and a long-underwear shirt

U.S. DEPARTMENT OF THE INTERIOR
NATIONAL PARK SERVICE
SUPPLEMENTARY CASE/INCIDENT RECORD

ORGANIZATION (PARK) NAME	CASE/INCIDENT NUMBER
Glacier National Park	8 0 1 9 9 8

LOCATION OF INCIDENT	DATE OF INCIDENT MO DA YR
Elizabeth Lake Foot Campground	1 0 0 3 8 0

NATURE OF INCIDENT

Bear Mauling Fatality

COMPLAINANT'S NAME	COMPLAINANT'S ADDRESS

RESULTS OF INVESTIGATION

Evidence Location
Scale 1" = 2'

#1 to #2 6'7"
#1 to #3 5'4"
#2 to #3 2'11"
#1 to #4 6'0"
#1 to #5 3'8"
#1 to #6 3'6"

Dimension of Disturbed Area
9'6" X 6'4"

Key
1. Skull
2. Left Boot
3. Right Boot
4. Femur
5. Pelvic Piece
6. Pelvic Piece
7. Leg Bone

Sketch of Body Site

SUBMITTED BY (SIGNATURE AND DATE)	APPROVED BY (SIGNATURE AND DATE)
Reed E. Date 10/12/80	Charles D. Sigh 10/24/80

Sketch of Larry Gordon fatality site, including dimension of disturbed area (indicated by dotted lines), in which were found bone fragments and a pair of boots.
ILLUSTRATION FROM CASE INCIDENT RECORD NUMBER 801998

U.S. DEPARTMENT OF THE INTERIOR
NATIONAL PARK SERVICE
SUPPLEMENTARY CASE/INCIDENT RECORD

FRANSON #10

ORGANIZATION (PARK) NAME
Glacier National Park

CASE/INCIDENT NUMBER
8 0 1 9 9 8

LOCATION OF INCIDENT
Elizabeth Lake

DATE OF INCIDENT
MO 1 0 | DA 0 3 | YR 8 0

NATURE OF INCIDENT
Bear Mauling Fatality

COMPLAINANT'S NAME

COMPLAINANT'S ADDRESS

RESULTS OF INVESTIGATION

Bloody
Wrong Side Out
Thermal Cotton
Under Shirt
white
5cm to 5.5cm
Teeth Index

Bloody
Wrong Side Out
Thermal T "Shirt
Du.
6cm
Teeth
Index

Bloody
Wrong Side Out
Blue Cotton
[Go Hike The Canyon]
Grand Canyon Nat. Park
5cm
Teeth
Index

Blue Levi Jacket
No Holes
Pockets Unbottoned
Sand & Gravel
in Right Pocket
Found on Beach

SUBMITTED BY (SIGNATURE AND DATE)
Rdo. & R. Franson   10/15/80

APPROVED BY (SIGNATURE AND DATE)
Charles B. Sigler   10/24/80

Sketch of Larry Gordon's clothing found at fatality site, including three shirts with bear teeth marks indicated at front of neck, and an undamaged blue-jean jacket. ILLUSTRATION FROM CASE INCIDENT RECORD NUMBER 801998 soaked in blood were found. This is the only blood that was found at either site. Between the shirts and the body site a Seiko self-winding watch was found with the time and date showing 1:30 p.m., Sept. 28. The watch had stopped. . . .

The skeletal remains were flown by helicopter to Chief Mountain where the coroner received them. Of note at the investigation scene was [the] noticeable lack of any struggle [at the] site, no blood and no heavily disturbed areas. Possible drag marks were found from the lakeshore to the willow thicket. The body site was quite disturbed, resembling a roto-tiller activity. The body appeared to have been buried and dug up several times. Bear scat samples from the immediate area were also collected. . . .

October 5, 1980: A search was begun in the Belly River area for the bear meeting the description given by the three treed hikers. Of special importance was the tag in the left ear. At approximately 0930 hours [9:30 a.m.] a large dark bear with blond hair over the hump and an ear tag in the left ear was sighted at the foot of Helen Lake by Rangers Bell and DeSanto. District Ranger Frauson informed DeSanto that the bear should be dispatched. At approximately 0935 hours [9:35 a.m.], the bear was terminated with shotgun slugs. . . . The tag in the left ear indicated #201, a male adult grizzly bear transplanted from the Many Glacier Valley in 1978 to the Valentine Creek drainage. The bear weighed 379 pounds. Measurement of the bear showed six feet, one inch from nose to tail tip. . . .

Of special note were three religious books all turned to areas [pages] between September 26 and 27. These were daily type passages designed to be read one day at a time. This indicates, along with the stopped watch, that Mr. Gordon probably died sometime on September 27. One passage on September 27 was underlined in blue ink corresponding to a ballpoint pen found in Mr. Gordon's possessions. . . .

Film found in Mr. Gordon's camera, which was later developed, had two photos of his campsite with items scattered around in similar fashion to the way it was found by park rangers on 10/3/80. Grizzly #201 was transported to Bozeman, Montana, to be autopsied. . . .

October 10, 1980: Final ground search at the campsite and body site. A pair of aviator sunglasses belonging to Mr. Gordon [was] found, as well as a piece of plastic peanut butter tubing [squeeze tube for hikers] matching a piece found at the initial investigation and search. A grid-type search of the shelf leading out into Elizabeth Lake was performed by Ranger Conrod with snorkeling equipment. Nothing relating to Mr. Gordon was discovered. The trap at the Belly River Ranger Station was tripped and left in place. . . .

Teeth prints on the religious reading material do match quite closely to the teeth of the bear, but due to varying pressures of jaw bite, etc., this proof is inconclusive.

"The bear weighed 370 [earlier indicated as 379] pounds (Lab No. 178351), 5–7 years," wrote the lab supervisor at Montana Fish, Wildlife and Parks to Glacier Park's superintendent on October 16, 1980. "Back fat 1¾ inches deep indicated good condition. . . . Conclusion: Nothing found on or in this carcass to indicate association with the incident of human mortality. . . . Examination of 16 bear scats reveals 9 scats contained from 5 to 90 percent (average 38 percent) of human tissue, bone, and/or clothing."

Scat #16 reveals that the bear may have had problems of his own: "Plastic baggies, wrappers—20 percent, Paper—5 percent, Bottle tops plastic—5 percent, *Perideridia sp.* tubers—60 percent, Debris, needles, dirt, duff—10 percent."

No human remains were found in Scat #16.

＿＿

What can we learn from Larry Gordon's tragic fate?

Glacier Park's Board of Review convened at 10:00 a.m. on October 22, 1980, at Park Headquarters, West Glacier, Montana. According to their report, "Laurence Byron Gordon probably was fatally mauled by a bear on either September 26 or 27, 1980, at a campsite at the lower end of Elizabeth Lake in Glacier National Park."

The report continues:

The possibility, though remote, exists that Mr. Gordon died from some other cause and was then consumed by the bear. . . . The camp was in some disarray. A sleeping bag, tent, and foam pad were scattered about, along with several other items. Some of the items were torn. There were no signs of a struggle. The only significant amount of blood was found on three pullover shirts near the willow patch in which Mr. Gordon's remains were found. A Seiko self-winding watch with a bloodstain was found. It had run down at 1:30 p.m., September 28. . . .

Deduction, using circumstantial evidence, indicates a strong probability that [grizzly bear] #201 was the bear that killed Mr. Gordon. The general description of the bear that treed the hikers matches #201. That bear was quite aggressive. Scat samples found in the vicinity of the fatal attack and the Glenn's Lake treeing incident contained human remains. The necropsy conducted by the Montana Fish, Wildlife and Parks laboratory at Bozeman showed no human remains in the suspected bear's intestinal tract. This may well have been because of the time lapse between the incident and the necropsy. Teeth marks in at least one book found in Mr. Gordon's pack match perfectly [*sic*] the dentition of #201. . . .

Conclusion

Mr. Gordon acted responsibly in that he obtained a camping permit and, further, had it revised when he discovered that a portion of his proposed route had been closed because of bear activity. He was receptive to the advice and information imparted to him by three staff members who were involved in issuing his permit. He followed his itinerary. His camp gear appeared clean. The only deviation from good camping practice was that his food cache was too close to what appeared to be his campsite, and it had not been secured out of reach of bears. . . .

In total, it appears that Mr. Gordon acted in such a manner as to reduce to a minimum the likelihood of a confrontation with bears.

The foregoing notwithstanding, this fatality, following close on the heels of the Eberly-Ammerman fatalities, places upon the National Park Service a heavy responsibility to vigorously reassess the bear management activity.

Discussion

Bears appear to show less "avoidance behavior" toward people within the Park than outside. According to Mr. [redacted], it has been "many" years since anyone was killed by a bear in Montana outside Glacier. (Subsequent search of the literature revealed that the last fatal mauling of a human by a bear in Montana, outside Glacier National Park, occurred in 1956.) Bears in Glacier have little reason to perceive man as a threat. This may be an evolving phenomenon involving gradual changes in bear behavior. . . .

The degree of feeding accomplished by the bears in the three fatalities this year raises the possibility that these bears were hungry and actually involved in predation.

"Death is swallowed up in victory." These words appear in the "evening" reading material Larry Gordon marked on September 26 at his Elizabeth Lake campsite.

We seek solace in wilderness, as Henry David Thoreau has written, and sometimes we don't even know we're seeking it until we find it. The hope is that Larry Gordon did find what he was looking for.

In the following chapter, a photographer spots a grizzly bear with an unusual complement of three cubs. Then, the grizzly bear notices him.

PART 4

FATAL SPRING–SUMMER OF THE GRIZZLIES, 1987

6

FINDING CHUCK

1987: THE ELK MOUNTAIN TRAIL GRIZZLY

He spotted the grizzly and first he saw two cubs, and then he handed me the binoculars and I saw them. . . . I said, Yeah, it's with three cubs. I looked through the binoculars some more as he was watching them through the camera lens and maybe taking a couple shots. And he commented to me at that point that the Lord had really been good to him to share seeing so many grizzlies in Montana.
　　　　　　　　　　　—The wife of Chuck Gibbs, interviewed
　　　　　　　　　　　　　　　　　　　by ranger, May 14, 1987

Fatality: Charles Gibbs
(Bear defending cubs; no action taken)

National Park Service–Glacier Park
Case Incident Record Number 870092
Location: Southwestern Glacier Park, Elk Mountain
Date/Time: Saturday, April 25, 1987, approximately 6:00 p.m.
Remains found April 26, 1987

She was golden-tan and beautiful. Even more unusual, she had raised three similarly tan young ones to near adulthood, despite the perils of food finding and the marauding of males. This family of four stayed close, exploring Glacier Park together.

Chuck Gibbs was a loving husband who carried his wife (recovering from surgery) twice across the stream on that final day. He was a photographer and a school bus driver, and he practiced the art of photography for art's sake, and because he needed extra money.

This Glacier Park grizzly mother and the man who loved to be out in nature—whether hiking, hunting (he was an expert marksman), or taking photographs—came together on April 25, 1987. That Saturday, the late-April Glacier Park sun shone upon Charles "Chuck" Gibbs and his wife [name redacted] at the far southwestern boundary of the Park, the temperature reaching the high 50s. The couple started up the Fielding Trail near the Fielding Patrol Cabin at about 11:15 a.m. Their plan was to hike to Ole Creek and then return. The sky was clear, with no precipitation. Nature seemed benign. They parked their camper truck on the access road, leaving their civilized comforts behind.

Born in Virginia, Chuck was a six-foot-tall Montanan with short brown hair and a mustache. He carried his camera bag, including a 400mm telephoto lens for close-ups.

At 2:00 p.m. Chuck and his wife arrived at Ole Creek, and at 3:00 p.m. left Ole Creek for the hike back to the trailhead. Their return hike was interrupted when Chuck spotted something on the southwest flank of Elk Mountain, high up beyond wooded brush. Chuck had an unusual ability to spot wildlife, either with the naked eye or through binoculars, even when the wildlife resembled nothing more than a dot. Movement of the dot caught his attention; even when at rest, his talent could spot the living creature.

"On Friday afternoon on entering the park," Chuck's wife said, "we stopped at the Goat Lick and he hiked quite a ways up the top of that mountain to photograph some goats that he spotted up there." Excerpts from her interview with the ranger [name redacted] on May 14, 1987, appear below.

Most of the people just kind of looked at the bridge, you know, from a distance, that was fine, but he got right on up to the top of the hill—I did not go with him at that time. I've been recuperating from surgery about three weeks ago, and I was just resting in the truck. And he came down and he was pointing it out to some local tourists, where all the goats were, and also looked over to the left and no one would have seen those, but he saw a herd of elk, and let people look through his binoculars at the elk too. They were kind of impressed that he could spot all those animals, you know. Real readily; [he] had a really keen eye in the woods. . . .

[It was] a beautiful afternoon on Saturday. We ate an early lunch around 11 o'clock and headed up the trail. . . . I kept hiking along very, very slowly, just taking my time and just enjoying the day. It was beautiful and just good to be out again. . . . He was going very slowly with me. At that time we came to a larger creek. I'd stepped across two previous creeks before the ranger cabin and got to that and I thought that was going to be my turning-around point, because I thought I wasn't quite up to fording the stream.

And he picked me up and carried me across. . . .

We headed on back, and he stopped and was glassing over to the left at some avalanche chutes that he thought, you know, looked like [they] could be promising for grizzlies. . . .

He thought with his naked eye that he had spotted a grizzly just from where we were looking back over to those clearings. It just looked like a dot, but you know, he's real uncanny about picking up things like that. I would have walked right back past the trail and never have [known] there was a grizzly within miles, and he spotted the grizzly, and first he saw two cubs, and then he handed me the binoculars and I saw them. . . . I said, Yeah, it's with three cubs. They were yearlings; they weren't this year's cubs, so they looked to be pretty good-size cubs. . . .

I looked through the binoculars some more as he was watching them through the camera lens, and maybe taking a couple shots. And he commented to me at that point that the Lord had really been good to him, to share seeing so many grizzlies in Montana. . . .

After we had sat there and watched the grizzlies and commented on how neat it was to spot them in the wilderness. . . . He was just kind of joking around [and] asked me what I would do, or said that if he was attacked, he would try to climb a tree, and said, What would you do? [. . .]

I said I'm not a good tree climber—but I'd probably give it a good try, too, if I possibly could. . . . You know, he just seemed kind of content just to see them—it was the first spotting of the spring, and [he] got real excited by that, and the fact that there were three cubs, which we had never seen before. . . .

He carried me back across the stream and constantly was asking me if I had any sharp pains or should we turn around. . . . I said No, I'm fine—just a little tired, just enjoying the hike. And as we were approaching back around the curve, I guess, close to the cabin . . . [he] said, I think I'll go up through this wooded brush and see if I can get a little bit closer and maybe get some good grizzly pictures. . . .

I said—you know, I wasn't about to stop him. . . . that's what he loves to do—and I said I'll just walk back to the truck and wait, and that was around 5:00 p.m. . . .

He knew he had plenty of daylight time. . . . It was really, really warm, like I said, on that exposure, when we spotted the grizzly, because she stopped and rested under a tree, looking for some shade, and the cubs were kind of just playing. . . .

And so I went back, I might have dozed a little bit, I just sat up in the cab and listened to the radio, and I think it was really [around] 7:30 that [I] just kind of started [worrying]. . . .

[By] 8:30 [p.m.] it's starting getting dusk, and he should be here soon—and 9:00 it was pretty dark, but maybe he got right to the edge of the trail and he would be there shortly after dark.

At 10:00 I said I'd wait till 10:15, and start looking for someone to contact, and remembered passing the Walton Ranger Station on the way in, assumed that might be the closest contact and phone. . . .

She arrived at the Walton Ranger Station, where rangers immediately responded to her plea for help, organizing a search party and requesting helicopter assistance. Of course, the light was gone and the night had arrived.

"[I] received a phone call from Ranger [redacted] at Walton who was reporting an overdue hiker in the Fielding area," wrote the Reporting Ranger (R/R) [name redacted] in the "Supplementary Case/Incident

Record," dated May 2, 1987. The time was "approximately 2345 hours [11:45 p.m.] on 4/25/87."

> It was decided that [name redacted] would hike into the Fielding patrol cabin and conduct a hasty search, taking proper precautions in bear country.
>
> R/R held briefings for the Flathead Co. Sheriff and dog teams as well as NVSAR [search and rescue]. The NPS Command trailer was dispatched to the scene to serve as a field command post. A radio relay was also established at the Walton Ranger Station to relay radio traffic between the search area and park headquarters.

"Requesting [name redacted] to Fielding to stay with wife," the Radio Transmission Log KOE 729, Walton Ranger Station noted on April 26. The time was now 1:45 a.m.

Finally daylight returned. At 9:00 a.m. three armed rangers set out to find Chuck Gibbs.

"We departed from the point last seen . . . and conducted a coarse [rough] grid, hasty search up the southwest flank of Elk Mountain in an effort to cut sign [spot evidence] of the victim and/or sow grizzly and cubs," wrote Ranger [redacted] in the Supplementary Case/Incident Record. The April 30 report continues:

> We spaced ourselves approximately 50 meters apart and kept ourselves intervisible [keeping each in sight of the other]. The perimeter of our search area was marked with yellow flagging. We were delayed twice to allow Flathead County Sheriff Dept. search dog handlers to establish their search area, and then continued our search.
>
> At approximately 1510 hrs [3:10 p.m.] at the 5,900-foot level on the southwest flank of Elk Mountain, I observed the body of the victim lying in a supine position in open ground approximately 20 meters to my right (east). I shouted for assistance from Rangers [redacted], and after they covered my advance with shotguns, I approached the body.
>
> I observed the body of a male matching the description of Gibbs and radioed the command post that I had an apparent Code 10-50f [fatality].

There was no pulse or respirations present on the body and rigor mortis had set in on the extremities. The pupils were fixed and dilated. The body had numerous frontal area wounds which appeared to have been inflicted by a bear. There were no drag marks or indication of a struggle at the location of the body.

Evidence at that location indicated that the victim had been dragged out of a tree and had attempted to fend off the bear while facing it. Wounds on the body were exclusively on the front of the body. Ranger [redacted] located the victim's blue camera bag containing extra camera body and lenses approximately 200 meters downslope. It appeared to have been purposefully placed there by the victim.

The body location and apparent attack site were marked and secured. The victim was airlifted from the site by a Malmstrom Air Force Base helicopter. Ground teams cleared from the scene at approximately 1730 hrs [5:30 p.m.].

Evidence—Clothing: The victim was wearing tan trousers, a blue and tan checked flannel long-sleeved shirt, a gray undershirt with red sleeves, blue/gray socks, a brown leather belt, and LaCrosse high-topped leather/rubber boots with round nubbed rubber soles. A black nylon/cordura shoulder holster was on the body but did not contain a weapon. It was under the victim's back and left side and also contained an empty and unsnapped leather ammunition dump pouch. . . .

I observed no bear tracks, scat or other sign in the immediate vicinity of the body. The victim's .45 semiautomatic Colt and camera were found at the apparent attack site on the ground. There were no spent bullet casings found at the scene. There was no ammunition recovered from the immediate vicinity of the body. . . . Photographs of the body and the scene were taken on-site.

On April 27, Ranger [redacted] "met with Mrs. Gibbs at the Bear Creek Ranch and conducted an interview, recorded on cassette tape, regarding events leading up to the incident." The ranger continues in his Supplementary Case/Incident Record, dated 4/30/87: "I then escorted Mrs. Gibbs and her friends to the trailhead per Mrs. Gibbs's request, then

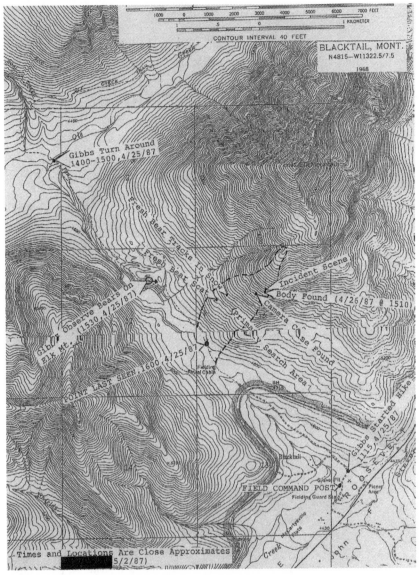

Map showing Chuck Gibbs's fatality scene, including point last seen, primary search area, camera case found, and body found.

ILLUSTRATION FROM CASE INCIDENT RECORD NUMBER 870092

back to a location where I could locate for Mrs. Gibbs, through binoculars, the incident location on Elk Mountain."

On April 28, "At about noon . . . [name redacted] called me to advise that [two names redacted] had searched the incident scene with a metal detector with negative results." No bullets or bullet casings were found. Although the gun recovered did not have a recently cleaned barrel, it was found that it was unlikely that the gun had been fired (and so neither the sow nor cubs had run off injured by a gunshot). This ranger report [name redacted] is dated April 30, 1987.

On April 29, "I conducted a patrol of the Autumn Creek Trail and found only one fresh bear track toward the lower end of the trail," wrote [redacted] in his Supplementary Case/Incident Record of April 30. "At noon I met with [three names redacted] and reported additional findings at the scene, including blood-soaked tree limbs approximately 18 feet up a tree and evidence of blood locations on the ground around the scene not noted before."

On May 14, a cause of death was reported, which the coroner gave as "hemorrhaging." The "Nature of Incident" was listed as "DEATH/ACCIDENTAL Bear Mauling."

What did the exhaustive investigation find?

On May 14, a "Summary of Investigation" was prepared by a Park employee, whose name was redacted. The time was given as 3:10 p.m. on April 26.

Mr. Gibbs's body was found at about the 5,900-foot level on the south aspect of Elk Mountain, about ¾ mile and 1,100 feet above the point last seen on the Fielding Trail. Mr. Gibbs was the apparent victim of a fatal bear mauling incident.

Evidence found at the scene included a blood trail leading directly downhill for about 150 feet from the base of two trees to Gibbs's location. Scattered about the base of these two trees were found a semiautomatic pistol with five rounds in the magazine and one round in the chamber (cocked and off safety); a roll of exposed film; two folding knives; a camera with a 400mm lens attached; six unspent rounds of ammunition; two cough drops and two cough drop wrappers; and a

U.S. DEPARTMENT OF THE INTERIOR
NATIONAL PARK SERVICE

SUPPLEMENTARY CASE/INCIDENT RECORD

ORGANIZATION (PARK) NAME	CASE/INCIDENT NUMBER
Glacier National Park	8 7 0 0 9 2

LOCATION OF INCIDENT.	DATE OF INCIDENT
Elk Mountain	MO 0 4 DA 2 5 YR 8 7

NATURE OF INCIDENT   DEATH/ ACCIDENTAL

Bear Attack, Search, Recovery

COMPLAINANT'S NAME	COMPLAINANT'S ADDRESS
Charles Gibbs	(b)(7)(C), (b)(6) LIBBY, MT.

RESULTS OF INVESTIGATION

MISC. FIELD OBSERVATIONS

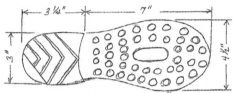

Boot print of Charles Gibbs (left boot) sketched
from track on the Fielding Trail, 4/26/87, by
(b)(7)(C),(b)(6)

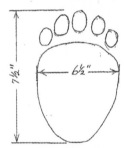
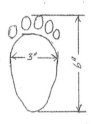

Sketches of fresh bear track found on snowfield on 4/26/87
approximately ¼ mile south-west of accident scene, by
(b)(7)(C),(b)(6).

(b)(7)(C), (b)(6)   5/2/87   APPROVED BY (SIGNATURE AND DATE)   5/5/87

Boot print of Chuck Gibbs (left boot) sketched from track on the Fielding Trail,
April 26, 1987. Sketches of fresh bear tracks found on snowfield on April 26,
approximately one-half mile southwest of the fatality site.

ILLUSTRATION FROM CASE INCIDENT RECORD NUMBER 870092

baseball cap. Another blood trail was found between the base of the most northerly tree ("tree #1") for about 20 feet east and at a right angle (across slope) to the fall-line.

In tree #1 several freshly broken branches were found up the tree to a height of 20 feet. Bear claw marks were found up the tree to a height of 14 feet. Hair from a bear was also found at 14 feet. A blood-soaked branch (not broken) was found at 16 feet up the tree. Several broken branches, green and dead, were found at the base of [the] tree, some stained with blood.

Approximately 150 yards below the body (200 yards below tree #1) was found a camera bag at the base of a tree. The bag was upright, closed, and contained a camera body, binoculars, film, lenses, and camera filters.

Two rolls of exposed film found at the scene (roll in camera and roll found at the base of tree #1) were processed by Kodak laboratories, and 40 slide photographs taken by Mr. Gibbs in the hours leading up to the time of his death were obtained. Thirty-nine of the photographs are of grizzly bear(s) and one photograph is of an Amtrak train passing "Blacktail Station" near the Fielding Trailhead.

On 5/13/87 rangers returned to the scene of the incident with prints of Mr. Gibbs's photographs and a camera with a 400mm lens to determine Mr. Gibbs's location when each photograph was taken. Mr. Gibbs's locations were determined in all but three places with very high confidence.

Results indicate that Mr. Gibbs photographed the bears from eight different locations on Elk Mountain, from a standing position, in the open (not concealed by rock or vegetation).

His first position was near the tree where the camera bag was found, and photographs taken here are believed to have been taken with a lens other than 400mm. The seven other photograph positions were within 150 feet of the incident scene (about 200 yards uphill from the first position). The farthest distance measured between Mr. Gibbs's positions and the bears was 280 feet; the closest was 168 feet, and was at the last photograph taken.

What happened to the golden-tan mother grizzly and her three golden-tan cubs? A "Report of Accident/Incident" under the letterhead "US Department of the Interior, Safety Management Information System," stated the following:

> Corrective action taken or planned. At this time it is believed the attack was provoked by the possible surprise encroachment on a grizzly bear. No action taken or planned at this time pending further investigation.

Would Chuck have agreed?

Chuck's wife, on the day after his disappearance, told Ranger [redacted] that "Her husband had a great admiration for grizzly bears, and would not have wanted the bear responsible for his death to be killed." (See Supplementary Case/Incident Record dated May 10, 1987, by Ranger [redacted] in Case Incident Record Number 870092.)

The four grizzlies are gone now, vanishing into the backcountry of Glacier Park. Their photographs remain.

The wife of Chuck Gibbs described that day of April 25, before the tragedy occurred, as a "beautiful afternoon." Where Chuck was found on Elk Mountain, a large cairn of rocks now stands.

—◆—

The following chapter solves the mystery of an avid hiker who went missing on his day off from work at Glacier Park.

7

FINDING GARY

1987: THE APIKUNI (APPEKUNNY) CIRQUE GRIZZLY

It seems as if my hearing has become more acute. I first heard the grizzly bear and her cubs, I first heard the bighorn sheep at Iceberg Lake, I first heard the sounds of the golden eagles' young crying from their aeries. Only after hearing them was I able to search them out and see them.

—GARY GOEDEN'S DIARY, JULY 22, 1987
(THE DAY BEFORE THE ATTACK)

Fatality: Gary Goeden
(No bear found)

National Park Service—Glacier Park
Case Incident Record Number 870092
Location: Apikuni Cirque
Date/Time: Thursday, July 23, 1987, morning
Remains found September 1, 1987

Gary Goeden had a passion for hiking, climbing, photography, and nature—its beauty, but also its harsh realities. He had already hiked and climbed over two hundred miles in the mostly vertical Glacier Park since arriving on June 16, 1987, for his job as night auditor at the Swiftcurrent Motor Inn, located near Many Glacier Hotel. His night-owl hours at the

Inn—from 11:00 p.m. to 7:00 a.m.—facilitated his outdoor adventures during the day. Gary would go straight from work to his next hike, then sleep in the late afternoon and early evening before returning to work.

On June 27, while hiking, he experienced a non-injurious encounter with a mother grizzly and two cubs, reporting this event to a ranger, who filled out a "Bear Sighting Form," below:

Specific Location: Grinnell Glacier Trail north of first switchback.
Time: 0915 [9:15 a.m.].
Identifying Marks: All 3 bears uniform medium brown.
Comments: Hiker came upon sow + 2 cubs on south side of Grinnell Glacier Trail, foraging. Hiker observed bear from 10 yards while ringing bell. Bear + cubs paid him no attention, continuing to forage. Hiker passed by continuing up trail and observed bears foraging for 45 minutes from further vantage.

Gary wrote in his personal diary on July 22: "I haven't hiked for three days now, and I'm starting to get on edge. Rain for over three days—snow in the peaks. . . . The boon of having mornings and afternoons off for hiking becomes a bore when it's raining and everyone else is at work. Even I can only read so long."

So it was with eagerness on July 23, after a rainfall from two to six inches the day before, that Gary set out for his next backcountry hike. The early-morning air was fresh and chilled, and the sky cleared in a few hours. His fellow employee, a young woman, came to breakfast at 7:10 a.m.; Gary, age twenty-nine, came in at 7:15, and was still there when she left the employee cafeteria at 7:30. She described him as a slender man, six-foot-two, with short, curly sandy-blond hair, earlobe-length sideburns, a small mustache, and tortoiseshell-framed eyeglasses. He wore a light blue T-shirt with dark blue trim and tan shorts. She mentioned that he was impressed with the Glacier Park goats and bighorn sheep.

Friends reported that Gary planned to hike to the Apikuni Cirque, and perhaps climb Mount Henkel. To reach the Cirque, Gary would repeat one of his favorite treks: the Apikuni Trail to the Apikuni Falls and Cirque. In his diary he kept his hiking schedule, which lists:

06-17 Appekunny Falls
07-01 Appekunny Falls, Scramble
07-02 Appekunny Creek, Scramble
07-10 Appekunny Falls

Even better, today—July 23—was Gary's day off. He did not need to hurry back. He was seen by another employee walking on the road with his blue visor and faded blue nylon backpack with black shoulder straps (with no waistband) at the Many Glacier Hotel intersection.

"Oh, he must have the day off," she thought.

This young person was perhaps the last to see Gary alive.

The trail to Apikuni Falls is a moderately strenuous two-mile hike. "It leads up to the desolate cliffs of Apikuni Mountain to visit a long and slender waterfall," writes Erik Molvar in *Hiking Glacier and Waterton Lakes National Parks*.

> The trek begins on Apikuni Flats, where grassy meadows offer views of the major peaks up the valley. . . . The path ultimately climbs onto rocky and barren slopes where only a few firs survive, and the bleached and gnarled skeletons of long-dead white bark pines rise mournfully to the sky. Apikuni Falls can be seen ahead, dropping through a cleft in the limestone walls. The path becomes primitive with steep, uneven footing as it navigates a rocky ravine to reach the base of the falls.[10]

In a grassy meadow along the way, a spring bubbling straight from the earth allows a hiker to fill up with water that is (at least, probably) pure. Perhaps Gary refilled his quart water bottle here.

The temperature now had risen to 71 degrees. From Apikuni Falls Gary hiked on to the Apikuni Cirque, in his words, for "a good scramble."

"The high cirque beyond is accessible to climbers via a little scrambling," writes Eric Molvar. "The enterprising bushwhacker who reaches the head of this tiny bowl is rewarded with views of Natahki Lake and the towering cliff walls surrounding it."[11]

Gary himself describes what a cirque is in his diary: "The glaciers [in Glacier Park] at one time were overwhelming, at least 2,500 feet deep in the larger valleys, and the crests alone remaining above level," Gary wrote on July 22 (one day before going missing). He explains further:

The cirque is the area at the head of the glacier that is subjected to glacial erosion the longest. The cirque was actually the basin where the glacier started eroding the rocks. Cracker Lake and Iceberg Lake are two of the best examples of cirque lakes.

Park personnel later discovered that grizzlies had frequented the area of Apikuni Cirque, leaving diggings and scat (droppings). Perhaps army cutworm moths (a protein-rich bear treat) flew to the Cirque during the hot day to rest, shaded beneath its pebbles.

It was here that Gary disappeared.

Because July 23 was his night off from work, he was not known to be missing until the next work night, on Friday, July 24.

At 11:30 p.m. Gary was a half-hour overdue. The Swiftcurrent Motor Inn manager "reported to the Many Glacier Ranger Station that the night auditor (Gary J. Goeden) did not return from a hike, or to show up to work at his scheduled time of 2300 [11:00 p.m.], 7/24/87." According to the Case Incident Record, dated July 28, the "Nature of Incident" is "Missing Person—Search."

The report continues:

Goeden reportedly stated to friends on Thursday morning, 7/23/87, between 0730 and 0745 [7:30 or 7:45 a.m.], that he intended to hike in the Appekunny Cirque and climb Mt. Hinkle [Henkel]. A detailed investigation and search was conducted from 7/25/87–7/28/87 without finding Mr. Goeden. During this time period, the search involved approximately 24 NPS personnel, a helicopter and pilot, three Flathead County Deputy Sheriffs, and three Flathead scent dogs.

On this date and time, the search effort is ongoing.

To ascertain Gary's state of mind, rangers interviewed scores of witnesses. In the case of a missing person, suicide is always a remote possibility.

MISSING

PLEASE HELP US LOCATE THIS PERSON

NAME: GARY J. GOEDEN
AGE: 29
HEIGHT: 6' 2"
WEIGHT: 165 LBS.

SWIFTCURRENT MOTEL EMPLOYEE
HOME: WISCONSIN

DESCRIPTION: CAUCASIAN MALE
SLENDER BUILD
SHORT, CURLY SANDY-BLONDE HAIR
EARLOBE-LENGTH SIDEBURNS, SMALL MUSTACHE
WEARS TORTOISE-SHELL GLASSES, VERY NEARSIGHTED

LAST SEEN WEARING LT. BLUE T-SHIRT W/ DK. BLUE TRIM
FADED BLUE CUTOFF SHORTS

POSSESSES TWO WINDBREAKERS — ONE BLUE, ONE BEIGE
BEIGE-BROWN FLANNEL SHIRT
VIBRAM BOOTS, APPROX. SIZE 9½
DK. BLUE DAYPACK
BRILLIANT BLUE CAMERA BAG, POSSIBLY CONTAINING
MINOLTA CAMERA AND SEVERAL LENSES

LAST SEEN NEAR SWIFTCURRENT MOTEL, THURS. 7/23, APPROX. 7:45AM
POSSIBLY HAD INTENTIONS OF HIKING TO APPEKUNY FALLS AND
CONTINUING ON TO CLIMB MT. HENKL

Missing person sign posted around Glacier Park describing Gary Goeden, his clothing and possessions, and point last seen, near the Many Glacier area's Swiftcurrent Motor Inn. ILLUSTRATION FROM CASE INCIDENT RECORD NUMBER 870092

"At about 0745 [7:45 a.m.], a campstore clerk talked to the subject, who seemed frustrated on learning from a ranger that several trails were closed," wrote Ranger [redacted] in a Supplementary Case/Incident Record, dated August 2. The subject supposedly stated that "if Appekunny is open, I'm going to do that, and then go over Hinkle [Henkel Mountain]. [Name redacted] stated that the subject seemed to be bothered by something. Other employees who saw Goeden on Thursday morning (such as [name redacted]) felt the subject was in a cheerful mood."

The report continues:

Ranger [redacted] searched Goeden's dorm cabin A-9 on Friday, and found: a white paint imprint of Goeden's lug sole boot, a tent, backpacker's stove, red frame pack, undeveloped film, numerous color prints, books, a cassette radio, and a loose leaf diary. The diary contained an entry indicating that he intended to hike over Siyeh Pass on 7/24/87 [the following day]. . . .

I also talked to another employee [redacted], who with three other employees hiked in the Natahki-Appekunny Cirque on Thursday from 4–8 p.m. [Redacted] said they did not see Goeden in the area.

On July 31, rangers, at some risk to their own lives, continued trying to find Gary. They looked for evidence in cliffs and waterfall areas in Apikuni Cirque. In a "Search for Missing Person" report dated July 31, a ranger [redacted] wrote: "The Drainage Basin Proper was searched en route back to Appekunny Falls Trail, along the entire water course. The waterfall below the lower lake is [approximately] 75 feet vertical, and the gorge is narrow. If the subject is in the pool at the base of the falls, he will not be visualized unless a rappel [with rope] were made directly into it. Loose rock conditions in the area above the pool would cause this to be a hazardous undertaking beyond reason."

Where was Gary?

"Major search areas continued until July 31, 1987," the Board of Inquiry reported, "and a scaled-down search continued [afterward]."

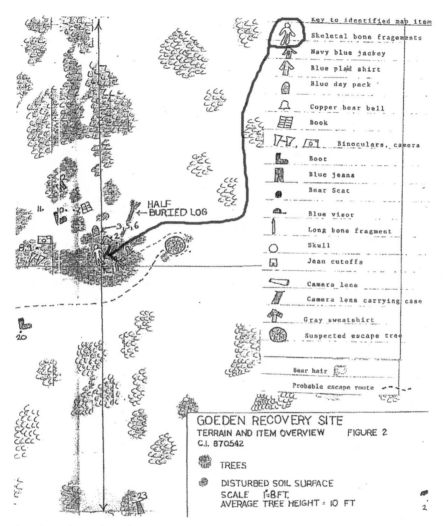

Key to identified map item

- Skeletal bone fragments
- Navy blue jacket
- Blue plaid shirt
- Blue day pack
- Copper bear bell
- Book
- Binoculars, camera
- Boot
- Blue jeans
- Bear Scat
- Blue visor
- Long bone fragment
- Skull
- Jean cutoffs
- Camera lens
- Camera lens carrying case
- Gray sweatshirt
- Suspected escape tree
- Bear hair
- Probable escape route

HALF ←BURIED LOG

GOEDEN RECOVERY SITE
TERRAIN AND ITEM OVERVIEW   FIGURE 2
C.I. 870542

- TREES
- DISTURBED SOIL SURFACE
SCALE 1=8FT.
AVERAGE TREE HEIGHT = 10 FT

Terrain and overview of Gary Goeden recovery site, showing location of skeletal bone fragments (see arrow) within trees near a half-buried log. Dotted line shows probable escape route toward suspected escape tree. Items found include clothing and copper bear bell. ILLUSTRATION FROM CASE INCIDENT RECORD NUMBER 870092

On August 2, the Case Incident Record reports, "Received 344 Statement from [redacted] that he climbed Hinkle [Henkel Mountain] on 7/23/87, Thursday, and that he noticed no other persons at the time he climbed up and down."

Then, on September 1, 1987, at approximately 2:00 p.m., an off-duty Glacier Park communications dispatcher and a friend discovered human remains. They hiked out and reported their find to rangers at 6:30 p.m.

"They described a boot, camera and blue pack lying on the ground in a scrub forest at the upper end of the cirque," Ranger [redacted] wrote in the "Case Summary," dated September 7, 1987. "On 9/2/87 at 0800 hours [8:00 a.m.], Rangers [redacted] hiked up into Appekunny Cirque, located and confirmed Gary Goeden's remains. . . . "The area is an open stunted pine/fir forest with bear grass predominating as the undergrowth. A small creek is actively flowing approximately 200 feet west of the location site. The winds in the cirque tend to swirl and shift from various directions. Bear diggings and scat of the year are numerous and widely dispersed throughout the area."

In a "Scene Investigation" report, dated September 7, Ranger [redacted] wrote that "A scene sketch and photographs are available for reference."

He continued:

The primary location site was determined by the greatest density of skeletal remains and personal property. Skeletal remains at the site consisted of ribs, sternum, and some cervical vertebrae, all partially covered by loose soil and branches. The personal property included a blue windbreaker jacket, a torn plaid flannel shirt stained with body fluids, and a blue "Caribou" daypack. . . . His eyeglasses, a film canister containing exposed film, a small bell, and a plastic bag containing an apple were found in the loose soil buried 2–6 inches below the skeletal remains.

Scene Reconstruction

The film recovered at the site from the victim's camera (11 frames), and the separately exposed roll, show a sequence of locations from the Swiftcurrent Motor Inn to a point less than ½ mile from the location site. . . . In summary, the photographs show that

1. He traveled east on the Many Glacier Road from the direction of the Motor Inn to the Hotel Junction and then on toward the Appekunny Trailhead.
2. He hiked up the Appekunny Trail and into the cirque above the Falls.
3. He continued into the cirque and climbed/hiked up an obvious left-sloping ramp into the upper end of the cirque.
4. Morning mist and shadows support that photograph #12 was taken prior to afternoon; and
5. That the last photos taken show his location at the top of the left-sloping ramp to be less than ½ of a mile NE of the primary location site. This is the victim's last known location based on photographs. . . .

Scene Reconstruction, cont'd.

1. A gray sweatshirt with red stripes on the upper arms was located slightly upslope and [approximately] 125 feet NW of the primary site. The sweatshirt has a jagged rip in the interior head lining. . . .
2. A blue visor cap (known to be Goeden's), as well as the sweatshirt . . . was located approximately 65 feet WNW from the primary site. The visor has large animal bites on the bill and is bloodstained. Human hair and bear hair was found at this location site. The soil and duff was compacted.
3. A pair of tan corduroy shorts was found in close proximity to the [camera] lens. The shorts had no body fluids on them.
4. Looking from the location of the lens ENE, a path of least resistance can be determined, and from here can be seen the tallest tree in the area (15 feet [approximately]). As the tree is approached from this direction, a freshly broken branch on the tree can be seen. On close investigation, it can be observed that the branch was broken in the direction of a pull that the victim would have attempted if trying to climb the tree. Scuff marks (possibly boot) were observed near the base of the tree, and freshly removed bits of bark were lying on the ground at the tree's base. No other scuff marks were observed further up the trunk, and there were no broken branches above the one described above.

It appears that the victim did not make it up the tree. Four other branches were broken off the tree where the victim may have tried to escape a bear by running around the tree in a counterclockwise direction. The broken branches (photographed) were all broken in the same direction, and it occurred this season as evidenced by the green foliage. The tree is less than 20 feet from the primary location site. There were no body fluids found on or near the tree. There are no drag marks leading to the primary location site.

In "Log: Events Involving Remains Discovery and Recovery," Ranger [redacted] writes that on September 2, the following occurred:

> 1145 [11:45 a.m.] Gary's girlfriend notified through return call to ranger station.
> She was also from Wisconsin and worked at Yellowstone Park.
> At 1830 [6:30 p.m.] Recovery crew returns to ranger station with remains.
> At 1930 [7:30 p.m.] Bodily remains released to Deputy Coroner for disposition to family. Property of value kept for inventory and shipping by Park personnel to family.

Confirmation of Gary's identity was accomplished with dental records.

The Board of Inquiry into Gary Goeden's death met, reporting their conclusion in a report dated September 30, 1987:

Conclusion

Based on evidence at the scene, the following scenario is probable: Gary Goeden hiked alone into the Appekunny Cirque area on July 23, 1987. He may have had a surprise encounter with a grizzly bear at the streamside. He apparently had contact and struggle with a grizzly bear at the location where his visor was found, and attempted to evade the bear by moving to the tallest tree in the area. Broken branches on the tree and scuff marks and grizzly bear hair at the base of the tree indicate he attempted unsuccessfully to climb the tree and struggled with a bear at this point. Goeden's remains were found less than 20 feet from the tree.

It should be noted that the responsible grizzly bear (or bears) were not found.

Fortunately, Gary was found, and his eloquent words at the beginning of this chapter commemorate him

In the next chapter, a Good Samaritan risks his own life trying to save a bear attack victim.

PART 5

FATAL AUTUMN OF THE GRIZZLIES, 1992

8

FINDING JOHN

1992: THE LOOP TRAIL GRIZZLIES

I knew that the attack was very recent. Because of that, I tried to determine where the bear went, and follow the blood trail off the main Loop Trail, in hopes that the victim would be alive and there would be something that I could do. I did have a bear [repellent] canister . . . and felt that, although this was a very dangerous situation, that I might be able to take some reasonable chance and help the guy.
　　　　　—"Good Samaritan" (name redacted), "Bear
　　　　　　　　Mauling Interview," October 4, 1992

Fatality: John Petranyi
(Mother bear and two cubs killed)

National Park Service–Glacier Park
Case Incident Record Number 92158
Location: Loop Trail, one-half mile south of Granite Park Campground
Date/Time: October 3, 1992, approximately 11:00 a.m.

Landscapes were what John Petranyi loved to photograph, not wildlife like bear, elk, or moose. His brother said he lived for his three weeks' annual vacation time, when he was set free. That was when John could enter those landscapes and walk in the unspoiled backcountry of beautiful parks, in Canada as well as the United States.

In Glacier Park, John left his car, a Mazda with Wisconsin plates, at the parking spot above the Loop Trail, and began hiking to the Granite Park Campground, where he could go on to visit the historic Granite Park Chalet. The views from the above-timberline Chalet are magnificent.

Of course, the Granite Park Campground is the site of Julie Helgeson's fatality in 1967's "Night of the Grizzlies." But John Petranyi, a seasoned forty-year-old, was hiking under the open sky of daytime. Surely he wouldn't encounter any danger.

Had others been attacked in the Granite Park area, after Julie Helgeson's attack?

The Petranyi Board of Inquiry Report issued a historic record of "Bear Maulings in Granite Park Chalet / Loop Trail Area" on December 17, 1992, including John's attack:

Date	Time	Location	Species	Sex	Cubs?	People
08-13-67	12:45 a.m.	Granite Park Campground	Griz	F		2 of 2
09-11-86	3:00 p.m.	Loop Tr. just below Petranyi Site	Griz	Unknown		2 of 2
08-18-89	4:00 p.m.	Loop Tr. ½ mi above Packers Roost junction	Griz	F	2 yrlg*	1 of 2
10/03/92	11:00 a.m.	Loop Tr. ½ mi below Granite Park Chalet	Griz	F	2 COY†	1 of 1

* yrlg indicates "yearling."
† COY indicates "cub of the year."

But John did not arrive at the Granite Park Campground, or at Granite Park Chalet.

He expected to see the comforting presence of fellow hikers along the way. The Board of Inquiry into the Death of John Petranyi states that "Approximately one-half of backcountry trail use in the Park is in the Granite Park / Many Glacier Valley area. Bears appear to be habituated to human presence during the heavy visitor-use period (July and August), and tend to avoid the trails and Chalet. However, as fall approaches and trail use declines, the bears may not be avoiding the visitor-use areas as before, and the probability of surprise encounters may increase" (page 3).

On that October 3, 1992, John was a colorful figure with his red day-pack and blue hat, carrying his blue camera bag and tripod as he hiked along the Loop Trail (known also as the Granite Park Trail). The trees and bushes along the way showed autumn yellows and reds, and John took photographs. The Loop Trail curves and changes elevation many times, causing poor sighting distance of what is ahead. At the site of the soon-to-come bear encounter, John stopped to photograph his view of Glacier Park's Heaven's Peak. The time was approximately 11:00 a.m.

John was not heard from again.

A report of "a possible bear attack near Granite Park Chalet" came in at 5:30 p.m. to the Glacier Park Communications Center.

"By the time of my arrival," wrote Ranger [redacted] on November 16, 1992, "Rangers [redacted] had flown to Granite Park and contacted the reporting individual, who had reportedly arrived at the scene shortly after the incident occurred." (See Good Samaritan's quote at the beginning of this chapter.)

In the "Bear Mauling Interview" conducted by Ranger [redacted] on October 4, the Good Samaritan related the following.

> Okay, I was in the Granite Park campground, having arrived there the night before the incident. . . . [I] did not eat dinner in the campground, so there was no food out.
>
> [The next morning] I noticed fresh cub tracks *over my fresh tracks* [emphasis added] in the trail. That indicated to me that sometime between 10 and 11 a.m. a cub had walked through my camp. I did not see any tracks of the accompanying adult, but that doesn't mean too much, of course. . . .
>
> I started out on my day hike. . . . I then went down the Loop Trail approximately 150 feet, at which point I saw evidence of a bear attack. There I saw a man's cap in the middle of the trail, a camera on [a] tripod with a lens cover on and the legs all folded, indicating no use of the camera, set off to the side of the trail, and with a red daypack laying

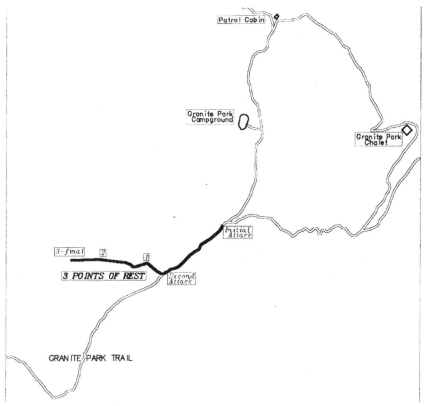

Overall view of John Petranyi attack and fatality sites along the Granite Park Trail, showing initial attack site, second attack site, and final point of rest, where he was found. ILLUSTRATION FROM CASE INCIDENT RECORD NUMBER 921583

in the middle of the trail. Upon backing uphill about 20 to 30 feet I noticed the major pool of blood in the middle of the trail, and then off to the trail to the right, looking downhill.

I proceeded then down the trail following bear tracks, right down the middle of the Loop Trail. Tracks and spots of blood were down, followed for about 150 feet down the trail. At that point, there was an indication of a scuffle, a lot of dragging and fresh marks in the trail. A boot lace was in the trail. . . .

I followed the blood trail about 150 feet into the brush, at which point I found the body. I say "the body"; I don't know if the victim was alive or not at that point. I felt for a pulse. I did not see any evidence of a pulse. The body was warm; the blood on his scars was starting to turn dark. At this point he had been mauled severely. . . .

I retreated fairly quickly and headed back to my campsite with the intention of getting a jacket to go back and cover him up, in case he was alive and warmth would do him some good. Upon going back up the trail toward camp I checked his daypack to see if he had a coat in there, which he did. I took that coat out and quickly returned to the point where I had seen the body in no more than 3 to 4 minutes, total distance of maybe, no more than, I'm guessing 500 feet, a couple hundred yards.

The body was not there by the time I got back in that amount of time.

The Good Samaritan then left his can of bear repellent spray and notes to warn others coming up the trail. Looking through his binoculars he was able to see people at the Granite Park Chalet, notified them, and left more warning notes on other incoming trails.

The Good Samaritan's account continues:

Then the rangers and I eventually went in to locate the body. We located the body by around maybe 1900 [7:00 p.m.]. The body had been drug another 150 feet from the site where I had observed it, pretty much in the same condition as far as any predatorial type behavior. . . .

We got back to the original site of the incident where the daypack was in the trail. The rangers were taking photographs, at which point we heard huffing, I guess you would say—grunting noises, and definitely some of that behavior where they jump up and down on their hind legs, kind of an aggressive type thing, from around a blind spot in the trail.

Eventually a sow and a cub . . . we only saw the front half of the sow and the cub . . . I would estimate at 350 lbs. range, female, which is a pretty big female. I would estimate the cub was a second-year cub. It was a large cub. . . .

The first time that the bear saw us, it stopped dead in its tracks and stood there. We probably observed the bear for less than 15 seconds. It backed around and sort of flanked us initially, back off to our left looking uphill, which is the side of the trail the body was on . . . We could hear the bear for maybe another 30 seconds out in the brush. After that we didn't have any further observation of the bear being in the area.

By now twilight was approaching. John's body was still lying where he had been found. "R/R [reporting ranger] photographed the point of rest and marked the area with flagging," according to that ranger's Supplementary Case/Incident Record, dated October 13, 1992.

The decision to evacuate the body in the morning was made because of the daylight hours left, and number of people it would take to do a carry-out, and the presence of the bear(s) still in the area. Rangers [redacted] exited the area, flagging the route as we went. At the site of the pack we stopped to try to get some ID of the person who had been attacked. While doing so, Rangers [redacted] were charged by a dark-brown-color sow and at least one cub. The cub was light brown in color with dark brown legs. The bears charged within 50 feet of Rangers [redacted]. At this time [they] left the area and hiked back to the patrol cabin.

October 4, 1992

The operation [to recover John's body] was delayed because of weather until 1100 hours [11:00 a.m.]. . . . While the first group was being flown in to Granite, they observed the bears near and on the body. The bears were a sow, dark brown in color, with a lighter color around the neck area. Two cubs of the year [had] lighter-color bodies and dark legs.

After leaving the patrol cabin the helicopter flew over the area of the body to chase the bears away from the area. The six rangers then started to enter the area for the body recovery and investigation. The bears kept coming back to the area and the helicopter chased them off and down the slope while rangers were in the area. The body was removed from the area by the helicopter and flown to headquarters. The rangers then took measurements and photos of the scene. The rangers were flown out that night from the Chalet.

On October 4, John's father was notified by [redacted].

"At approximately 1645 hours [4:45 p.m.], [redacted] returned a call stating that he had contacted the victim's father . . . and notified him of his son's death. [Redacted] spoke to [the father] briefly, giving him some details of the incident and the telephone number of Johnson's mortuary. At approximately 1900 hours [7:00 p.m.] [redacted] again contacted the victim's father and requested and received permission to release the victim's name."

The order of the discoveries on the trail and in the brush leading rangers to the body is detailed in an "Enlarged View of Incident Scene without Geographic Background," in the Case Incident Record. Accompanying the graphic (not shown) is the "Map Legend," which lists the following:

1. Junction of Loop and Granite Park Trail Cabin Trails
2. Victim's hat
3. Victim's camera and tripod (undamaged)
4. Victim's pack
5. Victim's glasses
6. Blood pool off the trail, 3 feet
7. Victim's wallet & point of initial attack
8. Beginning of scuff marks in the trail
9. Small pieces of flesh, #1
10. Small pieces of flesh, #2 & significant blood pool
11. Small pieces of flesh, #3 & significant blood pool
12. Victim's left boot lace
13. Victim's left boot
14. Victim's watch, in working order
15. Canadian coins, presumably from victim's pocket
16. Camera lens filter, also thought to be from pocket
17. Point of rest #1, where victim found by reporting party
18. Change of direction #1 in drag trail
19. Change of direction #2 in drag trail
20. Fragments of victim's shirt and direction change #3
21. Point of rest #2

22. Victim's sock
23. Victim's right foot at point of rest #3 (final)
24. Victim's left foot at point of rest #3 (final)
25. Victim's head at point of rest #3 (final)

The "total linear footage of incident area (wallet to trail to final point of rest) equals 1,188 feet, 9 inches."

The immediate task for rangers now was to find, if possible, the bears responsible. They had vanished somewhere in the backcountry of Glacier. "On October 10, I flew to Granite Park to assist the crew in locating and removing the suspect bears," Ranger [redacted] wrote in the November 16, 1992, Supplementary Case/Incident Record.

10/10   Morning—a non-target bear (male grizzly) is caught in snare trap. Bear is worked up and released.

10/11   Kruger [helicopter] spots target bear family in Bear Valley. Rangers [redacted] fly to site and shoot sow and cubs. One cub gets away. Search started for cub in Bear Valley with rangers [redacted]. No success. Cub spotted around 1800 [6:00 p.m.] near site of sow kill. Ranger [redacted] and [Stephen] Frye fly to area, shoot cub. Frye, [redacted] and bear cub flown out.

10/12   Removed all snares, flew everything out of Granite Park area and removed all personnel from scene.

10/13   [Redacted] drives the three bear carcasses to Bozeman for analysis [Wildlife Laboratory, Montana Department of Fish, Wildlife and Parks].

Someone stole the Loop Trail / Granite Park Trail "Bear Closure Sign" on October 17. Ranger [redacted] notes the following need: "Replace Bear Closure Sign." In his Supplementary Case/Incident Record, dated October 22, the ranger states: "On the afternoon of 10/17/92 park employee [redacted] reported that the orange trail closure sign [due to bear attack] posted at the Loop was missing and appeared to have been stolen. I responded at about 1600 hours [4:00 p.m.], and replaced the trail closure sign. The barricade rope which held the first sign appeared to have been deliberately cut in the middle and the sign taken."

John's camera film was found and developed for any information it could offer. "Photos developed from the victim's camera and camera bag," wrote Ranger [redacted] on October 19, 1992. "[They] gave no evidence pertaining to the incident, as they were scenic shots [. . .] of Chief Mountain as seen from east of Glacier National Park, other nondescript scenes, and Heaven's Peak as seen from the general area of the incident."

Inventory of John's vehicle included receipts of his tours through Canadian parks from September 19 through October 1, including Banff and Jasper National Parks and Head-Smashed-In Buffalo Jump. Then he entered Glacier Park. Rangers found the Glacier Park brochure about wildlife, which recommended that visitors "Enjoy Them at a Distance." John had trail maps for the following areas in Glacier that he perhaps wished to hike: Two Medicine, Many Glacier, St. Mary / Logan Pass, and the Lake McDonald area. Hindsight, for what it's worth, makes us wish he had chosen a different trail to hike that October day. A topographic map of Grand Teton National Park in Wyoming was found. Perhaps John intended to travel there next.

What was the extent of John's injuries?

The pathologist's report, dated November 9, 1992, indicated "Final Diagnoses: Body as a Whole—Exsanguination [blood loss], Multiple Injuries—Grizzly Bear Mauling." The report includes the following injuries, abbreviated here.

> There are several lacerations of the head. The right ear is absent and there is partial avulsion of the right eye. There are large lacerations on the right shoulder area with exposure of the underlying rib cage and the pleural cavity. There is absence of the right forearm.

What were the findings of the Board of Inquiry?

Glacier Park's Board of Inquiry into the Death of John Petranyi, dated February 5, 1993, states: "It is the opinion of this Board that the action leading to the death of Mr. John Petranyi was a surprise encounter between Mr. Petranyi and a female grizzly bear with two cubs-of-the-year and the bear's subsequent efforts to protect those cubs. This occurred on the Loop Trail approximately one-half mile below Granite Park Chalet."

The Board concluded that additional contributing circumstances included:

- The trail traverses a prime grizzly feeding area.
- Bears appear to be habituated to human presence during the heavy visitor-use periods (July and August) and tend to avoid the trails and the Chalet. However, as fall approaches and trail use declines, the bears may not be avoiding the visitor-use areas as before, and the probability of surprise encounters may increase.
- Mr. Petranyi was hiking alone in an area of known grizzly activity.
- Because the trail has many curves and elevation changes, poor sight distance at the location of the initial encounter may have been a factor.

Other bear maulings in the area where John Petranyi was attacked are identified in the Petranyi Board of Inquiry, on a page dated "December 17, 1992." "Bear Maulings in Granite Park Chalet / Loop Trail Area" (in addition to the report listed previously), clarifies the circumstances of injuries, below.

Granite Park Campground, 08/13/67, two people of two, 12:45 a.m., by "Grizzly female."

Loop Trail just below Petranyi site, 09/11/86, two people of two, 3:00 p.m., by "Grizzly, sex unknown."

Loop Trail ¼ mile above Packers Roost Junction, 08/18/89, one person of two, 4:00 p.m., by "Grizzly female with two yearlings."

Loop Trail ½ mile below Granite Park Chalet, 10/03/92, one person of one, 11:00 a.m., by "Grizzly female with cubs of the year."

One year later, in 1993, John's brother flew with a friend to Glacier Park. In his August 3, 1993, "Fatal Bear Attack Follow-Up," Ranger [redacted] wrote that he "met with the brother of bear mauling victim" for approximately two hours at the Park Headquarters conference room.

We discussed the incident at length, and I showed [redacted] the original report, evidence, and the video footage taken on the day of the recovery of John's body. As requested, I did not show the graphic images of the body to him. [Redacted] stated that he and his friend would probably hike up to the area of the incident within the next few days.

I provided him with various maps and informational brochures about the park and answered every question he had to the best of my ability.

And so, standing near the spot where John Petranyi encountered the mother grizzly and her two cubs, his loved ones delivered their final good-bye.

In the next chapter, Park employee Craig Dahl disappears in the Two Medicine Valley, surrounded by glacier-carved peaks. The year is 1998.

One year before, in 1997, in the same area, Park employee Matthew Truszkowski disappeared on a solo climb of Sinopah Mountain.

Is there a connection?

PART 6

FATAL SPRING–SUMMER OF THE GRIZZLIES, 1998 AND 2016

9

FINDING CRAIG

1998: THE SCENIC POINT TRAIL GRIZZLIES

First and foremost is the safety of all incident personnel. Crew should be prepared and geared up for a long search in rugged and steep mountainous terrain. Be aware of loose rock. Test all snow crossing areas for weak surfaces. This is Bear Country! Pay attention and make your presence known.

—CRAIG DAHL SEARCH, "INCIDENT ACTION
PLAN," MAY 20, 1998

Fatality: Craig Dahl
(Mother bear and two cubs killed—proven responsible)

National Park Service–Glacier Park
Case Incident Record Number 980106
Location: 540 feet belowScenic Point Trail, Two Medicine Valley
Date/Time: Last seen alive Sunday, May 17, 1998, at 2:00 p.m. in East Glacier
Death: May 17 or 18, 1998

Craig Dahl did not plan to hike alone. His girlfriend was meant to accompany him, but bad weather set in: a day of snow and sleet, followed by two days of rain. Even though it was May, snow remained underfoot—not surprising, since this was still considered winter in Glacier Park. When Craig's girlfriend checked in with him, he had already departed. Craig valued nature in the raw, and being out in white precipitation did not faze him. So he began.

The next day, Monday, was Craig's first day of work as a Glacier Park, Inc., employee. The twenty-six-year-old from Colorado would drive the red bus with its top open to delight visitors, and safely return them. But this day—Sunday, May 17, 1998—he wanted to enjoy his time off from work. Craig did not return.

An experienced outdoorsman, Craig had guided others on canoe trips in northern Minnesota and on backpacking trips in Colorado. He stood six feet tall with a slim but muscular build. He wore a daypack, and his curly, dark brown hair was covered by a stocking cap embroidered with the word "Avalanche" (a Denver hockey team). His brown eyes looked out from behind thick, teardrop-shaped lenses in wire frames. He started up the trail toward Appistoki Falls, "a short and delightful walk through a young forest to a waterfall above a series of cataracts and turquoise pools," as Alan Leftridge describes in *Glacier Day Hikes*. According to Leftridge,

> A large number of hikers use this trail. Many of the hikers have Scenic Point as their destination. [The mountains include] Scenic Point to the east, at 7,522 feet, Mount Henry to the south, at 8,847 feet, and Appistoki Peak, with an elevation of 8,164 feet, to the west. . . .
>
> *Winter in July*: Snow falls every month of the year in Glacier, often by surprise. The storms may be a novel experience for you, but consider the dangers, slippery footing, wet clothing, and freezing temperatures. There is an upside to these storms: You can contemplate the matchless beauty of the forests, meadows, streamsides, and mountains blanketed in snow.[12]

This day was certainly winter in May. Perhaps Craig was enjoying these snowy scenes as he hiked along. He was now almost one mile from the Mount Henry / Scenic Point Trailhead, following the trail as it crossed the southwest face of an unnamed ridge. After he reached timberline, Craig had no trouble navigating the cliffs and rocky terrain, which were mostly scree rocks and small patches of *krummholz*. Alan Leftridge defines the German word *krummholz* this way: "At timberline, trees such as alpine fir will grow in a low, gnarled, ground-hugging form" [to survive the winds].[13]

When Craig did not return by late afternoon, at the end of her work shift his girlfriend and three friends drove to Two Medicine to look for him. They found only his parked car, a tan 1984 Buick with Colorado plates, at the trailhead, and by 9:00 p.m. they reported Craig missing.

The next morning, May 18, Craig's employer noted that Craig did not report at 11:00 a.m. for his first day as a red bus driver. Official notification of his absence to Glacier authorities followed.

On May 18, a full-scale attempt to find Craig began.

"At approximately 2051 hours [8:51 p.m., the night before], Glacier Park, Inc. employees advised Ranger [Dona] Taylor of a missing hiker," stated Taylor's Board of Inquiry "Findings" report, dated June 25, 1998.

The initial lost person investigation started immediately. Due to the late hour and the concern for employee safety, the initial field search did not begin until the next morning, May 19, 1998, at 0700 hours [7:00 a.m.]. Six hasty[-search] team members were assigned trail segments in the vicinity of Mr. Dahl's vehicle to search initially. As the day progressed, the search expanded.

Initially, one helicopter was assigned to the search, and a second was in place later that evening. Dog teams were requested. Initially, the number of search team members was limited to preserve as much scent as possible. On the evening of May 19, 1998, after searchers had left the search area, Blackfeet Tribal Biologist [name redacted] determined that a female grizzly and two cubs were in the Appistoki drainage near the search area, through the use of telemetry [signals from the bear's radio collar]. [This bear, #235, noted by many visitors for being a striking blond with dark brown legs and mask, had a history of habituation to humans.]

[On] May 20, 1998, telemetry was used to determine if the grizzly family group was still in the area. They were located in the Aster Creek drainage. As search teams were briefed with their assignments for the day, three search dog teams were deployed from the Mt. Henry / Scenic Point Trailhead area.

A Glacier Park press release dated May 19 described "Missing Hiker in Two Medicine Area," with his name, description, and point last seen: "Sunday afternoon in the East Glacier area." At the bottom of the page, the press release states, "Note: *THIS IS NOT THE SAME MISSING HIKER FROM LAST YEAR. THIS IS A NEW CASE.*"

The year before, in 1997, another Glacier Park, Inc., employee, Matthew Truszkowski, failed to return from his hike in the same area. He had planned a solo climb of Mount Sinopah (which in Blackfeet means "kit fox"). As of 2019, Matthew remains missing.

At risk to their own safety, the searchers continued their exhaustive search for Craig. They were looking for any evidence, but particularly for color: Craig was reported to be wearing a long-sleeved blue shirt, blue jeans, black gaiters [wet-proof pant sleeves], black wind pants, dark teal windbreaker, black leather Scarpa boots, size 9. "Possibly has avalanche shovel (plastic, small)," which he could have used to shovel himself out if an avalanche had overtaken him. But he had only a medium blue nylon fanny pack, and certainly was not prepared to camp out overnight.

"Tuesday's ground and aerial search of ten employees grew to an expanded team of nearly 50 people Wednesday, largely due to volunteer help from several organizations," a press release dated May 20, 1998 stated.

So it was that a volunteer team of searchers found Craig's remains.

"At approximately 0915 hours [9:15 a.m.], Volunteer Team 2 advised the Command Post they had located Craig Dahl's remains and that it appeared to be a bear attack," the Board of Inquiry's "Chronology" report states, in the Supplementary Case/Incident Record from Ranger Dona Taylor, dated June 25, 1998. The report continues:

> Due to poor visibility (steep terrain and krummholz) in the area, searchers were advised to back out of the area safely in case the bear was still in the area. All search teams were advised to return to the Command Post; the search was over.

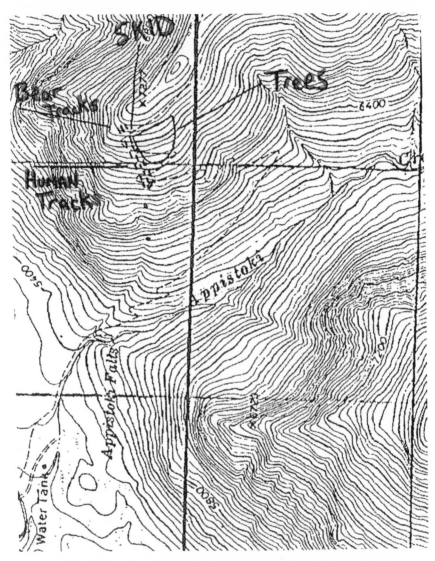

Map of Craig Dahl fatality scene, showing skid marks downhill from trail, trees toward which Craig may have headed for safety, human tracks, and bear tracks following in pursuit. ILLUSTRATION FROM CASE INCIDENT RECORD NUMBER 980106

Approximately seven people were involved in the site investigation and eight were protecting the perimeter. Craig Dahl's remains were flown out by helicopter.

The site, "a patch of krummholz located below an easy cliff band, was secured and the investigation team was brought to the location," states the "Summary," submitted by ranger Richard Mattson, dated May 24, 1998. His report continues:

Mattson, accompanied by [two names redacted], investigated the area above the site of the victim. A faint trail of disturbed rocks and patches of clear dried liquid (?) were followed upslope. Broken eyeglasses and pieces of cloth were discovered and their location flagged approximately 100 yards above the victim. No definite trail was observed in the cliffy area above this find. Above these cliffs, the terrain was mostly scree, with small patches of krummholz.

This area was traversed upslope. Several sets of tracks, which could have been made by humans or bears, were observed heading downhill in this area. Upon reaching the trail, approximately 540 vertical feet above the victim, tracks were observed heading downslope. These tracks were followed down for approximately 200 vertical feet, where a stocking hat was found under a small bit of krummholz. The hat, later positively identified by the victim's girlfriend, was collected and the site flagged. . . .

Broken cliffs above the victim are easy to get through, even when wet. No evidence of a "fall off the cliffs" was observed.

"We saw something," two hikers reported in reference to Craig Dahl. After widespread publicity concerning the death of Craig Dahl, and the place where it happened on May 17 [or 18], 1998, two hikers on the same trail on May 18 called about witnessing something of possible importance. By now it was May 28.

Ranger Richard Mattson wrote in his Supplementary Case/Incident Record, dated June 6, that he contacted these hikers by phone and asked them to describe what they saw.

[Redacted] stated that he and his friend hiked on the trail toward Scenic Point from the trailhead at Two Medicine on the afternoon of 5/18/98. At approximately 1400 to 1430 hrs. [2:00–2:30 p.m.], they reached the northern point of the second-to-last switchback. At this point they noticed tracks coming down from above. [Redacted] remained at the switchback and [redacted] followed the tracks uphill.

[Redacted] described the tracks as appearing to be a person running downhill, possibly being chased by an animal. He described the tracks as "skinnier" tracks, with a three-feet-wide "disturbed" area over them. He described the snow as being windblown, with no single animal tracks being visible. [He] followed this track for a distance, then moved to the north and paralleled these tracks close to the northern point of the highest switchback. He could see the tracks continuing above his highest point. [He] then returned to the point of the lower switchback.

[One of the two] found a pack about 10 feet north of the tracks in the snow and a little west of the lower switchback. The pack contained 3 Clif Bars, a water bottle, and a jacket. The tracks/disturbed area was seen continuing below the lower switchback.

They then returned on the trail to Two Medicine by 1530 to 1600 hrs. [5:30–6:00 p.m.], hung the jacket on the signpost, and kept the pack. [Redacted] stated that they talked about "reporting it" to a ranger, but that [redacted] "didn't think it was a problem," so they didn't. . . .

A map of the area, with the trail and trees marked on it, was faxed to [redacted]. He marked the site of the pack and the trail in the snow and then faxed it back on 5/29/98. This map is attached to this report.

A Glacier Park press release, dated June 5, 1998, stated that "Reports were only recently received from hikers who found Dahl's pack on the Scenic Point trail, Monday, May 18." The press release continues:

> At the time they found the pack, the hikers saw tracks in a snowfield. They stated they observed human footprints that appeared to be running straight downhill directly above where Dahl's body was later found. They also reported signs of disturbance through the snow near the human tracks, which may have been that of a bear running downhill. . . .

The hikers are returning Dahl's pack to park officials and have since cooperated in the investigation. . . .

Investigators suggest the following scenario: Dahl, who was hiking alone, surprised a family group of grizzly bears; fled; was pursued, killed, and then consumed.

Meanwhile, the search for the previously observed grizzly bear family group (the radio-collared mother and two almost-grown cubs) near the Craig Dahl attack site continued. In her "Incident Commander's Report," dated July 11, 1998, ranger Dona Taylor wrote that "During the investigation several bear scat samples were collected from the scene, along with separate bear hair samples. Hair and scat samples, along with known hair samples from the same grizzly family group who were located in the Appistoki drainage on May 20, 1998, were packaged and sent to the University of Idaho for DNA analysis."

Rangers monitored the grizzly family group while awaiting the results of DNA testing. Meanwhile, as grizzly mothers must do, the radio-collared bear left the ear-tagged cubs, forcing them to make their way on their own, as she sought out a male grizzly to mate with. The family group was no more.

But their individual depredations may have continued.

"On May 30, 1998, the park received the DNA results, positively identifying the grizzly female (mother) and the male cub on the fatality scene," wrote ranger Dona Taylor in her "Incident Commander's Report," dated July 11, 1998. "DNA matched the hair samples; also, human DNA was found in the scat samples."

Her report continues:

A management decision was made to remove the family group from the Glacier National Park population. Several people were contacted in regards to the management decision; bear biologists and Fish and Wildlife Service. . . .

It was soon apparent the grizzly family group had been separated by a large male grizzly. In order to positively identify the grizzly family group, it was determined to capture the bears, take DNA samples, and wait for a final management decision.

On June 3, 1998, a two-year-old female grizzly cub was snared near the foot of Two Medicine Lake. Hair and blood samples were sent for DNA analysis. The cub was placed in a culvert trap as a lure for the mother and/or sibling [without result; four days later this cub was euthanized].

On June 4, 1998, the female (mother) grizzly was shot and killed near No Name Lake. Both bears were examined, with Glacier National Park Bear Handling Forms completed and their bodies sent to Bozeman, Montana, for necropsy.

Glacier Park management reopened trails for hikers in the Two Medicine Valley on June 12. But soon after, there was a harrowing incident where people were charged by a young grizzly. "On June 24, 1998, at approximately 1425 hours [2:15 p.m.], received a report of a grizzly charging a large group of people near the pit toilet on the Upper Two Medicine Lake Trail," Ranger Taylor wrote on June 26 in her "Chronology" report. "Following is a report from the Glacier Park Boat Company interpreter [redacted]":

I returned from my Twin Falls walk with a group of 16 people. We arrived at the shelter at 1445 hours [2:45 p.m.] as a condensed group. One of the people shouted "Bear!" and I saw a young sub-adult grizzly running toward the group. The bear left his direction of travel, approximately 30 yards, and started north. I told my group of people to stay together in the shelter until the boat arrived and then to proceed on the boat slowly. I proceeded up the trail to the outhouse to see if anyone was there.

As I moved up the trail I noticed the bear following me 30 yards parallel to the trail and myself. I arrived at the outhouse and no one was there. Seconds later the bear appeared in front of me in the trees and charged me to a distance of 20–30 feet. The bear aborted its charge, stood on its hind legs and growled and clacked his teeth, and then took off into the trees. I walked down the trail to the shelter and helped the boat leave. I stayed at the shelter to wait for incoming hikers.

Approximately 5 minutes after the boat left I noticed the bear once again. He walked around for 10–15 minutes and then charged me again. He started his charge at about 50 yards away from my location. I attempted to climb on top of the shelter and fell. I noticed that the bear stopped his charge when I hit the ground. Two hikers witnessed the charge and my fall. The boat arrived back at the dock and we went back to the other side of the lake.

The above Glacier Park Boat Company interpreter should be commended for taking a number of actions to protect others at his own risk.

Ranger Taylor's "Chronology" continued. "Mr. [redacted] said that he viewed an ear tag in the bear. . . . Ranger [redacted] was assisted by three Tribal employees in searching the area thoroughly. But the bear was not seen again."

Rangers believe that the above aggressive grizzly which charged the crowd of sixteen people was the last surviving (male) cub. "On June 25, 1998, the remaining grizzly cub was located on the northwest slope of Sinopah," wrote Ranger Taylor in her "Incident Commander's Report," dated July 11, adding, "Rangers shot and killed the cub after positive identification. DNA samples were collected (tissue and hair) along with the ear tags and sent for analysis. Bear carcass remained in the backcountry (it is located well away from trails)."

And so the Two Medicine grizzlies—the striking blonde mother with dark brown legs and mask (known by some as "Chocolate Legs") and her two lookalike cubs—were removed from the Glacier Park bear population.

The Board of Inquiry into the Death of Craig Dahl was held on July 23, 1998. The "Location of Death" was given as "approx. 1 mile up from Mt. Henry/Scenic Point Trailhead, SW face of unnamed ridge which trail traverses." The "Summary" includes the following:

On May 17, 1998, Mr. Craig Dahl parked his vehicle at the Mt. Henry / Scenic Point Trailhead in the Two Medicine area. Information gathered during the investigation indicated that Mr. Dahl planned to take a hike in the Two Medicine area. Evidence collected during the investigation of Mr. Dahl's disappearance and subsequent death indicates that sometime during the hike he encountered three grizzly bears in the Mt.

Henry / Scenic Point area. Mr. Dahl's remains were located on May 20, 1998, at 9:15 a.m. Evidence further confirmed that three grizzly bears were involved in partial consumption of Mr. Dahl's remains.

"I'd like to express appreciation for your (EVERYBODY'S) search and rescue efforts, in rough terrain," Craig Dahl's cousin wrote to "#GLAC All Employees" on May 22, 1998. "As an EMT in northern MN, WI, teaching skills in Wilderness Survival to Boy Scouts, I hope to turn my grief into education for others."

A memorial ceremony was held for Craig's family, his fellow employees of Glacier Park, Inc., and his friends.

The "National Park Service Morning Report" on Friday, May 22, 1998, also noted that *"Due to the onset of the spring snowmelt, Park personnel have also resumed the search for GPI employee Matthew Truszkowski, who disappeared while en route to a solo climb of Sinopah Mountain in the Park's Two Medicine Valley last July (97-301)* [emphasis added]."

See also chapter 28, "Still Missing and Presumed Dead."

—⁓—

In the next chapter, a forest service employee rides a mountain bike just south of Glacier Park (but within shouting distance), and in the middle of the trail collides with a grizzly. The grizzly does not run away.

10

FINDING BRAD

2016: THE OUTER LOOP TRAIL GRIZZLY

At a speed of 20–25 miles per hour, there were only 1–2 seconds between rounding the curve, the victim seeing the bear in the trail, and impacting the bear.
—Interagency Grizzly Bear Committee, Board of Review Report, March 3, 2017

Fatality: Brad Treat
(Bear acted defensively, no action taken)

National Park Service–Flathead National Forest (bordering Glacier Park)
Case Incident Record Number: None (Interagency Grizzly Bear Committee Report)
Location: Outer Loop Trail at Half Moon Lake, West Glacier, Montana
Date/Time: Wednesday, June 29, 2016, estimated at 1:30–2:00 p.m.

If he had stopped for a coffee before heading out on his mountain bike on that forested, shrubby trail—if he had turned right instead of left where the trail forked—then perhaps actually colliding with a grizzly bear, in that disastrous split second, would not have occurred. Does this represent the true randomness of the universe? Or did Brad Treat believe, as some do, in fate?

From a bear's perspective (if such a thing exists), the area of collision is a complicated place.

Although West Glacier, where this occurred, is a small town, it's a major people hub, featuring Glacier's West Entrance, the Park Headquarters, and the West Glacier railroad depot. The Outer Loop Trail near Half Moon Lake, where Brad's tragic fatality occurred, is located in the Flathead National Forest. But at this location, the forest (bordering Glacier Park) contains private inholdings and homes, one of which belonged to Brad and his wife. The major Highway 2 bringing visitors north to Glacier is so close to the incident location that while on the forested trail, Brad could hear traffic noise.

The Interagency Grizzly Bear Committee investigated this incident. Its Board of Review Report, dated March 3, 2017, states that "This report relies heavily on the input of Brian Sommers, a criminal investigator and Wildlife–Human Attack Response Team (WHART) leader for Montana Fish, Wildlife and Parks, who was the lead investigator on this incident."

That Wednesday, June 29, 2016, three prior events (and a fourth event that may have occurred earlier) factored into Brad's encounter with a grizzly bear. The first event is the fact that this male "black-colored grizzly with white on its face" was previously captured on May 13, 2006, at Camas Creek in Glacier Park, but not for actions dangerous to people. The bear was captured, anesthetized, and handled as part of a research study, according to the Board of Review Report, issued by the Interagency Grizzly Bear Committee (page 10). At the time of the grizzly's capture, he was estimated to weigh 370 pounds and be eight to ten years old. This bear was noted to be uninjured when released after capture. Previous bear handling by people has been thought by some to possibly influence later bear behavior toward people. In 2016, the bear was estimated to be a fairly old eighteen to twenty years.

The second event is the fact that "This bear was also detected 5 times since 2009 in DNA samples collected in research studies in the general area of the incident near West Glacier, Montana. There was no DNA evidence from any other bears in the samples collected at the incident site" (Board of Review Report, page 10). This finding suggests that the

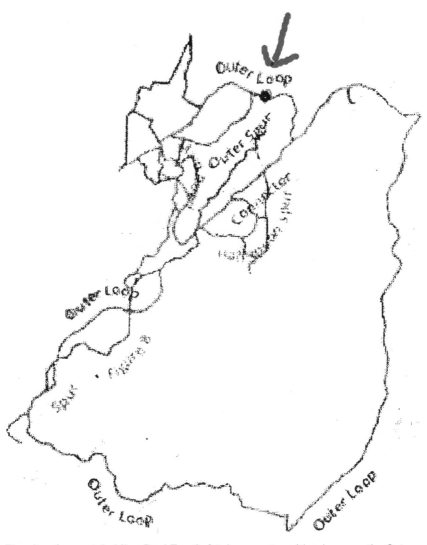

The site of mountain biker Brad Treat's fatal encounter with a bear, on the Outer Loop Trail complex near West Glacier's Half Moon Lake, just south of Glacier Park. ILLUSTRATION FROM THE INTERAGENCY GRIZZLY BEAR COMMITTEE'S BOARD OF REVIEW REPORT, MARCH 3, 2017

"black-colored grizzly with white on its face" was frequenting the area of the incident.

The third event is the fact that on the afternoon of *the same day as Brad's fatal encounter*, a grizzly charged a mounted horseback party from Swan River Outfitters, "a horse concession that used the trails in the incident area." (*Note:* This charge may have occurred just prior to the attack on Brad—estimated between 1:30 and 2:00 p.m.—but there is no definitive proof.) If it happened just after the attack on Brad, this could explain the agitation of the bear, possibly precipitating a second encounter.

The Board of Review Report (page 8) explains:

> They [Swan River Outfitters] reported that a bear had charged a group of their riders on the afternoon of the same day as the incident. . . . The description of the attack noted that at 1430 hours [2:30 p.m.] they were riding back toward their corrals when they observed a black-colored grizzly bear with white on its face, about 40 yards ahead of them. The bear charged to within about 6 feet and then veered off to the left and went a short distance off the trail and made noises and snapped its teeth. The bear then left the area and headed in the direction where they believed the incident with Mr. Treat had occurred. The leader of this horse ride said he estimated that this charge happened about 800 yards or so from where the incident involving Mr. Treat occurred, and he was sure it was a grizzly bear.

The fourth event—the fact that the grizzly for whatever reason was heading toward the incident site—is noted in the Board of Review Report (page 10). "There was a large grizzly track seen on the afternoon of the incident in mud in the trail by Tim Manley (MT FWP) [Montana Fish, Wildlife and Parks] on his way into the incident site." The report continues:

> This track was in the trail approximately [redacted] mile from the incident site, between the green gate and the incident location. This track appeared fresh and the bear was headed in the direction of the incident site. This may have been the bear involved in the incident.

The general area around the incident site is extensively used by grizzly and black bears throughout spring, summer, and fall. Within a 3-mile radius of the incident site, DNA samples from 6 different male and 3 different female grizzly bears were collected as part of USGS [US Government Survey] research studies conducted 1998–2011. In addition, between 1999–2016, 5 radio-collared male and 6 radio-collared female grizzly bears were located within this 3-mile radius.

So it was that on Wednesday, June 29, Brad and his companion rode mountain bikes toward the Outer Loop Trail. Brad, thirty-eight, had been a Forest Service law enforcement officer for the Hungry Horse Ranger District for the past twelve years, and like all law enforcement officers, had risked his life every day. He had also helped his fellow citizens by working on local search-and-rescue, swiftwater-rescue, and avalanche-rescue teams. His sister-in-law told ABC News that he "loved the outdoors and enjoyed hiking, kayaking, running, and biking." In fact, the Board of Review Report notes that Brad, his wife, and his dog had jogged this same trail earlier that morning. This area (which excludes engine-powered vehicles) is known as Green Gate Trails, and is not maintained by the US Forest Service. The trails are old logging roads maintained by its users, one of whom was Brad, who would regularly clear it of debris.

Brad and his companion that day (who had never before ridden a mountain bike) entered the extensive series of trails around Half Moon Lake. Perhaps they saw other people, who daily use these trails. Mountain biking is a relatively silent activity, and the gaze of the rider is often focused downward on the uneven terrain. According to the Board of Review Report, "Vegetation along these trails is in various stages of regeneration following past timber harvest."

Sight-distance is limited along the trail in many areas and at the site of the collision. Understory vegetation is composed of various shrub species, including buffaloberry, which was fruiting at the time. At the site of the collision and fatality, sight-distance is limited due to a curve to the right in the trail and vegetation along the trail. The area is close enough to Highway 2 that traffic noise can be heard through the forest from areas along the trail.

Meanwhile, the late-June sun shone on Brad's protective bike helmet as he and his companion enjoyed the trail. Neither carried bear spray nor firearms. Brad pulled ahead, riding faster downhill, rounding a right-hand curve and disappearing from his companion's view.

"Immediately after Mr. Treat disappeared," states the Board of Review Report (page 5), "his companion heard the sound of Mr. Treat and his bike colliding with the bear and the bear vocalizing and making a sound 'like it was hurt.'"

The report continues:

He described what he heard as a "thud" and an "argh." As his companion rode around the curve and stopped his bike, he saw the bear standing over Mr. Treat who was laying in the trail. The bear was broadside to the companion and on the left side of the trail. His companion described the bear as "very big, brownish-black in color, lighter than black." He described the hair on the back of the bear as "bristled up." His companion did not remember if the bear had a dished face or a hump or not, but he did describe it as "big."

His companion waited what he described as "probably within 30 seconds," trying to figure out what to do. His companion said the bear was "intent and focused on Mr. Treat" and did not seem to see or turn toward the companion at all. It appears that his companion was within 37 feet of the bear and Mr. Treat when he stopped his bike at the curve of the trail.

His companion waited for a "short time" and then decided to turn around and head back up the trail the way he had come to seek help. Neither rider carried bear spray or firearms or a cell phone. His companion said he was worried about the response of the bear should he try and "push" the bear off of Mr. Treat, since he had nothing with which to defend himself.

His companion turned around and headed back up the trail an undetermined distance until he heard the sound of vehicles on

Highway 2. At that point, he began bushwhacking toward the highway, carrying his bike. The closest distance to Highway 2 from where his companion went back up the trail is approximately 1 mile through thick forest. When his companion reached the highway, he flagged down a vehicle and was driven to a phone to call for help. The call for help was received by 911 at 1452 hours [2:52 p.m.].

At 4:03 p.m., the first responder to the scene, Glacier Park ranger Brad Blickhan, confirmed that Brad had died from an apparent bear mauling. In its "Investigation of the Incident," the Board of Review Report (page 6) states that "Initial investigators on the scene found Mr. Treat and his bike in the trail at the site of the collision."

His bike helmet was beside his body and it was in pieces after being bitten by the bear. [Further description redacted.] The impact of the collision that hurled the victim and his bike over the bear indicates the speed of the collision. The bike shoes victim was wearing (that clipped into the pedals of the bike) pulled bike over the victim and over the bear with the force of the impact, so that the bike landed farther down the trail. The front reflector was knocked off the bike at the initial site of the collision and was found in the trail on the other side of the victim from the bike.

Both the victim and the bike were found on the trail, indicating that there was no evasive action taken to steer to either side of the trail to avoid the bear in the trail. There were no skid marks in the trail, indicating that there was no hard braking before the collision. The lack of evasive steering and lack of skidding are further evidence of the surprise and high speed of the collision. The bear apparently had no time to move to avoid the collision. At a speed of 20–25 miles per hour, there were only 1–2 seconds between rounding the curve, the victim seeing the bear in the trail, and impacting the bear.

The force of the collision with the bear apparently propelled Mr. Treat's torso into the handlebars as evidenced by a straight-line bruise across the inside of the lower front part of his ribs. . . . The force of the collision that hurled Mr. Treat over the bear caused him to break both of his wrists and his left scapula when he hit the ground as he tried to break his fall with his hands.

No part of Mr. Treat's body was consumed by the bear, and the bear did not cache his body by covering it with dirt and debris, as is common for bears that are storing a food source and plan to return to it. There was no bear attractant at the collision site such as an animal carcass. The bear was not present when first responders arrived at the incident site, nor [did] any other bear [visit] the incident scene for at least 48 hours, as confirmed by remote cameras placed at the site.

Evidence of Bear Activity in the Area and Bear-Trapping Operations

After the initial on-site investigation, the WHART [Wildlife–Human Attack Response Team] decision was made not to set any traps to capture the bear because it appeared that the bear was acting defensively.

Just after dark on the day of the attack, a sheriff's deputy posting closure signs reported being "charged by a bear near the green gate." In response to that report, MT FWP [Montana Fish, Wildlife and Parks] set two culvert traps and remote cameras that night in the area of the green gate.

That same night Tim Manley (MT FWP) set two culvert traps and remote cameras in the area of the green gate. On the morning of June 30 (the day after the incident), Tim Manley made a helicopter flight with Two Bear Air Rescue to look for bears in the incident area using a forward-looking infrared (FLIR) camera. No bears were located. . . .

After further discussions with the sheriff's deputy who reported a charging bear, it was determined that the report of a charging bear by the green gate *did not occur* [emphasis added]. . . .

Based on this [autopsy] information [that Mr. Treat collided with the bear] and the fact that no bears were captured or photographed on the remote cameras, MT FWP decided that all bear traps should be removed from the area on July 1 after being set for 2–5 days.

Another bear sighting occurred on June 30, the day following the incident.

"A woman reported that she saw a 'big, black-colored bear' at 1100 hours [11:00 a.m.] near her driveway. This sighting was approximately 1.5 miles from the incident location and on the other side of Highway 2," adds the Board of Review Report. It continues:

> Natural aggression of grizzly bears toward humans most commonly occurs in 3 specific instances: 1) surprise encounters . . . 2) defense of a food source . . . or 3) defense of young. . . . Bears involved in such surprise encounters [as Mr. Treat's] are not captured or removed in most cases, even when the result of the encounter is serious injury or death to a human. Bears involved in surprise encounters have no record of repeated attacks on humans, nor is there any information that they are more dangerous because of their involvement in such an incident. . . .
>
> In a separate report, this Board of Review makes recommendations about how to improve safety for mountain bikers in grizzly habitat.

What then can be said of this fatal encounter? The Outer Loop Trail grizzly was allowed to go on his way. He vanished into (and hopefully will stay in) the remote backcountry. However, grizzly bears "aren't just in the backcountry anymore," said Gregg Losinski for the Interagency Grizzly Bear Committee. "They're going to expand into places that are biologically suitable," he continued, "which for grizzly bears is just about anywhere. But the expansion also has to be socially acceptable. It's not what bears are going to do, but what we allow them to do."

Rob Chaney in his 2016 *Missoulian* article "Bears vs. Bikes: Who's at Risk?" added that "The Interagency Grizzly Bear Committee has a precarious job: aiding the recovery of a wild predator that won't always cooperate with a human community that fears it."[14]

The issue of bears versus bikes has become a national concern. On October 8, 2019, Jim Robbins of the *New York Times* wrote that "Dr. Christopher Servheen, who led the committee that investigated Mr. Treat's death, said the accident prompted him to speak out publicly against recreational sports in the areas where grizzlies live." Robbins noted also that "The Trump administration recently allowed e-bikes, or electric bikes, to be used on all federal trails where bicycles are allowed."[15]

As for Brad, his loss is grieved. A memorial service at Kalispell's Legends Stadium honored him. Brad's sister-in-law, Melissa Treat, told ABC News that he was an "amazing man, an all-around stand-up guy, a devoted husband, amazing brother, loving son, and loyal friend. He would go above and beyond to help those in need."

———

The following chapters examine the circumstances of grizzly bear maulings, from near death to lesser wounds. Chapter 11 describes the near deaths of two hikers—a father and his daughter, Johan and Jenna Otter—who were attacked on a Glacier Park trail in 2005. Mr. Otter later wrote a book about the horror of their experiences.

PART 7

A CENTURY OF NEAR-DEATH AND SIGNIFICANT MAULINGS

11

FINDING JOHAN AND JENNA

2005: THE GRINNELL GLACIER TRAIL GRIZZLY

Terror in Paradise . . . Johan looked up. Jenna was running toward him. She had yelled something, he wasn't sure what. Then he saw it. The open mouth, the tongue, the teeth, the flattened ears. Jenna ran right past him, and it struck him—a flash of fur, two jumps, 400 pounds of lightning.

—THOMAS CURWEN, *LOS ANGELES TIMES*, REPRINTED
BY THE *MISSOULIAN*, MAY 31, 2007

National Park Service–Glacier Park
Case Incident Record Number 050695: Johan and Jenna Otter
Location: Grinnell Glacier Trail
Date/Time: Thursday, August 25, 2005, 9:00 a.m. (helicopter rescue at 1:55 p.m. and 3:10 p.m.)

Parental instinct can be an even stronger force than the will for self-preservation. In that subalpine landscape on the Grinnell Glacier Trail on August 25, 2005, an instinctive drive to protect one's offspring took over. Two family groups encountered each other five feet apart around a blind hairpin turn. The mother, a grizzly bear with two yearling cubs, attacked. The father stood his ground to protect his daughter.

The father and daughter are Johan and Jenna Otter.

The two estimate that the grizzly encounter occurred at 9:00 a.m., and, having seen no other people, that they might have been the first hikers on the Grinnell Glacier Trail that morning. This portion of the trail is only three feet wide, with a steep cliff face above the trail and steep drop-offs below. The trail itself follows zigzagging switchbacks, climbing 1,600 feet from the Swiftcurrent area from which Johan and Jenna had started to their goal: Grinnell Glacier. But as experienced hikers, father and daughter felt the confident traction of their boots on the red rocky ground. Better yet, they felt the comfort of each other's presence. And now, after a chilly start, the sky had cleared. With no breeze on the trail itself, the sun warmed their faces and hands. Just twenty-four hours before, "there had been snow on the ground at 6,000 feet, and low cloud cover, rain and sleet falling, and ambient temperatures of 40 degrees."

It was a "chance." In Glacier Park, when you get the chance of warm, sunny weather in the brief summer season, you go out and make the most of it.

Five minutes before, Johan had filmed a golden eagle. Johan liked to stop and use his video and camera gear, and now Jenna was urging him to catch up. The trail was too narrow to walk side by side. She stayed a few steps ahead, and was setting the pace. She was celebrating her graduation from high school, and their close father-daughter bond. He took two photos of her, standing tall and happy as they approached Grinnell Glacier, she in rolled-up blue jeans and a light green sweater, hatless, her hair black.

The family group of grizzlies—she, small and light brown, later described by Jenna as "honeyish," and her two yearling cubs—climbed up the opposite way on the same trail. They were now a quarter-mile above Thunderbird Falls. Where were they heading? Toward whatever it is that grizzlies do.

— ❧ —

That Thursday morning at 7:30 a.m., Jenna and Johan left their Swiftcurrent Motor Inn room, near the Many Glacier Hotel. In Johan's camera, rangers later found three photographs of a black bear in an identifiable location near the Motor Inn. In their room, rangers found and safeguarded some items of theirs, including a mounted "jackalope" (a fake jackrabbit head and antelope antlers), a horseshoe, and two black-and-white framed photographs. The father and daughter had arrived at Glacier Park from California, where Johan had emigrated from the Netherlands and was now a physical therapist with a PhD at Scripps Memorial Hospital. Jenna, having crossed that major milestone called high school, was a dancer moving toward college. Johan was a marathon runner, and both loved outdoor adventures; they had fitness levels that made trail climbing at altitude here in Glacier Park a pleasure.

Then the two family groups met.

⌒⌒

What happened next?

"Just prior to the attack [Johan and Jenna] had been talking and stopping along the trail, taking in the views, and did not remember much wind at the time," wrote Ranger [name redacted], after interviewing Johan by telephone in his Seattle hospital room on September 7, 2005. "He first saw the bear as Jenna stepped back away from the bear, which then lunged into his leg in less than a second" (Case Incident Record Follow Up report, dated September 11, 2005). The report continues:

> [Johan] immediately was concerned for his daughter and preventing her from being injured and trying to get away from the bear, which was tossing him about "like a rag doll." He tried to roll off the trail away from the bear, which was above him. He called to Jenna to get her to roll off the trail. The bear then came to him and attacked again, focused on his daypack, and [he] held the bear with his hand, trying to hold its mouth away from him for protection, and to keep it from going after Jenna.
>
> He reached for his bear spray, which had been in a mesh outer pocket of his daypack, but saw the can of spray lying on the ground, so instead, tried to protect the top of his head as the bear was repeatedly biting the top of his skull. He then tried to lie still, and the bear stopped.
>
> He intentionally fell down the chute a bit further where the bear couldn't get at him, and the bear walked away.

Shortly afterward he heard Jenna scream "Oh no," and then silence. He was unsure if Jenna had been killed or [if] the bear had left. After a brief time he called Jenna and she responded that she was okay, but also injured. Realizing the bear had left, they started yelling for help and taking assessments of the extent of [their] injuries. [Johan] scrambled up about three feet to a flat rock, and decided that due to the extent of his injuries, it was best he wait at the location for help.

Then there is Jenna's point of view. Ranger [name redacted] interviewed her, writing the "Initial Investigation" report, dated September 10, 2005. Jenna stated that she and her father "came around a corner and were within five feet of a grizzly sow and two cubs." The sow's eyes, she said, went wide.

The sow attacked within seconds. Jenna was in front of her father, but the bear attacked Johan first. Jenna was unclear on what happened between the time the bear attacked her father and the time it attacked her. After it attacked her, she fell or was knocked to the ground, faceup, and the bear stood on or over her and bit at her. She attempted to push it away, but then decided to "play dead."

As soon as she stopped moving, the bear glanced away, looked back at her, glanced away again, and then ran off. Jenna thought the entire incident lasted less than a minute. She was unclear about how she got down the steep slope to the area where her father was, but at some point she was possibly below him, and at another point she was possibly hiding in some brush. She may have had problems with her vision for some time as well. At some point, she located a can of pepper spray on the ground, but was unfamiliar with how to use it.

Johan and Jenna were out of sight of any hikers, and well below the trail. Into the vast emptiness around them, "separated by about fifty feet from each other," they kept calling "Help. Help. Help." Eventually a hiker coming up the same trail heard them and ran back down the trail to notify a naturalist-ranger leading a hike. After a complicated rock-climbing rescue was ruled out, a helicopter was called.

"On the flight in, the helo flew close by the face of the cliffs below the trail at the scene to give an overview of the situation," wrote Ranger [redacted] in "Results of Investigation," dated September 6, 2005. The report continues:

The injured (two) were on a ledge, separated by about 50 feet from each other, and there were park rangers and several other hikers assisting each injured [person] at the time. [Names redacted] were landed about ½ mile downtrail from the scene, and they took technical climbing gear with them uptrail to the scene. After depositing gear in a marshaling area above the injured's location, [redacted] was requested by park medic [redacted] to bring additional oxygen to the location of the injured male hiker [father]. . . . This [patient] was observed to have an extreme scalping laceration atop his head; his face was covered with dried blood, [and] he was resting in a supine position and was able to converse quietly. . . .

The daughter-victim . . . was in the company of volunteer Park visitors but without any NPS ranger with her. [Name redacted] saw that she was sitting up, yet suffering from a severe facial laceration/avulsion to her right cheek. She, too, had blood on her face, but not to the extent seen with the father. . . . At some point, park medic [redacted] took over as lead medic with the daughter. . . .

At mid-early afternoon . . . the decision was made to use the KRH Alert helo's "short-haul" capability. . . . Visitor-hikers who had been assisting were moved alternately far uptrail or downtrail away from the location of any possible accident arising from the technical helo short-haul operation. [Name redacted] and other rangers remained on the trail while [redacted] assisted the KRH flight paramedic load the first patient, the father, into the short-haul litter and get them airborne.

The short haul took the paramedic and his patient down valley to the Many Glacier helipad and then the ship returned immediately for the daughter. [Redacted] had gone down to the ledge following the first liftoff to assist in patient packaging of the daughter for the second flight out. Daughter was loaded and lifted out by the same short-haul procedure and was flown with the paramedic to the MG [Many Glacier] helipad. At this point, possibly about 1630+ hours [4:30 p.m.], rangers on scene began the escort of all remaining visitors out of the closed trail area and also began to take down all gear, anchor systems, equipment, and debris for carry-out. Climbing gear was gathered and flown out on the Park contract ship, *Minuteman*, which was waiting on the temporary helispot established ½ mile below the scene.

Also somewhere below the scene, the grizzly family group—the small honeyish-brown mother and the two nearly grown cubs—could not be located after extensive searching. They were thought to be "hiding away from human-trafficked areas."

An "Overall Summary of Incident and Conclusion," dated September 23, describes that "During or following the mauling, both [victims] fell or rolled off the edge of the trail, resulting in falls up to 65 feet total and necessitating a technical rescue."

The summary continues:

The trail in the area where the attack occurred consists of about three feet of trail tread, against a steeply sloping upper cliff face. Below the trail is a vegetated area of 10–15 feet, steeply sloping generally to the east. At the bottom of this slope are a number of alders, and below the alders is a vertical rock chute of about 20 feet. Below the chute is a steep, sloping area some 15–20 feet wide, consisting of broken slabs of rock with some vegetation. Below the slabs of rock is another set of vertical drop-offs, with some areas of less-than-vertical steep slopes and vegetation.

Evidence at the scene, as collected and photographed by rangers [names redacted] and as observed by responding rangers, indicates that Victim #1 [Johan] rolled or fell down the steep vegetated slope below the trail, possibly while struggling with the bear, and then fell down the first vertical chute; rolled or scrambled across the rock slabs; and then fell further down the vertical cliff, for a total distance of about 65–70 vertical feet. He then climbed back up a few feet to where he was originally found.

Victim #2 [Jenna] rolled or fell down the steep vegetated slope, then fell off the vertical chute, hid in some alders near the bottom of the chute, and was located near the alders on the rocky slabs, a total distance of about 30 vertical feet below the trail. . . . Victim #2 is then unclear as to how she got from the trail down the vertical chute, but stated to Ranger [redacted] that she watched the bear walk away after it attacked her. The bear at this point must have either been in the area of the steep vegetated slope, or down the rocky chute, and must have departed approximately northeast, either along the trail or along the steep slope above Grinnell Lake. There is no report of where the two cubs departed from, or to. Only Victim #2 saw the two cubs. . . .

All indications are that the encounter was a surprise encounter and the grizzly sow acted defensively, departing quickly after the perceived threat was neutralized. . . . No further action regarding the bears is planned.

But for the family group of humans, the agony of the long, long road to recovery followed. On August 29, a Public Affairs Office fax noted that the "male victim remains 'in intensive care, but is improving and conscious.'" At one point, Johan thought he was dying.

Jenna's less-serious injuries allowed her to be treated at the Kalispell Hospital in Montana, but Johan had to be flown to Harborview Hospital in Seattle. "My head had to be cleaned and covered to prevent infection," Johan wrote in his 2016 book, *A Grizzly Tale: A Father and Daughter Survival Story.*

Between 60 and 80 percent of my scalp was gone, and the wound was down to the bone. Two arteries that run in that area had been torn off, but the jacket that I had covered my head with had sealed those wounds very well, which had kept me from bleeding to death. The hole in my right forearm had torn tendons that needed repairing. A claw that had penetrated my eye socket had torn a muscle and caused a fracture of the wall of the eye socket. . . . Below the neck I had more than twenty wounds large enough to need serious care. Dirt was everywhere, and [the wounds] were slathered in bear slime.[16]

One year after the attack, following many reconstructive surgeries, Johan Otter revisited the Grinnell Glacier Trail with park ranger Gary Moses, who had helped rescue him.

Three years after the attack, Johan and Jenna visited with friends, including some whom they had not previously known, but who had helped find and save them that day on the trail.

No bears were sighted on those trips.

"Since the attack at Glacier," Johan Otter wrote in his book, "I have found greater meaning in the notion that we live our lives for our families and loved ones. This concept—keeping loved ones safe—seems to resonate deeply for a lot of people when I give my bear story presentations, especially for parents. We all say that we would give our lives for our children, but many of us have never had to do that, so we don't really know."[17]

The following chapter tells the story of two women hikers who encounter and surprise a grizzly in 2003. "The trail led us into a large patch of scrub," one wrote, "which we attempted to bash through, looking for the elk trail. But alas, we scared a bear to our east—uphill—gnashing at us."

12

FINDING KATHRYN AND KELSY

2003: THE PIEGAN PASS TRAIL GRIZZLY

Patient 1: Impact pain to chest, LF arm & sprain to LF ankle. Also bear spray exposure & puncture to back. LF ankle swollen and abrasion with ecchymosis; puncture wound to RT scapula area; lacerations on mandible area [jaw]; ecchymosis to LF upper arm. Suspect fracture/sprain of LF ankle; deep puncture with tissue damage from blunt object.

Patient 2: 0–4x wide puncture wounds to LF scapula area, 1x puncture wound to LF arm, 1x puncture wound to LF pectoralis area. Very agitated and discomforted by bear spray exposure. Suspect deep puncture wound with extensive tissue damage due to mechanism of injury. Blunt trauma to LF forearm.

—Paramedic, "Mechanism of Injury: Bear Maul," transfer to ambulance to Browning Hospital

National Park Service–Glacier Park
Case Incident Record Number 030735: Kathryn Hiestand and Kelsy Running Wolf
Location: Piegan Pass Trail, ¼ to ½ mile off trail
Date/Time: Saturday, September 27, 2003, approximately 2:00 p.m.

Imagine growing up as they did, with Glacier National Park as their backyard. The beauty and even the dangers are part of what you see. The timeless granite and the shrinking glaciers support meadows and forests full of wildlife of every kind. But you belong there, too.

Then came the bear attack that September 27, 2003. Afterward, they were forced to hike five miles before a fellow human heard their calls for help and found them. The alternative was a night in the backcountry, with the smell of blood all over them. Some experts believe a grizzly can smell blood from two miles away. Imagine the struggle to walk as fast as you can while bleeding, agonized from inadvertent bear spray, and battling going into shock. Kathryn Hiestand, forty-eight, and Kelsy Running Wolf, twenty, accomplished just that.

The two women took one trail that Saturday afternoon in September, and their six friends from Many Glacier Hotel took another. All were to meet in the backcountry at Three Ponds / Mount Allen and celebrate a great day. Then they would hike back to Many Glacier together.

The six friends from Many Glacier hiked on Cracker Lake Trail and through Snow Moon Basin to Mount Allen. At the appointed meeting place at Three Ponds, they did not see Kathryn and Kelsy. Eventually they returned to the Many Glacier Hotel, but now they were worried. Where were the two women?

Kathryn and Kelsy were experienced hikers and carried bear spray. The morning was bright at 10:45 a.m. as they parked their car at Siyeh Bend on the Going-to-the-Sun Road. They hiked the Piegan Pass Trail four and a half miles, which is rated "Moderate," and stopped to appreciate the view from Piegan Pass. This is a popular trail; as Kathryn later wrote on her "Interview with Victim(s) and Witness(es)" sheet, the two women saw "People @ Pass. 3 guys ahead. Never saw again."

Describing this area and the view from Piegan Pass, Erik Molvar writes the following in *Hiking Glacier and Waterton Lakes National Parks*:

> The trail begins at Siyeh Bend on the Going-to-the-Sun Road, at a scenic crossing of Siyeh Creek. The open meadows and tiny fir trees are left behind quickly as the trail climbs onto well-drained slopes covered with tall spruce and fir trees. . . . Bearing left, the trail to Piegan Pass crosses a small creek and ascends onto the talus slopes of Cataract Mountain.

The trail curves around to the head of the basin to reach the high col of Piegan Pass. . . . Mountain goats are frequently seen capering on rocky slopes and in grassy parklands around the pass, and marmots may be seen ambling along in rockslide areas. Looking northward, the Bishop's Cap crowns the Garden Wall on the western rim of the valley, while Mount Gould can be seen in the distance.[18]

But then the two hikers made a decision which, in retrospect, they should not have made. They left the trail.

"Below Piegan Pass on north side and just before trail goes into trees," Kathryn wrote (in her October 8 "Interview"), "we left the trail out of the riverbed. Headed southeast and then east toward the base of the slopes that connect [Mount] Siyeh and [Mount] Allen." They planned to contour [follow] around the base of Mount Siyeh and Mount Allen, and then to meet their friends at Three Ponds. In her "Interview," Kathryn described what they saw:

Terrain is open with patches/mats of subalpine scrub. We approached an elk trail [that] basically parallels Piegan Pass Trail, but way above tree line. The trail led us into a large patch of scrub which we attempted to bash through, looking for the elk trail, but alas, we scared a bear to our East—uphill—gnashing at us.

We could not see it. It immediately charged us as we turned away. It pushed—shoved me into a subalpine fir, but I had at least been able to get out my bear spray.

As I lay against the tree, I turned to spray the bear who by now was biting Kelsy's left shoulder as she tried to curl up. Two sprays did reach the bear.

Whether it left due to spray or simply satisfied it had put us in our place, who knows. But it left as quickly as it came—encounter was no more than 10–15 seconds. We left ASAP and returned to trail.

What exactly happened to Kathryn and Kelsy, and where?

The Case Incident Record reported by Ranger [redacted] on October 8 provides more insight. Ranger [redacted] had Kathryn "point on a USGS quad map the location of the incident. She indicated UTMS: 5400. 8N x 303.2E, elev. 6,800 feet." The report continues:

> The elk trails they were following kept dead-ending in scrub. [They] were hiking about 5 feet apart from each other and talking loudly about the trails and asking each other if they [could] see another way to go. They also had shouted out a couple "Hey, bears," but mostly the noise they made was in the form of loud talking.
>
> At approximately 1400 hours [2:00 p.m.], while searching for the continuation of the elk trails, they both heard a woofing sound and the sound of gnashing teeth. They said it sounded to be about 20–30 feet away, and at this time, they were [still] hiking about 5 feet apart from each other. They both instinctively turned and started to run, but didn't get more than 5 feet (or 3 steps) when the scrub stopped them.
>
> Kathryn had also realized in this time that running was the wrong thing to do. She had, in those 3 steps, drawn her bear spray and had started to turn toward the bear when it hit her from behind, knocking her into a subalpine fir tree. Kathryn remained on her feet, hitting the tree with her sternum. The bear then left Kathryn and hit Kelsy, who stated that she thinks the bear bit her shoulder and pulled her to the ground. When she hit the ground, she was able to curl up into a ball and cover her head with her right hand. The bear, however, was standing on her left arm.
>
> Kathryn had, by this time, regrouped and sprayed her bear spray at the bear, or [unwittingly] Kelsy. Although she sprayed at the back of the bear, she hoped that it would turn toward her and get some in the face. The bear never turned, but instead ran off in the direction it [had come] from. Kelsy was aware of the bear leaving because it stepped off of her left arm, but she couldn't open her eyes at this point due to the bear spray.
>
> Both women were carrying food in plastic containers ["Interview" states "veggies"]. . . . Both women have lived in the local area and have hiked extensively in Glacier National Park and are very familiar with bears, safety in bear country, and are familiar with all of the Park's bear literature.

Kathryn had a severely swollen and painful ankle, a laceration on her chin, and puncture wounds on her right scapula. Kelsy had 6 puncture wounds: 4 to her left scapula, 1 to her left arm, and 1 to her left pectoral area. She also had a swollen and bruised wrist where the bear had stood on her.

The two women stayed in the area of the attack for about 5 minutes, recovering from the bear spray and making sure the bear was really gone. They then returned to the Piegan Pass Trail and hiked the full distance to the Many Glacier Boat Concession Road (about 5 miles), where they yelled for help as they walked. Parties unknown to Kathryn picked the women up and brought them to the ranger station.

The two women were examined and treated by a paramedic, who transferred them by ambulance to Browning Hospital in nearby Browning, Montana, just east of Glacier Park.

What kind of bear was it?

In answer to the "Interview" questions, Kathryn wrote that the bear was a "grizzly—light color—small to medium?" The grizzly "seemed to be all one color, but we saw it only very briefly." The bear "was perhaps sleeping [?] in subalpine fir." She reported that no cubs or other bears were seen. The "Interview" continues:

Question: Was bear surprised?
Answer: Yes—or perhaps it heard us and we merely came too close.
Question: What were bear's immediate actions upon sensing people?
Answer: Woofing and [chomping] [of teeth].
Question: Apparent reason for bear's behavior?
Answer: I believe we simply got too close to his space.
Question: How did bear leave the scene?
Answer: Ran in the direction it came—uphill and to the east.
Question: What seemed to make the bear leave?
Answer: Personal opinion—the reprimanding was complete. Satisfied threat was gone.

Night of the Grizzlies attack victims Julie Helgeson and Roy Ducat drew this sign, "Glacier Park Employees Need Ride," to hitchhike to the trailhead. Julie's brown hiking boots are at the top and Roy's black and white sneakers are to the right. Their campsite belongings are shown here. PHOTO FROM CASE INCIDENT RECORD NUMBER 679050

The culvert trap set for any intruding bear at the far end of the Many Glacier Campground, prior to Mary Pat Mahoney and her friends setting up their tents. No bear was caught in the trap. PHOTO FROM CASE INCIDENT RECORD NUMBER 761630

Mary Pat Mahoney's red sleeping bag, extensively torn by the attacking grizzly bear, which dragged her away while she was still in the sleeping bag.

PHOTO FROM CASE INCIDENT RECORD NUMBER 761630

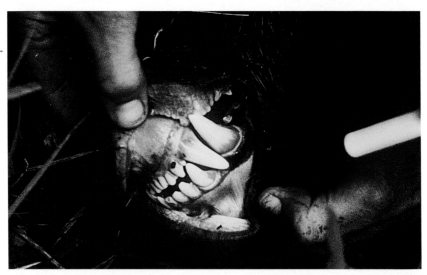

After Mary Pat Mahoney's fatality, this photo was taken by flashlight, checking for blood on the teeth of one of the Twin Grizzlies. (Both bears were shot and killed at the scene.) No human blood was found in either bear's mouth.

PHOTO FROM CASE INCIDENT RECORD NUMBER 761630

Chuck Gibbs himself took this photograph of the mother grizzly and cubs moments before the bears' fatal attack. PHOTO FROM CASE INCIDENT RECORD NUMBER 870092

After the fatal bear attack on John Petranyi, his bag, camera tripod, and blue hat are found on the Loop Trail near the trail junction in the Granite Park area. An armed ranger searches ahead. PHOTO FROM CASE INCIDENT RECORD NUMBER 921583

John Petranyi's hiking boot is found without its shoelace (pulled loose by the bear during the attack). PHOTO FROM CASE INCIDENT RECORD NUMBER 921583

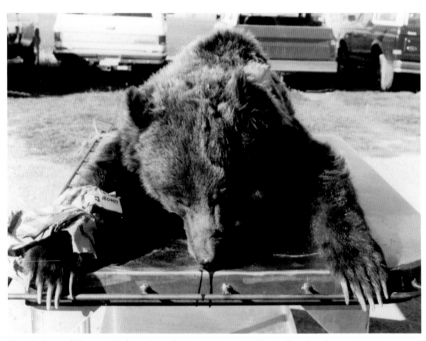

Head view of the adult female grizzly, shot and killed after its fatal attack on John Petranyi. PHOTO FROM CASE INCIDENT RECORD NUMBER 921583

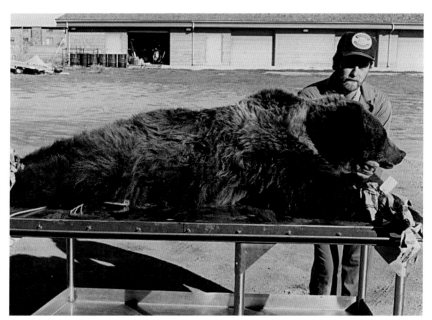

A ranger stands beside another view of the adult female grizzly, shot and killed after its attack on John Petranyi. PHOTO FROM CASE INCIDENT RECORD NUMBER 921583

View of John Petranyi's second attack site, looking up the Loop Trail. Petranyi's hiking-boot lace, torn loose by the grizzly, is shown in the left foreground of the photograph. PHOTO FROM CASE INCIDENT RECORD NUMBER 921583

Above: The Craig Dahl fatality site along the Scenic Point Trail, taken from a helicopter (trail can be seen in center of the photograph). PHOTO FROM CASE INCIDENT RECORD NUMBER 980106

Right: A close-up of the fleece jacket Craig Dahl may have had on at the time of the attack. PHOTO FROM CASE INCIDENT RECORD NUMBER 980106

Left: A ranger digs into a large mounded area, where the bear may have cached Craig Dahl's remains under dirt and vegetation. PHOTO FROM CASE INCIDENT RECORD NUMBER 980106

Below: The adult female grizzly involved in the Craig Dahl fatality, after being shot and killed. PHOTO FROM CASE INCIDENT RECORD NUMBER 980106

This view looks generally north along the Otters' hiking trail. A ranger stands at the point where Johan and Jenna Otter fell. When the Otters first encountered the bears, the bears may have been in the area of the large rock in the foreground. PHOTO FROM CASE INCIDENT RECORD NUMBER 050695

Below: Johan Otter's blood is visible on the side of the rock wall. This is the area from which a bear hair sample was taken. (The hair can be seen near the top of the photograph, attached to the wall.) PHOTO FROM CASE INCIDENT RECORD NUMBER 050695

It is important to note that successful use of bear spray while a bear attacks you is very difficult, and takes courage. It does not resemble your trial spray into the bushes. Ranger [redacted] writes (under "Notes" on the "Interview" sheet) that Kathryn "remembers being focused on finding [the] bear's head and shoulders before spraying it, and that the bear was on the other side of Kelsy, so she could not determine its side, other than it seemed to have a large head."

Both women were painfully affected by the spray and its blowback, but Kelsy was in agony from being caught by spray more or less directly as the bear attacked her. Emergency room staff began to treat their wounds and try to decontaminate them from the effects of the bear spray at the Browning Hospital in Browning, Montana, just outside the park.

In a Supplementary Case/Incident Record, date not given, Ranger [redacted] notes that he interviewed Kelsy's mother on September 30, 2003. The mother stated that Kelsy "felt burning on her legs, arms, and face from the bear spray. . . . The doctor wiped water and Dawn soap on her extremities as well as placed her in a shower to remove the spray. The burning was unbearable, and they had to stop treatment. After calling poison control, the doctor wiped milk on Kelsy's extremities and this gave her some relief."

The two women had their wounds surgically cleaned and bandaged by the emergency room staff. Unfortunately, no beds were available at the hospital, and they had to be released.

On September 28, the next day, Kelsy returned to the Browning Hospital emergency room with her mother. Kelsy "was readmitted to the hospital after suffering from extreme pain from her puncture wounds," wrote Ranger [redacted] in the above-noted Supplementary Case/Incident Record. "She was admitted to Room 258, where her wounds were packed and re-dressed and she was placed on an IV. . . . She was given pain medication."

So what does bear spray feel like to the sprayed bear? Unfortunately, no grizzly has been able to provide details of what it experiences from encountering bear spray. But some researchers have been willing to test it on themselves, and report a very unpleasant, but, of course, nonlethal, experience.

A Glacier Park news release dated September 29, 2003, concluded with this: "Park managers feel the attack was consistent with a defensive response on the part of the bear, rather than a predatory attack, and no wildlife management actions are planned. Park rangers have posted the Piegan Pass Trail for bear frequenting, and closed the north side of Piegan Pass to the junction with the Grinnell Lake trail to off-trail hiking."

The next chapter follows the first of two grizzly bear attacks on the same man, in two different national parks—Glacier Park, and then Yellowstone Park. In 2010, the survivor, Jim Cole, published *Blindsided: Surviving a Grizzly Attack and Still Loving the Great Bear.*

13

FINDING JIM

1993: THE FLATTOP TRAIL GRIZZLY

That brings me to the subjects of fear and craziness. When people find out what I do and what I've experienced, many of them ask me if I'm afraid of the grizzly bear now, or if I'm nuts to still be out there in bear country.

—JIM COLE IN *BLINDSIDED: SURVIVING A GRIZZLY ATTACK AND STILL LOVING THE GREAT BEAR*, WITH TIM VANDEHEY

National Park Service–Glacier Park
Case Incident Record Number 931476: Jim Cole
Location: Flattop Trail near Fifty Mountain Campground
Date/Time: Wednesday, September 29, 1993, approximately 3:15 p.m.

After a surprise bear attack on September 29, 1993, one friend helped the other—who was severely injured—to hike out more than ten miles to find help. The words of attack survivor Jim Cole and his heroic friend Tim Rubbert are reported below as they were tape-recorded on the same evening as the attack. This is as close to contemporaneous as possible. (***Note:*** The Reporting Ranger [R/R], name redacted, changes the first-person accounts given by the two men to "COLE" and "RUBBERT.")

The ranger's report, in his Supplementary Case/Incident Record, dated October 1, 1993, tells us that "The interview was conducted at Kalispell General Hospital. . . . [It was begun] at 2155 [9:55 p.m.] and concluded at approximately 0030 [12:30 a.m.].

The conversation with COLE was interrupted periodically to allow medical treatment to be accomplished. This accounts for the brief interruptions in the taped recording. There was also one interruption of the interview with Tim Rubbert, when his wife arrived at the hospital. . . .

R/R spoke first with COLE, who was not under any medications at the time. COLE began the interview by stating that he had been hiking in the park for nearly 20 years, and was aware of the dangers inherent in that activity. He also related later that he had worked in research projects with wildlife, and knew of animal behavior. Both stated they were avid hikers, and often did long day trips like the one they were undertaking that day [25-mile round-trip]. . . .

COLE and RUBBERT were in agreement that the orange "Grizzly Frequenting" and "Campsite Closed at Fifty Mountain" signs were in place on the signboard, and they both noted that when they began the hike at about 0715 [7:15 a.m.], they did not see much sign of bear activity on the hike up, until they reached the Fifty Mountain Campground Area. There they stated [that] they observed diggings and scat, but did not see wildlife, other than one golden eagle. They continued up the trail toward Sue Lake, about one-quarter of a mile above the campground, where they stopped and ate lunch at about 1420 [2:20 p.m.].

They then began the return part of the hike, and had passed through the campground, en route back to Packers Roost. The attack occurred approximately halfway up the incline, which starts just after the meadow and creek below the campground, and continues nearly to Flattop. They stated that they had been talking just prior to the incident, but were not yelling. Due to the perceived lack of fresh bear sign, RUBBERT admitted that they were "a little relaxed" and probably not making much noise. COLE was approximately 10 yards in front of RUBBERT on the trail, as RUBBERT was stopping occasionally to glass (with binoculars) the open hillsides, looking for wildlife.

At about 1515 [3:15 p.m.], they got the first indication of the bear, which was described as "a long hissing sound" when they both saw the animal. It immediately charged COLE, who was only about 10 feet away. COLE saw the bear coming, turned his back, and began to get down into the fetal position, as RUBBERT yelled for him to do so. COLE was just off the trail when the bear hit him from behind, and pinned him on the ground. COLE was unsure of what transpired next, but RUBBERT had an unobstructed view of the incident. The bear grasped COLE's head in its mouth as COLE screamed once, and then bit COLE's left wrist when COLE unintentionally raised that appendage.

RUBBERT said that then he pulled out his canister of bear spray (which both hikers were carrying) and began to walk toward COLE, as the bear was standing over him. RUBBERT did not feel that the animal was aware of him, and in an attempt to distract the bear, he fired a short burst from the canister. He was concerned that he may hit COLE with the spray, so did not direct it directly at them. Upon hearing the spray, the bear looked at RUBBERT and immediately charged toward him. RUBBERT then began to spray at the bear, and continued as it charged directly into the fog pattern emitted from the canister. RUBBERT said that [the] bear's head was "totally engulfed in" the spray at about 5 feet from him when it stopped the charge, and immediately ran away from the scene, and was not observed again.

RUBBERT then went to COLE and they both moved about 50 feet away, where they used COLE's first-aid kit to treat the wound. RUBBERT poured some hydrogen peroxide on the wounds, placed dressings on the bleeding scalp and wrist, then wrapped the head with an elastic bandage. They noticed a tear in COLE's daypack, a laceration in his scalp, puncture wound of the left wrist, and slight scratches across his left shoulder blade. COLE's watch came off at the attack site, and some packaging debris was left at the spot where they dressed the wounds. [Names redacted] were able to retrieve these the following day.

Before leaving the scene, they noted that the bear had come from the left of the trail (east), where there were some small, short, alpine trees, and some rock cliffs immediately behind the trees. They saw some digging there, and feel that this is what the bear had been doing at the time of the incident. The ground vegetation in the area was cured [dried], low grasses, but the tree/cliff area the bear was in was also shaded.

Both stated vociferously that the incident was a surprise encounter, and COLE said that they "had the bear cornered," and that it was a "mutual surprise." RUBBERT described the bear as a grizzly sub-adult, about 250 to 300 pounds, and uniformly light brown. He based the species observation on the prominent hump, dished face, and general appearance of the animal. He was able to recite the differences between the species, and said that he had [experienced] many sightings in the past. He also stated that it looked very much like the bear in the Monte Dolack poster of the Pine Butte Swamp. COLE was unable to provide much [of a] description of the bear, as it happened too quickly. They continued later to state that they did not want the Park to take any management action against the bear.

When asked about the weather at the time, both felt that it was clear and sunny, and if there was a breeze, it was a light one, and the direction was unknown. Neither had on any sunscreen, bug repellent, topical creams, or items with scent. The only food they had in the packs at the time of the attack was some granola, an apple core, and some "Power Bars," along with water. They had no other possible attractants with them. They did not see another hiker the entire day, nor did they encounter uniformed NPS personnel.

Both men then hiked out to their vehicle at Packers Roost. RUB-BERT carried COLE's pack, and COLE did feel weak and considered stopping partway out. He drank some water and ate a few "Power Bars," which gave him the energy to continue to the vehicle.

After they arrived at the trailhead, their attention focused on get-ting COLE to the hospital as fast as possible. They drove with the vehicle flasher lights on until they reached West Glacier. They stopped at the public phone between the gas station and the photo shop, and called the incident in on the 911 line, requesting a police escort to the hospital. Flathead County alerted their patrol units of this and notified the Park dispatcher of the incident. At the phones, COLE and RUB-BERT encountered Dr. [name redacted], a vacationing physician, who did a brief assessment, and consulted with Kalispell emergency room staff, who approved the private transport.

R/R [reporting ranger] arrived at the hospital 45 minutes after the victim, and was able to immediately begin the interview. Doctors described the wounds as:

1) A 4- to 5-inch laceration of the scalp, nearly midline, in the back of the head;

2) One puncture wound of the left wrist, which broke one of the small bones in the wrist; and

3) Some abrasion of the left scapula.

COLE was admitted after surgical cleaning of the wounds and suturing, but was released at about 1200 [12:00 p.m.] the next day.

R/R spoke via telephone to COLE on Thursday, 9/30/93. He was in good spirits, and was complimentary of the news coverage and [informative] way that the park dealt with the information management. He said that he would be back in the Park soon, after about one week of doctor-ordered recuperation. His watch was left in the Communications Center for retrieval at his convenience, as agreed upon.

And what about Glacier Park's other hikers/campers who might run the risk of encountering the same bear?

The Details report in the Case Incident Record states that trails were closed, and "arrangements were made for [names redacted] to fly in via the *Minuteman* helicopter to investigate the scene of the attack [and look for the bear]."

At approximately 0915 [9:15 a.m.] [redacted] piloted Kemper and Bell to the 50 Mtn. area. [Redacted] placed a note at the "Campsite Closure" sign for the [name redacted] party of 2 that had a backcountry permit for Flattop Campsite on the night of the 30th [September 30, 1993]. The note was for the eventuality that contact couldn't be made, to warn the party of Bear Danger, the area closure, and to redirect them out the Highline Trail toward Granite Park.

On the flight over the 50 Mtn. Meadows, a grizzly sow and 2 cubs were observed. Each in the family group was dark brown with blond highlights. Also observed was a solitary grizzly. This bear was dark brown with blond highlights, particularly over the hump and shoulders. Size was difficult to tell from the air, but the bear appeared to be a medium-sized adult, approximately 250–300 pounds. No other bears were observed in the area.

[Names redacted] were dropped on top of Flattop Mountain to hike down the switchbacks toward 50 Mtn. to find and investigate the attack site. They would then meet [redacted] in the meadowy area near the 50 Mtn. Spike Camp just off the NE shoulder of Flattop.

[Names redacted] first came upon the site where Rubbert had administered first aid to Cole. There were blood spots, some bloody gauze bandages, and bandage wrappers. Approximately 50 yards downtrail (toward 50 Mtn.), after following blood spots in the trail, the bear spray trigger guard was found, and the scene was reconstructed from there.

In general, the area was very open and grassy, with a few clumps of stunted fir trees among a series of rocky ledges. The trail offered clear views with occasional trees near the trail's edge. The trail was a section of gentle upgrade (for the victim). Mt. Kipp was a clear open view to the NE. Overall bear activity in the area was very minimal.

The Initial Attack occurred near a small, thick clump of trees. There was a spot of blood on a rock in the trail. The Final Resting Point was off the trail approximately 9 feet to the right, where Cole's watch, blood spots, and knee indentations were found. There were large scratches in the dirt just feet away.

To the left of the trail there was a very small disturbed area underneath a tree and along a rock ledge. It could not be conclusively determined to be bear activity; it appeared more likely to be activity of a squirrel. (Possibly, the bear was just getting started on it when it was surprised.) If the bear had been behind the trees (uptrail from the hikers), it would very likely not have been observed by the hikers until the hikers were adjacent to the trees. At that point the bear would have been 10–15 ft. from the lead hiker (in this case, Cole). A small disturbance to the soil approximately 10 ft. from the trigger may have been where the grizzly encountered the bear spray and subsequently left the area.

After the investigation was complete, [names redacted] proceeded down the trail to the helicopter. One last stop was made near Flattop Campsite to place a "Campsite Closed" sign, and [redacted] were clear of the Great Northern Helispot by 1210 [12:10 p.m.].

A physical barricade trail closure was placed at the Stoney Indian junction on the Waterton Valley Trail closing the Highline Trail. The

Fifty Mountain Campground closure and Flattop Mountain Trail closure were also moved to the Stoney Indian Trail junction at this posting.

Due to the surprise nature of the encounter, no Glacier Park management action was taken against the grizzly bear, and this was what both Jim and Tim wanted. To want otherwise would be "Bearanoia," according to Jim. In his book *Blindsided: Surviving a Grizzly Attack and Still Loving the Great Bear,* Jim includes a verse of his song, "Bearanoia."

> With fear as the fabric woven in mystery
> Generations pass down sensational folklore
> Now hikers are yelling with cowbells and air horns
> And leaving their common sense parked at the door.[19]

But common sense did tell Jim (as he told his friends) that from now on, during future hikes in bear country, the forty-three-year-old would carry not one but *two* canisters of bear spray.

This intrepid hiker went on to suffer a second bear mauling when he was fifty-seven, in a second national park (Yellowstone). Even though he was much more severely wounded on this occasion, he again managed to hike out to find help—this time, alone.

Jim's second bear attack is described in the book *Taken by Bear in Yellowstone.* The day began "just after dawn that Wednesday, May 23, 2007, when Jim Cole parked beside Yellowstone's Hayden Valley. He surveyed the open valley, looking for animals to photograph. From the elevated rise of the roadside turnout, grizzlies could sometimes be spotted below, foraging on grasses and sedges beside the silver meanderings of Trout Creek."[20]

Jim then stepped down into bear country.

How did the attack happen?

Jim told Yellowstone special agents Dan Kirschner and Justin Ivary "that the attack came while he was walking downhill. He said that while hiking down a slope, he glanced left, then right." The Yellowstone Case Incident Record Number 071114 continues.

[Jim] said he saw a bear charging him. He said a "mother bear is point blank charging." He also saw one cub for a split second. He said that there may have been a blind spot, down the hill, where [the] mauling took place.

[He said] that the bear was in full charge with no chance to get spray [that was] carried on [his] belt (indicates 2 canisters). During mauling, [he] was trying to get to spray, but arm was not working—thinks bear injured his shoulder when he was driven to the ground. He said he then saw the bear leave with a cub and they ran away from him in the same direction that the bear had approached, and at same speed [at which] she had charged.

That after the mauling, he remembers a "faint perception of sun" which he used to find [his] way back to road.

Two passersby in a parked car found him approaching the Park's busy main Loop Road. "We saw a man walking out about 150–250 yards," they handwrote for park investigators. "I figured he was doing research or something."

Watching him through binoculars, it looked like he was wearing a mask. Lost sight for a while. Drove to Trout Creek, saw him sitting on bank. Just looked through binocs and realized his face [was] covered with blood. As he walked across creek, he yelled, "Help. Help. I've been attacked by a bear." I helped him to side of road. My wife called 911. Others stopped to help.

Park ranger Richard T. Fey responded to the scene. In his report, he described what he saw:

His nose and nasal cavity appeared to be gone, so was his mandible and most of the soft tissue around it. It appeared that his eyes were missing. It was difficult for me to recognize facial landmarks! I recognized his eyebrows. Everything below that was unrecognizable.[21]

After seven hours of emergency surgery, Jim was placed on a ventilator. He faced numerous reconstructive surgeries, from which he did recover.

Taken by Bear in Yellowstone concludes this incident by noting, "As for the bear and cub, Yellowstone spokesperson Al Nash said on Thursday, May 24, 2007, that 'We are not at this time planning any management action against the bear. From the little bit of information that we have, it appears he [Cole] surprised the bear and was attacked.'"[22]

Jim Cole died at home, at age sixty, on July 22, 2010, from natural causes. Seventeen years had passed since his first mauling, which occurred in Glacier Park in 1993.

In the next chapter, "Finding Frances and Rob," we learn of a California couple who was mauled by a grizzly near the same place that Jim Cole was mauled—Fifty Mountain Campground.

FINDING FRANCES AND ROB

1984: THE FIFTY MOUNTAIN CAMPGROUND GRIZZLY

What a horrible thing to watch this animal eat you alive.
            —Frances Lordan, as told to Brian Kennedy

National Park Service–Glacier Park
Case Incident Record Number not available: Frances Lordan and Rob Hilligoss
Location of incident: Upper Highline Trail near Fifty Mountain Campground
When did it occur: Tuesday, September 4, 1984, approximately early evening

Rob Hilligoss had read an article in *Outside* magazine praising the unique sights in Glacier Park, and now he and Frances Lordan were here to see for themselves. The California couple had backpacked more than eleven miles the day before, from Granite Park Chalet to the Fifty Mountain Campground, in the center of the Park. So today, Tuesday, September 4, 1984, was a welcome rest day.

Frances and Rob felt the comfort of five other hikers who had set up camp beside them at Fifty Mountain. So they left their gear behind, and shoulders feeling weightless, walked farther on the Highline Trail, seeking a better view of the surrounding mountain peaks. The campground's name, Fifty Mountain, is said to derive from the unique views from here of fifty mountain peaks. Frances and Rob turned around and started back through a stand of trees, less than a mile from the campground and now off trail. Two deer silently passed.

Then came loud sounds of woofing and growling, and the pounding of feet. Rob saw the silver-tipped grizzly first, about seventy-five feet away. The bear was catapulting straight for him, and he told Frances to head up a tree. Rob climbed a tree, but two times the grizzly pulled him down. He climbed back up again.

Frances couldn't find a tree to climb and ran across a small clearing toward more trees. The silver-tipped grizzly pursued Frances now, and Frances tried to protect herself by covering the back of her neck with her hands as the bear took her down.

"He bit me several times on the shoulders and then pushed me over," she told Brian Kennedy of the *Hungry Horse News*. "We both rolled down a small hill and I bounced up."

This time, Kennedy writes, "the bear charged on all fours and bit her in the leg. She was wearing shorts and she watched the bear bite her thigh and swallow the flesh. 'What a horrible thing to watch this animal eat you alive,' Frances said. 'All I could think of was that woman in Yellowstone Park who was killed by a bear earlier this summer.'" (Swiss backpacker Brigitta Fredenhagen was camping alone in Yellowstone when she was dragged from her tent and sleeping bag.)

But here in Glacier Park, Frances fell and rolled into a protective ball as the grizzly launched a biting attack on her back. To distract the bear, Rob yelled from his tree. The bear swung over to him and climbed fifteen feet up and pulled him down for the third time.

"I felt like a drowning man," Rob told reporter Kennedy. "This is it. I'm dead."

Frances "wedged herself between two trees. The bear left Rob and hunted for Frances but couldn't find her," Brian Kennedy wrote. Once more Rob climbed his tree, and now saw the grizzly running away. Could it be true? The attack appeared to be over.

In her tree perch Frances started to black out, so tied herself to the trunk using the sleeves of her sweatshirt. The grizzly returned and Frances could see it from her perch, but it ran away again and this time did not return. Was it over?

"People at the campground heard their cries for help and cautiously walked to their rescue," Kennedy reported. "They helped Frances out of the tree. With their help she walked most of the way back, not giving out until she was in the tent. 'It was really frightening because we thought the bear would come back at any second,' she said. They moved the tents closer together and kept a smoky fire burning all night."

There were five other campers now, waiting out the night, plus Frances and Rob. It was, they said, a long and a very cold night. The group had no way to call for help. The darkness made them unable to see the trail, and made it too dangerous to hike out and seek help. And they assumed the bear was still nearby, ready to attack again at any sign of movement.

Both Frances and her companion, Rob, lay there, suffering from the shock and pain of their injuries. Frances's injuries were by far the most severe. Kennedy reported that she received "a gaping hole in her right thigh, where the bear tore out a piece of flesh the size of her hand. She also had a puncture wound in her left shoulder from a bite." The grizzly had bitten Rob severely on the left ankle, in its attempt to pull him out of the branches where he had climbed for safety.

The five other campers attempted to comfort the two victims and to relieve their pain. They tried sprinkling cayenne pepper on Frances's leg, and this did seem to stem the bleeding. The two Canadian campers contributed their pain pills, which included aspirin and codeine, and also antibiotic pills.

Frances did not sleep that long night, as she felt colder and colder as the hours passed. In response she kept moving and contracting her fingers and toes, willing them not to lose sensation and chance frostbite.

" 'I'm amazed at how brave she was,' Rob told reporter Kennedy. 'She never cried or complained.' "

Finally dawn arrived, and light spread among the tents huddled together. At 6:30 a.m. three of the party started hiking out to find help, fearing at any moment the sounds or sight of the grizzly reappearing. Two campers remained with Frances and Rob, helping and comforting them as much as they could.

Near Ahern Mountain, the three hurrying down the trail encountered a trail crew, one of whom rushed on through the early morning to reach the Granite Park Chalet, arriving about 10:30 a.m. At last, communication. At the Chalet a park radio was available, and after another hour, at about 11:30 a.m., Frances and Rob heard the *whump-whump* of a park helicopter's rotor blades. A two-member medical team arrived to check on their condition, along with two rangers.

" 'It was so good to hear that helicopter,'" Frances related to Kennedy. " 'You knew you had made it then.'"

When asked by the rangers, neither Frances nor Rob could give any reason why the grizzly had attacked. Nor could the rangers find an immediate explanation. Frances and Rob "didn't want the bear harmed 'unless it was always this vicious,'" writes Kennedy.

Frances's injuries required hospitalization and surgery, followed by plastic surgery and skin grafting. Rob's ankle-bite wounds became painfully infected. But eventually Frances and Rob found their physical wounds healing. The shock of the experience, however, was to remain with them permanently. Frances told Kennedy that " 'It was difficult to imagine something so terrifying could happen in such a beautiful place.'"[23]

But perhaps there was a partial explanation for the silver-tipped grizzly bear's aggression that day. A possible identification of the bear was made.

"Grizzly near campground matches description," reported the Glacier Park news release, later that September of 1984.

GLACIER PARK—Park rangers saw four grizzly bears in the Fifty Mountain Campground area last week after Tuesday's attack.

One of the bears, a sow with two cubs, matched the description of the grizzly that Frances Lordan and Rob Hilligoss said attacked them, although they reported not seeing any cubs.

Rangers said those three bears and another grizzly were not aggressive, and no management action was planned, since the attacking bear could not be positively identified.

The campground remains closed but should open later this month, Park officials said.

—◦—

The following chapter, "Finding Roscoe and Teresa," describes two near-death maulings which occurred in 1976. Park visitation had surged, and according to Glacier Park officials, more visitors encountered more grizzlies, with a record-breaking number of injuries to humans (as well as one fatality; see chapter 3, "Finding Mary Pat").

15

FINDING ROSCOE AND TERESA

1976: THE STONEY INDIAN PASS GRIZZLY

The bear chewed his leg first, then moved over Black's chest and laid on him, face-to-face. Black said he could feel the heartbeat of the bear, and that the bear had bad breath.
—Ranger interview of Roscoe Black at Kalispell Regional Hospital, Montana

National Park Service–Glacier Park
Case Incident Record Number 761586: Roscoe Black and Teresa Waden
Location of incident: Stoney Indian Pass Trail, between Stoney Indian Lake and Pass Creek Junction
When did it occur: September 9, 1976, approximately 4:00 p.m.

September's late afternoon turned golden, the sky a bowl of blue as the party of three colleagues enjoyed the fall colors while hiking down the Stoney Indian Pass Trail.

They had hiked from Chief Mountain Customs (Canada), and at 4:00 p.m. were approximately three and a half miles west of Stoney Indian Pass. "The Stoneys [Indians]," notes author Jack Holterman, "are a small branch of the Assiniboines."[24]

Roscoe Black, manager of the St. Mary Lodge and facilities at St. Mary Village (east of Going-to-the-Sun Road), and two women members of the St. Mary dining room staff, had no desire to see grizzly bears.

They may have chosen a different trail if they had known that Stoney Indian Pass was the site of Glacier Park's second documented grizzly bear attack, which occurred in early August 1956. Anthony "Toby" Johnson was asleep in his sleeping bag that summer, alongside his friend. Toby awoke to terror: A lone bear, believed to be a grizzly, was biting him. The bear bit through the makeshift lean-to shelter and Toby's sleeping bag and poncho. This dawn attack is believed to have been possibly predatory in nature, meaning that the bear was exploring Toby as prey. Toby screamed and flailed. Fortunately, this disturbance caused the bear to run off. Toby and his friend hiked out on their own and reached safety (see chapter 23, "Finding Toby").

But that was in 1956. This was Glacier Park in 1976, when a record-breaking number of bear-caused injuries to people took place. Tragically, one of these would be a fatality (see chapter 3, "Finding Mary Pat), occurring just days after the attack on Black and Waden.

But this was yet to happen on the day Roscoe Black, thirty-six, and Teresa Waden, twenty-one, hiked the Stoney Indian Pass Trail. They were walking with a third friend, a nineteen-year-old woman, who by now had fallen behind. The corners of the trail were brushy, and this friend could no longer see Roscoe and Teresa. Suddenly, she heard terrifying sounds from up ahead.

"I was hiking 5 min. behind Roscoe and Teresa. . . . I heard Teresa scream and I hid in the bushes," wrote the young woman [name redacted]. In addition to being interviewed by ranger Oakley B. Blair once she had safely returned to the women's dorm at St. Mary's Lodge, she also provided a handwritten report, excerpted below:

> I left the bushes approx. 10 sec. [later] and came upon Roscoe and Teresa around a bend in the trail. Teresa was sitting on the ground off the trail; Roscoe was limping up the trail toward me. . . . The bear had apparently gone down the trail (so Roscoe said), and I didn't see him. Roscoe then told me to run down the trail (making noise) and get help.
>
> I ran into two backpackers a little ways down the trail (they hadn't seen the bear). They returned with me and helped organize things and figure out what to do. . . . [Name redacted], (one of the hikers), stayed

behind to assist Roscoe and Teresa, while [name redacted] (the other hiker) came with me to the Waterton Ranger Station to get help, and a helicopter.

What happened next?

Another hiker (a third-year medical student from Indiana) was one of many whose altruism, now sometimes called "pro-social behavior," helped to save Roscoe and Teresa's lives. Altruism is at its apex when persons help others while putting themselves at risk. For example, instead of running away, according to the Case Incident Record, "Two hikers came up the trail [to help] in the same direction that the bear had fled." Ultimately three groups of hikers and many Park Service personnel on "Hazard Duty" helped.

What would you do if you were out in the backcountry with an attacking bear nearby?

The third-year medical student wrote the following:

Teresa Waden was going into shock. Roscoe Black was dazed but otherwise alert. I elevated Teresa's legs and covered both victims with clothing and sleeping bags. I next checked Teresa's 2 tourniquets [placed by earlier hiker], one located at the knee and the other located just above the wound on the calf. The tourniquets were made of cotton T-shirts. They were on for 10–15 minutes before I cut them off. Teresa complained that her leg was going numb, but after removing the tourniquets, the feeling returned. At 4:30 I gave Teresa ½ grain of codeine with APC. I had both victims drink water. I gave another ½ grain of codeine at about 5:30 p.m. to Teresa and continued comforting and clothing the victims to keep them warm and reassuring them that their wounds were not bad.

Roscoe Black's wounds consisted basically of bad puncture wounds on both sides of the right shoulder. The right leg had a large slice [off] the outside of the thigh. I covered the thigh wound with a clean T-shirt. Teresa's wound consisted of the right calf being partially torn from the leg. . . .

Roscoe said that Teresa told him *she thought the bear was going to eat her up*, and that she did not know why the bear left [emphasis added].

Sketch map shows the site of Roscoe and Teresa's mauling. The arrow in the center of the page points to the location where the bear attacked, along the dotted line indicating the Stoney Indian Pass Trail.

ILLUSTRATION FROM CASE INCIDENT RECORD NUMBER 761586

Two more hikers, a man and his wife, described hearing shouts for help, and they too rushed to help (even though they were the ones coming up the same path the bear was running down). "We had been hearing shouts and were not sure [if] they were of human or bird in origin. As we got closer, we were sure they were human," they handwrote on September 10 when interviewed by Ranger Blair at St. Mary's Lodge. Their account continues below.

> I realize now that it was [human] noise, in case we were a returning bear. As I came around the corner of the trail I saw Roscoe and then Teresa lying on the trail, wrapped in sleeping bags. At first I realized that something was wrong, I then realized that they [had] been injured. . . . [names redacted] had gone to Goat Haunt for help. Roscoe said that they should be getting back any time. I asked if they needed anything and they replied, "More 'down,'" so we contributed our sleeping bags. . . .
>
> We stayed with Roscoe and Teresa until the helicopter came by and signaled by moving out into the open, signaling with brightly colored garments. . . . Teresa was very shaken by the experience and did not want to talk about what happened. However, Roscoe had a very clear mental picture of the events. He hoped that the bear would attack only him and let Teresa get up a tree. He finally kicked the bear and it let go, but then pulled Teresa out of the tree she had started up by her boot or leg. . . . Roscoe stayed in fairly good spirits the whole time we were with them both. He even tried to keep Teresa's spirits up and refused codeine for himself, saying that the codeine should be saved for Teresa. . . .
>
> Roscoe said that "*he thought he was a goner,*" but the bear left [emphasis added].

And finally Roscoe himself, despite his pain and injuries, was able to tell what happened. Later that evening, Kalispell Regional Hospital emergency staff stabilized him, and investigating ranger Clyde M. Fauley interviewed him. Ranger Fauley wrote the following in his "Interrogation of Victim—Bear Mauling" report, below.

Mr. Black, Ms. Waden, and Ms. [redacted] had hiked from Chief Mountain Customs and at 4:00 p.m. were approximately 3½ miles west of Stoney Indian Pass, when the group encountered a grizzly bear. Mr. Black said he and Ms. Waden were about 10 feet apart with Black in the lead. Ms. [name redacted] was about 70 yards away, taking pictures.

Black came around the corner in a brushy area and the bear was up on the bank to the right of the trail. The bear grunted, then came toward Black and knocked him down backwards. The bear chewed his leg first, then moved over Black's chest and laid on him, face-to-face. The bear then chewed into Black's shoulder. Black said he could feel the heart-beat of the bear and that the bear had bad breath. Black got his foot up and kicked the bear, [which] then went after Ms. Waden, who was climbing a tree. She had thrown her pack with sandwiches in the trail, but the bear passed the pack and grabbed her from the tree. [The] bear then turned, stood up, came down again, walked a few steps, glanced at Black, and took off down the hill.

Black heard Ms. Waden's screams, but could not move to assist her.

In the meantime, [the third friend] headed for Goat Haunt Ranger Station. She met another party [names not known, except for two], who continued on up to the injured victims. A second party also arrived on the scene, and Black said one of them was a third-year medical student who had bandages, etc. with him, and administered good first aid. Black did not know the names of these people.

Roscoe Black's injuries were lacerated right shoulder, thigh, back, and hand. Apparently no broken bones. Ms. Waden received a severe lacerated calf of her right leg.

Black described the bear as a small, 3- or 4-year-old, about 225 pounds. The bear was black/gray, silvertip grizzly. He said that all of his injuries were from bear's teeth. Very few claw marks.

He said the first party to arrive after the incident heard the bear taking off down through the brush.

The bear had no ear tags. There was no wind. Black said the group had been talking and making noise prior to attack. He feels now the bear knew they were coming and was waiting for them around the corner. . . .

Ms. Waden was not permitted visitors so I did not interview her. Black said I could go see her anyway. He said she was still upset and did not want any interviews with news reporters, so I decided not to interview her at this time.

The "search and rescue" attempt to find Roscoe and Teresa unfolded as follows. Ranger Oakley B. Blair, at the Goat Haunt Ranger Station, wrote that at 1730 hours [5:30 p.m.] he was notified "that two people had been attacked by a bear and were injured. Mr. [redacted] stated that the location of the incident was approximately 1½ miles below the Stoney Indian Lake backcountry campsite."

The ranger's Supplementary Case/Incident Record continues:

Ranger Blair contacted District Ranger Robert Frauson and informed him of the incident and requested a helicopter and EMT to assist in the rescue.

A Mountain West helicopter took off from West Glacier at approximately 1900 hours [7:00 p.m.], with Ranger Bell (EMT) and a nurse from Kalispell Hospital, and landed at Stoney Indian campsite at approximately 1922 hrs. [7:22 p.m.]. Ranger Bell and the nurse made contact with the victims at approx. 1950 hrs. [7:50 p.m.] and began administering first aid.

Rangers Blair and Oltman were airlifted from Goat Haunt Ranger Station to Stoney Indian campsite and made contact with Ranger Bell and the victims at approx. 1955 hrs. [7:55 p.m.]. Ranger Oltman and Blair began to evacuate Teresa Waden to the helicopter and arrived at the helicopter at approx. 2140 hrs. [9:40 p.m.]. The helicopter lifted off for Kalispell Hospital at approx. 2145 hrs. [9:45 p.m.]. Ranger Bell evacuated Roscoe Black, with assist of 2 hikers, to the second helicopter. . . . Helicopter lifted off for the Kalispell Hospital at approx. 2155 hrs. [9:55 p.m.].

Ranger Blair asked the following questions of Teresa Waden [while she was being rescued].

Blair: "What caused the bear to attack?"

Waden: "I don't know."

Blair: "Did you surprise the bear?"

Waden: "I guess; it came out of the bushes."

Blair: "Did you have food in your packs?"

Waden: "Yes, but the bear did not touch our packs."

Blair: "Did you have bear bells on your packs?"

Waden: "No."

Investigator corroborates Teresa Waden's answers. Their daypacks were not molested by the bear, and their packs did not have bear bells on them.

(Addendum: Of the 9 people in the rescue party, 7 or 8 were using bear bells on their packs.)

To warn and protect any other persons in the area, rangers implemented the following (among many safeguards). "An 18-inch spruce log was rolled across the Stoney Indian Trail at the junction, and a plastic 'grizzly frequenting area' sign on a plywood board was nailed to the log," rangers noted the next morning, at 8:00 a.m. "With a grease pencil, 'Trail closed for season, grizzly mauling 2 mi ahead 9/9/76, Goat Haunt Ranger Station manned until 9/30' [was] written on the sign. Patrol was then made to Goat Haunt Ranger Station with a stop to check the campground at Kootenai Lake. The three hikers [names redacted] continued on to 50 Mt. as on their schedule."

What about the grizzly bear, which was not seen again after the ensuing commotion of rescuers and helicopters?

Since the attack was determined to have been defensive in nature, due to a surprise encounter with Roscoe and Teresa, no management action was taken.

Later, after the September 23, 1976, fatality of Mary Pat Mahoney, Roscoe testified in person about his mauling to the Board of Inquiry, regarding the death of Mary Patricia Mahoney (see chapter 3).

When interviewed by rangers later, the third-year medical student who helped Roscoe and Teresa added the following to his handwritten report: "I would like to take this opportunity to tell the Park Service how wonderful, efficient, kind, knowledgeable, etc., that I think they are. I was and still am very impressed by their efficiency. Thank you, Jerry,

Brian, Oak, and the rest whose names I didn't learn. You are great! [Name redacted], 8/10/76."

———

In the next chapter, two campers in the remote backcountry are attacked by a grizzly, which drags one man away while still in his sleeping bag.

16

FINDING WILLIAM

1976: THE LOGGING LAKE GRIZZLY

The bear persisted in chewing on Schweighofer. The bear dragged Schweighofer approximately 10 yards while he was still in his sleeping bag and tent.

        —FIRE GUARD WARREN J. PHILLIPS, FIRST RESPONDER

National Park Service–Glacier Park
Case Incident Record Number 760805: William Schweighofer
Location: Logging Lake / Midway Campground
Date/Time: July 16, 1976, approximately 8:30 a.m.

Two months before the death of Mary Pat Mahoney—in a similar predatory attack—the early morning of July 16, 1976, began with terror for William Schweighofer.

Deep in the roadless backcountry, he and his friend were in their tent at the Logging Lake / Midway Campground. The early light brightened, reflecting on the peaceful waters of Logging Lake. "Far from the scores of tourists traveling Going-to-the-Sun Road, Logging Lake receives relatively few visitors. The trail takes you through an undisturbed forest to a regenerating forest [after 1988's Red Bench Fire]," writes Alan Leftridge in *Glacier Day Hikes*, "and finally to a typical North Fork lake set amid towering peaks."[25] Adds Erik Molvar, in *Hiking Glacier and Waterton Lakes National Parks*, "Wildlife is abundant along the entire length of the trail. Deer, squirrels, and even mountain lions inhabit the forested valley, and the call of the loon is frequently heard on Logging Lake."[26]

And bears?

What happened next is described by investigating ranger Jerald L. Polzin in the Case Incident Record, dated July 18, 1976.

At approximately 0830 [8:30 a.m.], July 16, 1976, a bear, identified as a grizzly, hit the tent of William Schweighofer, and [name redacted]. Schweighofer yelled at his partner to stop [thinking his partner had hit him]. The bear then bit Schweighofer. [Redacted] got free of his sleeping bag and the tent and threw rocks and yelled to scare the bear away.

The bear persisted in chewing on Schweighofer. The bear dragged Schweighofer approximately 10 yards while he was still in his sleeping bag and tent. Schweighofer got away and he and [redacted] ran into the lake [Logging Lake]. The bear was at the campground approximately 1 hour. Both men yelled and threw rocks at the bear as long as he stayed. The bear left around 0930. [Redacted] applied a bandage to Schweighofer's upper left arm.

[Redacted] stated that Schweighofer passed out once and was going into shock. Schweighofer took two sleeping pills to relieve the pain.

[Redacted] left the campground at 10:30 a.m. to find help.

Between the Logging Midway Campground and the Logging Patrol Cabin, [redacted] met two parties: the [redacted] party—2 people; and the [redacted] party—2 people. Both parties proceeded up the lake trail to help the victim.

[Redacted] reported the incident to fire guard Warren Phillips at the junction of the Logging Lake Trail and the trail to the patrol cabin at the foot of Logging Lake at 11:45 a.m. Phillips was packing supplies for the patrol cabin with 2 horses. At the time of the report, Phillips was talking with the [redacted] party.

Phillips sent [redacted] to Polebridge Ranger Station [R. S.] for help, first-aid supplies, and a litter. [Redacted] reported the incident to Cindy Mish at Polebridge R. S. at 1305 [1:05 p.m.]. Phillips and [redacted] proceeded up the lake to the campground with first-aid supplies. They arrived at the site at 12:40 p.m. When they arrived, the [redacted] party had been there for five minutes.

Schweighofer was alert and sitting up and was very stable. . . . Phillips transported Schweighofer and [redacted] by boat to the patrol cabin at the foot of the lake. They arrived there at 1340 [1:40 p.m.]. The camping equipment was packed on one horse and Schweighofer was helped on the other horse.

This party proceeded down toward the Logging Lake trailhead. Party met rangers Stevlingson and Polzin, who were en route to assist Phillips approximately 1½ miles from the trailhead at 1545 [3:45 p.m.]. . . .

Jack Fewlass, district ranger, sent a helicopter with rangers Bud Sanders and Art Sedlack with EMT equipment and litter to Logging area. Stevlingson and Polzin proceeded from Kintla Lake R. S. to Polebridge R. S., picked up a litter, and went to Logging R. S.

From there they proceeded up the Logging Lake Trail 1½ miles, where they met the Phillips party. Polzin then went back to Logging R. S. to report the condition of the victim to Fewlass and arrange landing of the helicopter at the ranger station area for further first aid and transportation of the victim to a hospital. Stevlingson escorted the Phillips party down the trail to the ranger station. They arrived at Logging R. S. at 1620 [4:20 p.m.].

The helicopter landed at the same time in the streambed across from Logging Creek Campground. Schweighofer was transported across Logging Creek on horseback. Blood pressure of Schweighofer was taken and was normal, 120/80. An additional compress was placed on arm over original bandage (left arm).

Sedlack made the decision to fly Schweighofer to the Flathead Health Center. Helicopter left Logging R. S. en route to Kalispell at 1645 [4:45 p.m.].

Injuries to Schweighofer were puncture wounds: 1) left shoulder area, 2) left upper back area, 3) upper left arm, 4) left hand, 5) base of head, back side.

Ranger J. De Santo then interviewed witnesses for further information as to what had occurred. On July 18, 1976, De Santo wrote in a "Supplementary to Case Incident #760805" that [names redacted] "were hiking up the Logging Lake Trail about 10:30 [a.m.], 16 July 1976, when they met [redacted] coming down the trail."

[Redacted] informed them that his partner had been mauled by a grizzly and asked them to continue to Midway Campground to help while he went on for help. [Names redacted] dropped their packs and went on. When they got to Midway, the injured person had already been evacuated, so they returned to their packs (about ½ to 1 mile up lake from campground at foot) and *met a bear rummaging in their packs* [emphasis added].

They described the bear as a grizzly, brown in color, and about 8 feet tall. The bear ripped up [redacted's] pack and in the process, 2 camera lenses were lost (Zeiss 105mm and Zeiss 37mm); $30 in bills was also lost, and a negligible amount of food [was] lost, apparently devoured.

The 37mm lens was found by Polzin and Phillips and returned to [redacted]. Total loss incurred [was] approximately $150, with an additional damage to pack of $15. Grand total: $165.

The second party of those who courageously helped William Schweighofer was also interviewed by Ranger J. De Santo. He wrote on July 18 that "[Names redacted], both from Illinois, were hiking from foot to Midway [Campground] on Logging Lake Trail on 16 July 1976, when they met a man shouting (as they said) that his friend had been mauled.

De Santo's report continues:

He asked them to help the injured party while he went for help. They went on to Midway, found Schweighofer sitting there ("maybe in shock"), and with injuries to his back, arm, and hand. They sat with him until the boat with Forestry Tech Phillips arrived and, in the meantime, rounded up his equipment. [Names redacted] said they were told by Schweighofer that Schweighofer and [redacted] had watched the bear for 45 minutes before the bear moved in on them. [Names redacted] saw the bear and described it as brown to cinnamon in color, and they were not sure it was a grizzly.

Two rangers arrived to help the victim by helicopter. Rangers Bud Sanders and Art Sedlack wrote in the Case Incident Record on July 26, 1976, that they were "flown by helicopter to Logging Lake area."

> We patrolled the valley from Logging Ranger Station to Grace Lake. At 4 p.m. we received a radio message that the victim was at Logging R. S. The victim was checked for bleeding and shock. He was stable but complained of pain. We put a large bandage over the wound in his left triceps. The superficial wounds from neck to left hand looked well cared for by [ranger] Warren Phillips. [Name redacted] and Sedlack took victim, William Schweighofer, to Kalispell Regional Hospital.

And what about the grizzly William had encountered?

Ranger Polzin wrote on July 18 that "a patrol was made from North Fork Road to Logging and Grace Lakes by Polzin and Phillips. Drainage was cleared of all people. No bear was sighted. Tracks seen from Grace Lake to Foot of Logging Lake. Time: to 2200 [10:00 p.m.] on 16th. Returned to Polebridge 1730 [5:30 p.m.] on 17th."

No information remains in the Case Incident Record as to the follow-up condition of William Schweighofer, or the location of, and decision made, regarding the responsible bear, which had vanished into the backcountry.

It should be noted that William's friend and many others (both visitors and National Park Service personnel) helped William, at some risk to their own lives, without knowing whether the grizzly was gone or if it would return.

Why 1976? The next chapter, "Other 1976 Encounters," supports the Mary Pat Mahoney fatality Board of Review report: "The evidence is that there were more people–bear encounters within the park this year, and in the Many Glacier area, in particular, than in any previous year."

17

OTHER 1976 ENCOUNTERS

About halfway down from the [Ptarmigan] Tunnel, a lady ran up to me from behind. She asked me where the bear went, and I told her, the bear went into the campsite.

She then got excited, and she said she left her 20-month-old baby and her [illegible]-yr.-old child at the campsite with the babysitter, who was 17 yrs. old.

—RANGER R. E. MILLSAP, JULY 12, 1976

National Park Service–Glacier Park, 1976
Case Incident Records (handwritten) Numbers 761614, 769678,
761008, 761290, 761374, 761416, 761593, and one illegible
Locations: Various within Glacier Park
Date/Time: See individual encounter reports.

Four days after the last encounter on September 19, 1976, in this chapter, Mary Pat Mahoney was dragged from her tent in the Many Glacier Campground and killed.

The encounters described in this chapter begin on July 11 and end on September 19, 1976. Why did Glacier Park experience such a rise in reported bear encounters and attacks in the year 1976?

The answer is still unknown, but that year saw a rapidly escalating visitor presence and its attendant problems, some of which are highlighted below.

JULY 11 ENCOUNTER: THE PTARMIGAN TUNNEL GRIZZLY

Many anxious visitors witnessed this encounter, reported by Ranger R. E. Millsap on July 12, below.

About fifty meters below the old campsite [near Ptarmigan Tunnel, a trail blasted through rock], he [the grizzly] slowed to a walk. . . . Then the bear walked into the old campsite, and disappeared from view in subalpine firs. I then began to walk down the trail from the Tunnel toward the old campsite, to keep him in view, since there were forty-two day hikers at the Tunnel, and another estimated thirty to forty below at different locations around the lake and on the trail.

About halfway down from the Tunnel, a lady ran up to me from behind. She asked me where the bear went, and I told her, the bear went into the campsite. She then got excited, and she said she left her 20-month-old baby and her [illegible]-yr.-old child at the old campsite with the babysitter, who was 17 yrs. old. Mrs. [redacted] said she met her babysitter at the Tunnel, and she asked the babysitter where her kids were, and she said she left them in the old campsite with some visitors. So the mother got worried, and that's when she caught up to me.

We got to the first snowfield and saw fresh tracks in the snow, which was level. The front paws measured 5 inches by 5 inches, which was consistent with tracks measured earlier in the day in mud near the Ptarmigan/Lake Trail junction. The rear track in snow measured 5 inches by 10 inches, which was also consistent with tracks measured earlier in the day. Therefore, this bear probably frequents this trail.

Mrs. [redacted] and I then proceeded to the old campsite where we discovered no one there. We proceeded down the trail and caught up with visitors who were running, from Helena and Grand Rapids, Michigan. They said they were among thirteen visitors picnicking at the old campsite when the bear walked among them while they ate their food. They scattered, and some visitors picked up and left down the trail. Then, they said, the bear left the campsite, walked in the snow, circled behind the picnic area, and raised its head as if to smell their food.

Most said they did not think the bear was aggressive; however, a few felt threatened just because the bear came near them. They all indicated that the bear made no aggressive noises, such as "woofing" sounds, "snorts," or charges of any type.

Mrs. [redacted] and I proceeded down the trail, and we did not find the kids until we got to Ptarmigan Falls, where we discovered the visitors had removed her children for their own protection.

Ranger Shewmake swept all people out from the Tunnel after the decision was made to close that trail. He followed the bear tracks in the snow until [they] disappeared. He stayed in the area until about 1845 [6:45 p.m.], observed no more bears, and returned to the ranger station.

JULY 11 ENCOUNTER: THE RED ROCK FALLS GRIZZLY

Ranger Fred Reese investigated this "bear confrontation," as he wrote in his report. Location: "Red Rock Lake, near head of lake, July 11, 1976."

At approximately 1700 hours [5:00 p.m.], 7/11/76, near Red Rock Falls, Many Glacier Subdistrict, [names redacted] were walking toward Many Glacier from Red Rock Falls. They were within 100 yards of the falls when a grizzly bear came out onto the trail, about 100 feet in front of them, and started walking toward them on the trail. They slowly backed up the trail. The grizzly increased his pace somewhat and the two people turned and ran approximately 100 yards to the creek, waded the creek just below Red Rock Falls, and climbed a tree on the opposite bank of the stream. The grizzly walked to the creek side and waded around in the water, apparently not noticing them at all. After about 5–10 minutes, the grizzly walked across the stream (not close to the tree that the people were in) and disappeared up the hill in the direction of Grinnell Point. The two people waited another 10 minutes in the tree, then descended the tree and hiked back to Many Glacier. They did not see the bear during the return hike.

On 7/12/76 at 0930 hours [9:30 a.m.], I, Fred Reese, hiked to Red Rock Falls area to determine if the bear was in the vicinity of the

Falls–Trail area. I arrived at the falls at 1000 hours [10:00 a.m.] and spent some time (15 minutes) looking around for any sign of the bear and could find nothing. The trail is posted, "Grizzly Frequenting the Area."

JULY 13 ENCOUNTER: PATROL OF PTARMIGAN LAKE BASIN

Note: The number of visitors to Glacier Park, particularly near Ptarmigan Lake and drainage, is illustrated by the report below, when Ranger [name redacted] patrolled the area. He also tallied the impressive amount of wildlife he saw.

On 7/13/76 between 1300 and 2100 [1:00 p.m. and 9:00 p.m.], I patrolled the Ptarmigan Lake basin and observed no signs of grizzly bear activity.

The trail closure sign was to be removed on the evening of 7/13/76; however, a rescue was initiated near Redgap Pass and manpower was depleted. The trail closure sign was taken down 7/14/76, approx. 1330 [1:30 p.m.] by Ranger Fred Reese.

The foot patrol into the area by Penttilla produced observation of 48 visitors on the trail. 22 males. These contacts were made between Swiftcurrent and Iceberg Lake. 26 females.

31 Bighorn sheep near Ptarmigan Lake, with 9 of the 31 this year's young. 1 male ram, young. 6 goats—3 this year's young.

JULY 13 ENCOUNTER: THE JOSEPHINE LAKE GRIZZLY

Note: This encounter is handwritten and is only partly legible. The encounter occurred on July 13, 1976. Ranger Millsap writes on July 14 that "at approximately 1400 [2:00 p.m.], the Many Glacier Boat Concession called to report that a blondish and brown grizzly weighing approximately [unreadable] was seen above the trail near the upper end of Josephine Lake. He said the bear was 'aggressive,' and he said that 'something had to be done about the bear problem.'" [The rest of the report is illegible.]

JULY 19 ENCOUNTER: THE HIDDEN LAKE GRIZZLIES

Note: See "Encounters of the Twin Grizzlies" later in this chapter (page 222).

This July 19 Hidden Lake Grizzlies incident may in actuality be related to the Mary Pat Mahoney fatality. This adult mother bear may have been the grizzly that killed Mary Pat. At the time of this July 19 appearance, the mother grizzly was still accompanied by her twin near-adult cubs. After the Mary Pat fatality, the two cubs on-site at the Many Glacier Campground were shot and killed. The adult mother bear (if she was there) was never found.

The brief paragraph remaining on this incident appears below.

"Occurs about dusk at Hidden Lake. Three hikers camped illegally. Grizzly with two cubs run through their tent. The hikers retreated toward Logan Pass Visitor Center, are discovered about midnight by patrol ranger, no injuries."

JULY 27 ENCOUNTER: THE MANY GLACIER CAMPGROUND GRIZZLY

This incident occurred on July 27. Ranger [redacted] wrote that "at 2345 hours [11:45 p.m.], Mr. [redacted] came to my trailer in the Many Glacier Ranger Compound and notified me that an apparent bear had ripped open his tent, while he was away for the day."

The report continues:

His tent is located in Site 87, Many Glacier Campground.

I went to the site with Mr. [redacted] and noted that the side of the tent appeared to have scratches on it, like that of a bear. A sleeping bag had been removed from the tent and was on the ground about 30 feet from the tent; it was not damaged. No food was in the tent. A check by foot of the campground revealed no sign of any additional problems at 0430 [4:30 a.m.]. Upon talking with the visitors in the campground on the following morning, no one saw a bear in the campground on this evening.

AUGUST 15 ENCOUNTER: THE ICEBERG LAKE TRAIL GRIZZLY

This incident appears in the Case Incident Record as a "bear molestation without injuries." On August 15, ranger Terry Penttilla wrote the following.

Two persons [redacted] reported to me at the Many Glacier Ranger Station that a grizzly bear charged them, was aggressive, and the two gals ran up the trail a short distance and observed the bear still behind them.

They then dropped their packs and continued running up the trail toward Ptarmigan Falls. They stated that they found a tree and climbed it. The bear then stood up on its hind legs and leaned against the tree, then dropped down on its legs and remained in the area, always watching the girls. Then it finally wandered uphill toward the slope of the Hotel. This incident was reported to me to have happened on the Iceberg Lake Trail in the vicinity between Ptarmigan Falls and the Swiftcurrent Motor Inn.

The two women who encountered the grizzly above wrote their own first-person accounts of the incident.

Account One: As we were walking along the trail toward Ptarmigan Tunnel, [redacted] turned around to tell me something and quietly said, [redacted], there's a bear. Run! We ran a few hundred yards with our packs. The bear was about 15 to 20 feet running behind me. We dropped our packs and I tripped over [redacted]. When I turned around, he [the bear] was 5–10 feet behind. I took off like a shot. The bear stopped momentarily to sniff the packs, then continued to chase us. We ran quite a ways until [redacted] spotted a tree with small stumps sticking out. We climbed to the top with the bear following right behind. He stood up on his hind legs but couldn't get at us. He walked to the path, looked, came back to us, went to the path, then up the hilly side of the trail a ways. He stopped to look back many times. He stood up in the heavy brush and just watched us. We eventually climbed down when we couldn't see him, then tried to go within the brush and head over to the trail. We got stuck, returned to the trail, and saw the ranger. He sent someone to find my cousin Dave, who was hiking ahead, and walked us back down.

Account Two: As we were walking along the trail toward Ptarmigan Tunnel (we were about 3 or 4 miles from it), I was in front and [redacted] in back of me. We were carrying large packs when I turned around and saw a bear come out of the brush and charge us fast!

I told [redacted] to run, so we started to, but after 100 feet we dropped our packs, hoping to stall the bear—now he was 20 feet behind. I did not know [redacted] had tripped over her pack. He was still close, so we ran as fast as we could quite a ways, when I saw a tree I thought he could not climb. So up we went, and he came right behind us. [He] stood up and growled, then stayed there awhile, then walked to the path watching us as he went up the brush about a football field away. After 20 minutes, [he] watched us closely. He was very mean, and we stayed in the tree, praying, crying, confused, so we got down and started toward the creek, and then we froze almost and thought it was endless, so we started to come back toward the path. I saw a ranger hat and ran as fast as I could, tripping—crying, because someone finally came. My girlfriend was caught, so we went back to her after I found the ranger. Our friend [redacted] was ahead and did not know we were charged or anything. He was about 1 mile ahead of us.

AUGUST 20 ENCOUNTER: THE ICEBERG LAKE TRAIL GRIZZLY, NUMBER 2

A report "[r]eceived by Mary Ann Penttilla and investigated by Ranger R. E. Millsap on August 21, 1976," listed the incident as "grizzly molestation."

Mr. [redacted] stated he was walking alone toward Many Glacier on the Iceberg Trail, and passed Ptarmigan Falls, and was on the edge of the [illegible] before the trail breaks into open country. Below the trail in a gulley he saw a "grizzly" which was "350 lbs." in size. The bear was 20 yds away at the time. The man stayed still. The bear came up to the trail, and walked toward Mr. [redacted], who retreated toward Ptarmigan Falls a "few feet."

The bear continued to walk toward the man. Mr. [redacted] would stop and the bear would stop. They did this routine twice. Then he threw his can and water bottle at the bear who was about "20 feet" away. The bear then stood up and reached his claws high above his head. He said the bear "reached up more than [illegible] with his claws." Then the man yells, and the bear goes up the hill into the brush, never to be seen again. He said the bear was definitely a blond color all over, and when he stood on all fours, he was about a yardstick high.

ENCOUNTERS OF THE TWIN GRIZZLIES

And now comes the saga of the Twin Grizzlies, who were at the scene of Mary Pat Mahoney's fatality, but were not proven to be involved. Both were shot dead. These near-adult-size cubs were seen earlier in the summer, accompanied by a mother bear. Apparently the mother bear forced them out on their own as she came into fertility again, and she was seen without the cubs and mating with a large male grizzly. Some persons have suggested that this mother bear dragged Mary Pat from her tent and killed her. The twin cubs may have approached the mother bear again temporarily, at the time of the attack at Many Glacier Campground, but the mother bear may have driven them off yet again.

Between September 14 through September 23, 1976, the Twin Grizzlies were involved in the following incidents. On September 23, the fatality of Mary Pat Mahoney occurred at the Many Glacier Campground, where the Twin Grizzlies were shot and killed.

First Twin Grizzlies Incident: Iceberg Lake, the Night of September 14–15

Ranger Fred W. Reese submitted his report on a "bear molestation . . . reported several days after the occurrence by a secondhand source," on September 20, 1976, in Case Incident #761614.

This report is made up only to inform on the bear activity; as it is completely second- and thirdhand information, it is impossible to determine the facts at this time.

Reportedly on the night of September 14–15, 1976, two grizzly bears came into an illegal camp at Iceberg Lake. There were 6–7 people and two horses at this camp. The people had taken no precautions concerning their food, as it reportedly was in the packs on the ground. The bears ate some food from the packs. The people got up and moved their horses away from the area. The next day this group evidently went into the Belly River country from Ptarmigan Tunnel.

This is, as far as is known, the first of the several incidences involving the two grizzly bears and food sources. The illegal camp seemed to create the problem, or have been the initial impetus.

Second Twin Grizzlies Incident: Ptarmigan Lake, September 17

This report, written by Fred W. Reese on September 20, 1976, is included in Case Incident #761614, "bear molestation":

On September 17, 1976, at approximately 1500 hours [3:00 p.m.], near Ptarmigan Lake, the two dark brown grizzly bears traveling together were hiking down the trail, being "pushed" along by some hikers that were above them two switchbacks on the Ptarmigan Tunnel Trail.

[Names redacted] were resting just 100 yards below the outlet of Ptarmigan Lake on the trail and saw the bears coming down the trail. They took their packs with them for a few yards off the trail, uphill, dropped the packs, and proceeded to climb up the hill until they came to some cliffs. [They] climbed a short distance up the cliffs and waited at that point.

The bears came down the trail, smelled the food in the packs, and went to the packs and tore them open and ate the food. They remained at that location for about one-half hour and then left. The bears went off the trail, down to the creek, and onto the west side of Crowfoot Mountain and disappeared.

There was no injury to any person. [There was some] damage to the backpacking equipment.

Third Twin Grizzlies Incident: Many Glacier Campground, September 19, 11:30 a.m.

This incident, described in the report as "bear molestation," occurred on September 19, 1976. Ranger Fred Reese investigated the encounter in his report, dated September19, 1976.

> At approximately 1130 hours [11:30 a.m.], September 19, 1976, at Many Glacier Campground, three people sighted grizzly bears in the campground. The bears went through the camp very quickly and left within a very few minutes, going west. There were two bears, both 250–300 lbs., very close in size.

Fourth Twin Grizzlies Incident: Iceberg Lake, September 19, 12:00 p.m.

This account was submitted by Ranger Fred W. Reese on September 20, and occurred on September 19, 1976. The incident became Case Incident Record Number 761614.

> At approximately 1200 hours [12:00 p.m.], September 19, 1976, at Iceberg Lake, trail crewmen Corey Shea and Wayne Bird sighted the two dark brown grizzly bears.
>
> They were feeding very near to the bridge at Iceberg Creek, just below the lake. The two men ran up the hill toward "Shangri-la" bench to avoid the bears. The bears did not follow them. The two men noticed a very high number of grizzly diggings on the way up to and in the area of the "Shangri-la" bench.

Fifth Twin Grizzlies Incident: Fishercap Lake, September 19, 12:30 p.m.

Ranger Fred Reese, who described the Twin Grizzlies at Many Glacier Campground incident above, also wrote this report, included in Case Incident #761614, of the same Twin Grizzlies, this time at Fishercap Lake, just one hour later.

At approximately 1230 hours [12:30 p.m.] September 19, 1976, at Fishercap Lake, which is two-tenths of a mile west of Many Glacier Campground, the two grizzly bears were again seen.

[Name redacted] was sunbathing near the outlet of the lake; the two bears came by her to within a few feet, smelled her, and proceeded on down the south shore toward the inlet of the lake. Within ten minutes [names redacted] saw the two bears come out of the brush near the head of the lake. The two men started to run down the north shore of the lake with the bears trotting behind them. The one man [redacted] ran into the lake and lay down in the water to "play dead." The other man climbed a tree near the shore of the lake.

One of the two bears went into the edge of the water and took hold of the man's wader boot and shook it with his mouth. [Redacted] yelled out and the bear released the boot and left the lake; [the bear] climbed the tree, on the opposite side of [redacted], and was at a point directly across from [redacted] in the tree. [Redacted] dropped out of the tree and ran into the lake. The two men then discarded their waders and swam down the middle of the lake. The bears did not follow. They left the lake at the far end at the same point where Miss Kent was standing. The three of them ran through the brush the two-tenths of a mile back to the campground. The trails in the area were closed and a check was made which did not reveal the location of the bears.

Sixth Twin Grizzlies Incident: Fatality of Mary Pat Mahoney at the Many Glacier Campground, September 23

See chapter 3, "Finding Mary Pat."

In the next chapter, the date is 1975, one year earlier than the above encounters and incidents. A family of four, including two small children, are attacked by a grizzly as they hike the Grinnell Glacier Trail.

18

FINDING A FAMILY OF FOUR

1975: THE GRINNELL GLACIER TRAIL GRIZZLY

The father, struggling to protect his daughter from a repeat attack, grabbed the animal by the neck and punched it in the jowls.
—RANGER BOB FRAUSON AND NATURALIST DAVID CASTEEL

National Park Service–Glacier Park
Case Incident Record Number not available: Peterson family
Location: Grinnell Glacier Trail
Date/Time: Thursday, August 7, 1975, approximately 9:00 a.m.

Dawn's early light shone on the Peterson family—the parents, along with eleven-year-old Karen and seven-year old Seth—that August 7, 1975, as the experienced hikers started out on the Grinnell Glacier Trail, apparently the first to hike it that morning. Foot traffic of many others could be expected to follow, as this is a popular midsummer hike in the Park. It is also choice bear habitat.

What did this trail look like to the four Petersons as they walked along in 1975, anticipating no trouble?

"The trail soon enters a lodgepole pine forest which has come in since the 1936 crown fire," writes the Glacier Natural History Association in 1978's *Hiker's Guide to Glacier National Park*. Then the trail climbs. "Avalanche chutes can be seen on some of the far slopes. These are characterized by open, shrubby areas between forested slopes. The paths left by avalanches create a greater variety of habitats which account for a greater diversity of animals and plants."

Avalanche chutes are prized by grizzlies for this diversity of forage. The trail then passes north of Grinnell Lake, which reflects a brilliant turquoise blue, and climbs up the glacier-piled rocks called a moraine. "Grinnell Glacier covers 121 hectares (about 300 acres)," notes the *Hiker's Guide*, "and is the largest in the park. Above and to the right of Grinnell is The Salamander. These were once a single glacier, but *due to warming trends* [emphasis added], they became smaller and eventually separated."[27]

The Peterson family of four, after enjoying these glacier views, then turned back to retrace their steps to the trailhead. The trail descends now in a number of switchbacks, and the confident Karen, eleven, was leading the way, ahead of all three of her family members by perhaps one hundred yards. Her mother brought up the rear. The wind blew strongly as Karen passed a grove of alder trees, perhaps preventing any creature within from hearing the sounds of the approaching hikers.

In a blur of motion, a golden brown grizzly charged out of the trees and attacked Karen. The grizzly grabbed the eleven-year-old by her head, its jaws flailing her small body first to the right and then the left. Her father ran forward to see the grizzly throw Karen twenty-four feet in the air.

"The father, struggling to protect his daughter from a repeat attack, grabbed the animal by the neck and punched it in the jowls," relates former ranger Bob Frauson and former naturalist David Casteel. "The grizzly bit down full bore on the father's left arm, breaking it. Then as the father delivered another punch, the bear bit his other arm. The man let loose his grip on the grizzly, which turned and swatted first at the son, then charged the mother, who had heard her family's cries."[28] The son, Seth, only seven, was bitten and torn on the back of his head. The mother escaped injury. Finally, the bear crashed away into the brush.

The Petersons were making their way, all four close together now, back toward the trailhead, when Ranger Bob Isdahl, who was leading a nature hike, found them. A physician, Dr. George Cole, was in that party, and he administered first aid to the grievously wounded eleven-year-old, the seven-year-old, and the father. The mother, who had brought up the rear of the family hiking party, was not injured—at least, not physically.

Isdahl and Cole accompanied the traumatized Peterson family all the way to a hospital in Cardston, Alberta, where they were able to arrive that same Thursday, still in the morning hours.

"[Three] members of Illinois family injured by bear," read page 1 of the August 7, 1975, *Daily Inter Lake*. "Girl has surgery following attack," the Glacier Park press release stated on the same day. Karen suffered a fractured skull, broken nose, and cuts to the chin and forehead. She underwent immediate surgery, lasting for hours.

Her father was treated for a crushed and broken left forearm and badly lacerated hands. The son, Seth, was treated for puncture wounds and lacerations on the back of his head. Mr. Peterson told investigating Park officials that the attacking golden brown bear had the distinctive grizzly bear hump over its shoulders, and weighed about 250 to 300 pounds.

The Park Service's management assistant Dick Munro informed the public that this was the first reported bear mauling of the season. He added that the previous year, in 1974, a sow grizzly had attacked a medical doctor, who sustained a severe laceration to his arm that required eighteen stitches.

What does the Grinnell Glacier Trail look like today?

Five and a half miles one way, and starting near the Many Glacier Hotel, the trail was recently described by the *Missoulian*'s Sherry Devlin as "rising through forests of subalpine fir, across alpine meadows, along cliffs with panoramic views of high-altitude waterfalls and majestic peaks, up and over a terminal moraine to the foot of one of the park's largest remaining glaciers."[29] The trail remains to this day one of the most popular and scenic hikes in Glacier Park.

<hr>

In the next chapter, the year is 1974. Is it possible to find some humor after a bear mauling (once one has successfully survived)? "Finding Gordon" relates what happens after a professor encounters a mother grizzly with cubs.

19

FINDING GORDON

1974: THE FEATHER PLUME FALLS GRIZZLY

It was so incredible that I simply couldn't believe it was really happening, and perhaps that is why I felt no fear. I stood there thinking, "She'll know I'm not afraid, and she'll know I mean no harm, so she will veer off and return to her cubs." There was an unfortunate divergence of opinion about that, and she quickly closed the gap between us.
—GORDON EDWARDS, QUOTED IN *THE GRIZZLIES OF GLACIER,*
BY WARREN L. HANNA

National Park Service–Glacier Park
Report of Accident/Incident: Field Report No. 74-36—J. Gordon Edwards
Location: 100 yards off trail, just below Feather Plume Falls
Date/Time: July 25, 1974, 2:00 p.m.

Once there was a naturalist who became a Glacier Park ranger. He was known to be kind and caring, and at Glacier Park, he found something he had not found before. Perhaps this was something he didn't even know he was looking for.

This ranger identified 1,500 species of insects among Glacier Park's mountains (he called himself a Glacier Park "biological collaborator"). He became a mountain climber and wrote *A Climber's Guide to Glacier National Park.* He eventually found his naturalist niche as Dr. J. Gordon

Edwards, professor of entomology at the University of California at San Jose.

But he never stopped returning to Glacier Park.

Years later, when he was sixty-three, Gordon Edwards extended his hand to a lady grizzly in Glacier Park who took it, but then gave it back (requiring fourteen stitches).

Gordon described this bear incident—which took place at 2:00 p.m. on July 25, 1974—in Field Report 74-36, bringing his sense of humor even to a left-handed bear bite. The Field Report describes the event as "Caught between Jaws of Grizzly."

Gordon was bushwhacking, he said, one hundred yards off trail (which is *not* recommended), just below Feather Plume Falls. He was only one and a half miles from Josephine Lake, where a boat launch returned visitors to Swiftcurrent Lake, and then Many Glacier Hotel. In 1976, Glacier's first park naturalist, George C. Ruhle, warned in his guidebook that the trail to Feather Plume Falls "passes through grizzly country. *Keep alert, and try not to startle an animal by taking it by surprise.*"[30]

Good point there.

Gordon described what happened next in his Park document, titled A Grizzly Bear Held My Hand, which was included with the Field Report and is excerpted below:

> It was a spectacular day, with traces of fresh snow brightening hundreds of snowfields and glaciers. After a morning of report-writing I found myself free of duties about noon . . . I photographed spectacular Feather Plume Falls. A strong wind was blowing the water back up over the lip of the falls, providing a great spectacle of silvery spray against the blue Montana sky. I decided to climb through the brush to the steep little meadow just below the falls and take some more pictures.
>
> The steep hillside was forested above the trail, and between the trees were dense masses of false huckleberry (*Menziesia ferruginea*), forming a nearly impenetrable thicket four to six feet high. After five minutes of bushwhacking up that hillside I could see the steep little meadow above, with a necklace of snow at the cliff-base near the waterfall. While in the brush I had been clearing my throat every 15 to 30 seconds, which is my

customary method of alerting bears to my presence. Now that I could see the meadow and the open route to it, I stopped my throat clearing and looked about me, admiring the woods, the tremendous walls on both sides of the valley, and the silvery waterfall still high above me. . . .

Suddenly a fury of sound exploded a short distance to my right. Small trees and bushes were thrashing about wildly, branches were snapping and tearing, and a panic-stricken chorus of "yipping" filled the air. The effect was similar to that of two or three large dogs chasing their tails in those bushes, but of course I realized the sounds were being made by startled bear cubs, instead. That was quickly confirmed by the addition of a new and more awesome sound . . . a horrendous snarling combined with an ominous series of "bawling" noises. . . . She burst into view not 40 feet away, bounding toward me over the bushes at full speed, and she was a *grizzly*! [. . .]

I leaned forward and told her in fairly quiet tones, "No, no, not *me*! I won't harm your cubs or bother you!" She failed to be impressed, and came bounding on, now within 20 feet of me. There was an interesting telescoping of time during the final seconds of her charge, and I found myself thinking many thoughts while standing there, waiting for her to reach me. I said to myself: "This is amazing. I feel no fear. And they say wild animals can sense that, so this bear will know that I'm not afraid and also that I mean no harm. And knowing that, she will probably swerve off and go past me, then return to her cubs." I also observed with fascination the minute details of her movements as she drew nearer: "She certainly is heavy. It's amazing how the bushes break under her weight like cobwebs." And then, "No wonder bears can roam through these bushes so easily, for they just mash them all down as they go!"

My thoughts were halted by the realization that the grizzly was now only 7 or 8 feet away and was not swerving or slowing at all. . . . Acting instinctively, I abruptly raised the handle of my ice ax and placed the metal-tipped end of the shaft in the center of the grizzly's chest. At the same instant I took a quick step to my left and shoved very hard on the ice ax. The bear was running at full speed, with loose footing, and she tried to turn toward me just as her momentum was carrying her too far past me. My feeble shove was therefore enough to move her 250 pounds sideways and roll her down the steep brushy slope for about 10 feet. . . . She was again on her feet, coming straight up toward me with a quizzical look on her face. This time she was not running. She took a huge leaping bound, then stopped and cocked her head to one side and looked at me, then repeated that procedure. As she made four or five more leaps, pausing a second or two each time, I found myself thinking again.

I still felt no distinct fear, but I didn't know how to break through her antagonistic behavior. I kept talking to her, very calmly and with as much reassurance as I have ever expressed at any time in my life, but I failed completely. A final thought suddenly impressed me. "She sure was nonchalant while charging toward me," I recalled, "just like a huge dog bounding through a weed field to bark at a passing car."

Then it struck me. "She acted like she had done the same thing before, as though she knew exactly what to expect when she reached me!" I then recalled that a camper had disappeared from the shores of Grinnell Lake the previous month (just ¼ mile away), leaving his tent, fishing gear, and expensive equipment. His body was never found, and his identity remained unknown. "Perhaps he had met this same grizzly, and that explains her remarkable attitude toward me!" [See chapter 28, "Still Missing and Presumed Dead."]

But now she was preparing for her final leap. I again raised my ice ax and placed the pointed end of the handle toward her chest. She suddenly lunged violently upward, completely surprising me with her strength and speed. The flat head of the ice ax (which I was holding in my hand) struck me on the chest with great force and knocked me backwards. So powerful and abrupt was that blow to my body that, as I was propelled backwards, my left hand flipped out suddenly in front of me. Instantly the bear snapped at that hand and grabbed it between her front teeth. It all happened so fast that it was a tremendous surprise to me when I saw my hand in the bear's mouth! The entire hand felt instantly numb, just as fingers do when caught in a car door.

My greatest concern at that moment was not fear for my hand, but rather was a fear that the bear might stand up and swat at me with her forelegs while holding my hand in her mouth. Such a blow, with those long claws, can completely disembowel a person!

To avoid that possibility I immediately dropped the ice ax and fell to my knees in front of the grizzly, where I began to yank my hand out of her mouth. As we confronted each other, with my face only a foot from hers, I talked to her constantly and soothingly, saying: "Come on, now, let go of that hand. I'm not going to hurt you" (as though I could!). I repeated that message over and over, very calmly and quietly, speaking directly into her eyes with the same attitude and inflection a person uses when attempting to get a folded newspaper out of a big dog's mouth without tearing it.

As I spoke, I also kept patting her sharply on the nose and about the eyes with my right hand, but being careful not to slap hard enough to hurt her or antagonize her. That confrontation lasted for 30 or 40 seconds. I realized that if she "bit down" she could easily remove my entire hand, and I kept watching my fingers (which extended out of the left side of her mouth) and hoping in an abstract way that I wouldn't see them drop onto the ground.

Back and forth we yanked, in that uneven tug-of-war. And then all at once my hand came out of the animal's mouth! Why did she let go, instead of biting down? [. . .] I can never know for certain, so I have stopped trying to figure it out.

I only had a glimpse of my bloody hand as she released it, for I did not dare take the time to examine it more carefully. Before the grizzly could make another move, I took the initiative, instantly deciding to "play dead" (everyone in Glacier National Park does that, and it is very often effective). Before the bear could make another move, I flopped flat on my face with my back to the bear, and went limp and motionless. As I fell forward I crossed my wrists above my head so I could apply pressure on that left wrist in an attempt to reduce the flow of blood from the mangled hand. The ruse was gratifyingly effective.

Although the grizzly acted rather frantic behind me, she never touched me again. Snarling ferociously, she would run a few feet away, then rush back and snarl and bawl right over my neck, then run away a little further, then come thundering back to hover over me again. She continued that erratic behavior for several minutes as I lay there, motionless and helpless. . . . After the sow had made half a dozen rushing returns to my prostrate form, I finally heard the snarls getting further and further away. Eventually I heard her breaking off branches in a thicket 40 or 50 feet uphill from me, and after not hearing her for another 15 seconds or so, I turned my head to look for her. She was out of sight!

Quickly I got to my feet, picked up my ice ax and camera (happy to see that I could still use my fingers), and went straight down the hill as rapidly as possible. After a hundred feet I began to feel safer, for I doubted she would follow me that far. My first act upon reaching the trail was to laboriously take several pictures of my own hand, "for the record." Since the fingers did move easily, I wasn't much concerned about the punctures and slashes, the clicking noises in my wrist, or the squishing sensations that accompanied every movement of the fingers or wrist.

I hurried down the trail to Grinnell Lake, savoring the glorious feeling of just being alive. I had already pondered the feeling that I would have paid $100 for that experience, *if* I could have been convinced in advance that it would have the outcome that it did. What a memorable adventure!

Gordon hiked back to Josephine Lake, boarded the tourist boat there toward Many Glacier, and rangers were notified by park radio. He and his wife then drove to Cardston, Alberta, where, he wrote, "The talented Canadian doctors sewed up five of the punctures, shoved the fatty extrusions back into them to fill up the holes, prescribed some antibiotics, and released me."

Gordon was able to laugh about all this later, and others joined him. The front page of his hometown newspaper, the *San Jose Mercury*, carried this headline: "Bear Rips SJS Prof," followed by "Plays Possum, Lives." Someone at the university made a bumper sticker and placed it on his car: "World's Oldest Living Bear Wrestler," and Gordon left the bumper sticker there.

After this bear encounter, Gordon never again climbed alone. When he was asked what to do if a grizzly attacked, Gordon always replied, "I have no idea what to tell them!"

Gordon died on July 19, 2004, of a heart attack while just outside Glacier Park, hiking up Divide Mountain with his wife, Alice. He was eighty-four. Their daughter Jane was leading a climb of Mount Cannon at the time of her father's death.

A feature titled "Remembering J. Gordon Edwards" was included in the winter 2005 issue of Glacier Park Foundation's *The Inside Trail* newsletter. The authors note: "He was a legendary mountaineer and one of the most distinguished and famous figures in Glacier's history." A Dave Shoup photo shows "Gordon Edwards leading a group on the Ptarmigan Wall, as always the consummate host, freely sharing magical places with those of us who had the incredible good fortune to share time with him."[31]

—·—

The next chapter describes a severe mauling of a lone camper/hiker which occurred on the Going-to-the-Sun Road, within sight of the Logan Pass Visitor Center.

20

FINDING BOB

1968: THE GOING-TO-THE-SUN ROAD GRIZZLIES

The sow grabbed (bit) his leg and pulled him from the tree and both tumbled down the steep, snow-covered slope. The sow bit Hahn's hand three times while they were rolling and sliding down the slope.
—Bob Hahn interview by Ranger Frauson, en route to Cardston Hospital, Alberta

National Park Service–Glacier Park
Case Incident Record Number (not available): Robert Hahn
Location: Going-to-the-Sun Road within sight of Logan Pass Visitor Center
Date/Time: Monday, May 20, 1968, approximately 10:00 a.m.

Bob Hahn loved hiking and camping in national parks. He was a seasonal naturalist ranger in Yellowstone Park the summer of 1967 (and a teacher in Canada during the school year). While photographing flowers in Yellowstone in 1967, he looked up and saw a grizzly bear approaching him. He climbed a nearby tree. The bear walked to the tree and stood on its hind legs, looking up at Bob. Bob took movies of this grizzly action.

In Glacier Park, Bob had hiked extensively. While camping, bears had torn up his tent and equipment on two separate occasions in the North Fork area. But still he returned.

Now it was a year later, in 1968, on Sunday, May 19. At 9:00 a.m., Bob was left off by relatives at the Many Glacier area to once again hike and

Bob Hahn's campsite near Siyeh Creek, from which he left on the morning of the bear attack that occurred on the popular Going-to-the-Sun Road. Three rangers later took down the camp and returned the items to Hahn.
PHOTO FROM CASE INCIDENT RECORD (NUMBER NOT AVAILABLE)

camp in the Park. Bob was well equipped to navigate the snow and cold he encountered—but can one ever be prepared to encounter a mother grizzly with her yearling cub?

"Hahn said he had hiked alone from Many Glacier on the previous day (Sunday) over Piegan Pass and had planned to continue over Siyeh Pass and down Baring Creek," wrote ranger Robert N. Frauson in his memorandum to the chief ranger, "Subject: Bear Mauling (Grizzly) of Robert Hahn on May 20, 1968."

But heavy snow conditions changed Hahn's plans, so he went down Siyeh Creek and camped about ¼ mile from the Going-to-the-Sun Road.

On Monday morning, he left his camp on the [Piegan] creek and hiked over snow up the Going-to-the-Sun Road toward Logan Pass. Just after he rounded the curve where you can see the Logan Pass Visitor Center, he saw a grizzly sow and cub quite a distance up the road, toward the East Side tunnel.

Hahn stopped at this point and observed the bears with binoculars and took telephoto movies with an 8mm Zoom for one-half hour as the bear moved closer. Then, when the bears were 50 yards away (more like 65 ft on a later check), Hahn stood up so that he would be seen by the bears. The cub was a few paces closer than the sow.

The sow stood on her hind legs and then charged. Hahn then made a dash for a tree 15 feet away (more like 30 ft). He and the sow reached the tree at the same time. The tree was actually too big to climb. The sow grabbed (bit) his leg and pulled him from the tree and both tumbled down the steep, snow-covered slope. The sow bit Hahn's hand three times while they were rolling and sliding down the slope.

Hahn managed to stop his 200 ft. slide and the sow slid further down the slope. Hahn angled to a tree and climbed it. The sow returned and climbed the tree, biting his climbing boots and legs. The sow fell from the tree.

Hahn climbed higher; the sow re-climbed the tree, biting at his feet and legs. Hahn was kicking at the sow and hanging on. The sow then pulled the left boot from his foot and fell from the tree a second time. The sow had climbed the tree to a height of about 20 ft. to get at Hahn the second time.

The sow left the area and the yearling cub was not seen from the time of the initial charge.

Hahn stayed in the tree for about one-half hour, then came down and climbed the slope back to the road, retrieving his dark glasses, movie camera, and binoculars. [With severe lacerations to his legs and hands], he hiked down to the Jackson overlook (where the locked gate was) and was given a ride to [redacted] by a Lethbridge couple.

How badly was Bob injured?

After the attack on Bob Hahn, this "Trail Closed" sign, hand-lettered with "Grizzly Bear Problems," was posted at Siyeh Bend on May 20, 1968. Note the extent of the snow. PHOTO FROM CASE INCIDENT RECORD (NUMBER NOT AVAILABLE)

Ranger Frauson's memorandum, dated July 31, 1968, also detailed some of Bob's injuries. "On the afternoon of May 20, 1968, about 1:30 p.m., Frauson received a phone call from [redacted] requesting first-aid assistance for a man mauled by a bear."

Frauson gave first aid to Mr. Hahn, which consisted of applying large four-inch compresses to his left lower leg (rear), right lower leg (front), and three two-inch compresses to his left hand. . . .

Frauson instructed [Ranger Bill] Colony to close the area above Siyeh Bend by posting our "Trail Closed" sign.

Ranger Bill Colony "phoned to CRO" the following information (also noted in a memorandum of May 20): "[Hahn] received puncture wounds on both legs. His hands were clawed up, but all joints work. The bleeding was stopped when we got down to St. Mary, where Bob Frauson took him to Cardston Hospital. His people were coming down from Cardston to pick him up today. Bob Frauson will watch for them on the way. He will also take care of the camp near Many Glacier."

Grizzly bears sometimes seem to enjoy and "play in" the snow. Below are some interesting details on that behavior, in Ranger Frauson's memorandum, "Follow-Up Action on the Hahn Grizzly Bear Mauling by Rangers Colony, Wood, Stonestreet, Gale, and Frauson," below.

May 20, Monday: Rangers posted the area, "Closed to Travel."
May 21, Tuesday: Three rangers returned to the mauling site to look for the sow and cub.

A lone wolverine was seen in the area.

The patrol was made up through the East Side tunnel to Lunch Creek.

Bear tracks were seen in the mauling area.

On the return from the patrol, a lone mature grizzly was seen above the Road. It saw the patrol, and each observed the other for three hours at close range.

The grizzly was never antagonistic.

It slid down snowbanks like a skier.

It climbed small leaning conifers and laid astraddle the treetop and watched the rangers.

It laid on its stomach in the snow and cleaned its fur, all the time watching the rangers. It then departed the area upslope, diagonally away from the rangers.

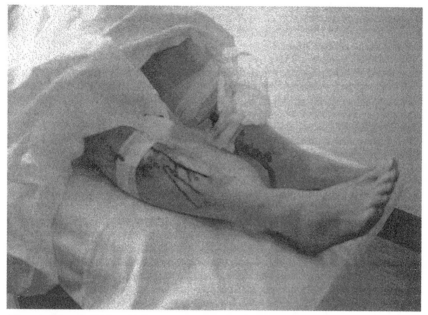

After the attack on Bob Hahn, a ranger took this photo of the bleeding injuries to Hahn's legs while Hahn recovered in Canada's Cardston Hospital.
PHOTO FROM CASE INCIDENT RECORD (NUMBER NOT AVAILABLE)

May 22, Wednesday: No patrol, heavy snowstorm.
May 23, Thursday: Three-ranger patrol into area, heavy avalanche all around area. No tracks.
May 24, Friday: Two-ranger patrol to area. No tracks.
May 25, Saturday: Two-ranger patrol to area. No tracks.
May 27, Monday: Closure signs removed from area.

"Biological aspects concerning Piegan Creek grizzly incident [the Robert Hahn mauling]" are outlined in research biologist C. J. Martinka's memorandum to the superintendent, dated May 23, 1968, below.

Grizzly bears, like other animals, restrict most activities during their lifetime to a definable area called a home range. During certain times of the year, particular sections of the home range may be heavily utilized while other portions [are] not visited at all. Similar use patterns would

Bob Hahn climbed this tree's ladderlike limbs to try to escape the attacking grizzly bear. The bear climbed after him twice, first biting his boots and legs (and falling off), and then climbing again to a height of twenty feet to get at Hahn. The bear dragged him from the tree.

PHOTO FROM CASE INCIDENT RECORD (NUMBER NOT AVAILABLE)

be expected every year and probably result from ecological requirements of the individual bear.

According to our monitoring records, a grizzly sow with a single cub was observed five different times last October near Piegan Creek [close to the site of Robert Hahn's mauling]. This may have been the same bear involved in the attack. There were no reported sightings of a single sow and cub in that area, however, prior to October. These data suggest that the area occupied by the female may change during summer and would hopefully be to an area receiving little or no visitor use. Should this be the case, there is a good chance that another problem might not develop should destruction not be possible.

Data from two other recent incidents (1963 and 1965) involving hikers and females with cubs may also be of value. In both cases the bears were not killed after the incidents and future problems with these bears not recorded. This suggests that the attacks were defense actions of the moment, and demonstrates that individual bears do not necessarily become a menace to visitor safety after an attack.

Was any action taken against the mother bear and her cub?

Chief park ranger Ruben O. Hart added this comment in his memorandum, dated May 21, 1968: "Mr. Hahn told District Ranger Frauson that he did not want any harm to come to the sow grizzly as a result of this attack. He felt that he was intruding into the bear's domain, and the bear should not be held responsible for her actions, which were natural under the circumstances."

The Park Service determined that this attack was defensive in nature, and no action was taken against the female grizzly and her yearling cub.

Ranger Frauson's memorandum adds, "This sow hadn't read the articles and publications that mature grizzlies cannot climb trees."

In the following chapter, we see that being a Glacier Park ranger does not prevent one from getting severely mauled by a mother bear with cubs. Also severely injured in this attack were ten-year-old Smitty, and a Swedish woman hiker.

CHAPTER 21

FINDING FIVE (INCLUDING A TEN-YEAR-OLD)

1960: THE OTOKOMI LAKE GRIZZLY

[Ranger] Nelson turned sharply, just in time to see the bear start tearing skin off the back of [ten-year-old] Smitty's head. Then she turned him half over and raked her claws across his face; and finally, she picked him up and threw him so that he landed on his back. Nelson, now standing behind an old and rotten tree, began shouting to distract the animal.

—ALBERT RUFFIN, "ATTACKED BY A GRIZZLY BEAR: THE ORDEAL OF A BOY ALL BUT EATEN ALIVE," *LIFE* MAGAZINE, AUGUST 27, 1965

National Park Service–Glacier Park
Case Incident Record Number 600045: Ranger Alan Nelson, Ranger Edomo Mazzer, Smitty Parratt, Brita Noring, and Gote Nyhlen
Location: One mile south of Otokomi Lake, Rose Creek Trail
Date/Time: Monday, July 18, 1960, 3:45 p.m.

This is "[t]he story of five hikers set upon by America's most fearsome beast—the grizzly," wrote Albert Ruffin in *Life* magazine in 1965. The events occurred on July 18, 1960.

What really happened?

Three hikers—two off-duty Glacier Park rangers plus a ten-year-old boy—headed to Otokomi Lake, climbing through Douglas fir and thimbleberries. The Rose Creek Trail to Otokomi Lake "soon makes several switchbacks as it continues to climb," writes the Glacier Natural History Association. "The lake lies in a glacial amphitheater and is bordered by steep, gray cliffs and subalpine meadows. The creek and basin were named after Charles Rose, an explorer whose Indian name, 'Otokomi,' translates as 'Yellow Fish.' The name was misspelled as 'Roes' by early cartographers, which accounted for the different spelling [Rose or Roes] on the maps."[32]

Just ten days before the grizzly encounter, Glacier Park records indicate that on the "Roes" Creek Trail on July 8, 1960, a grizzly mauled a lone hiker, resulting in lacerations (he survived). But now, on July 18, there was, presumably, safety in numbers.

So it was that the group of three arrived at Otokomi Lake at noon, where the two rangers, ages twenty-seven and thirty, got busy fishing alongside ten-year-old Smitty Parratt, son of another ranger. At the lake they met a couple, two schoolteachers from Sweden, Brita Noring, thirty-eight, and Gote Nyhlen, forty-two, who were also enjoying Glacier Park.

By midafternoon, the five chose to return together on the same trail, and were one mile from the lake, headed for the St. Mary area. The path narrowed and they could only walk single file.

"My roommate Ed Mazzer, a seasonal ranger, and Smith Parratt, the son of a seasonal park ranger, and I [with the Swedish couple] started down the trail to St. Mary," said ranger Alan Nelson. His words, "as told by Alan Nelson," were reported by United Press International, and reproduced in Montana's *Daily Inter Lake*.

Mazzer and the boy were ahead. They had just rounded a bend when Mazzer saw the bear and two cubs. He shouted "bear." We all scurried and tried to get up trees.

Mazzer ran off to the left and the boy dashed off to the right, and tried to find a tree. But the bear caught up with the boy and pounced on him. She started chewing and tossing him about and shaking him.

I ran behind a small tree and hollered and screamed at the bear. She came after me. I tried going up a tree, but it was rotten and the branches kept breaking off. I got up about four feet when the bear grabbed me by the back end with its mouth. It threw me down and tried to roll me over on my back. It tore all the clothes off my back and the upper part of my legs.

Meanwhile, Mazzer and the Swedish couple were climbing up trees. The lady was the last one up and the bear charged, leaped up, and caught her foot. It pulled her out of the tree and mauled her.

We all lay still for 20 minutes, pretending we were dead. Then about a half-hour later, the two men who were not hurt came down from the trees, checked those of us who were hurt to see if they could help. Then they ran four miles to a junction where they got help.

The attack occurred at four o'clock. It was 7:45 before the first party arrived, and the rest of the rescue party arrived at 8:00 p.m. They carried us down to the road and we were taken to Cardston to the hospital.

That 10-year-old boy didn't even cry. He's a stout-hearted little guy. A real trooper. They don't come any better.

This is my second summer as a seasonal ranger, and it's the first time I've seen a grizzly bear. I'll come back again next year. The number of bear incidents when compared to the number of automobile accidents is insignificant.[33]

Glacier Park records categorize the injuries suffered as "major" injuries, times three persons, with "severe multiple lacerations and bites, especially to Noring and Parratt."

The resident physician at Many Glacier Hotel detailed some of these injuries in his/her "Report of Rising Sun Bear Accident—July 18, 1960." (*Note:* The Rising Sun Campground was used as a first-aid station. The physician's report is excerpted below.)

At 6:55 p.m. a call was received from the ranger station at St. Mary's that there had been a bear accident up in the mountains, and that the ranger crews were proceeding to bring the victims down to the Rising Sun Campground area, and medical attention was requested. The nurse and I responded and proceeded to Rising Sun, where we set up an emergency first-aid station in the Rising Sun Campground. The ranger crews were on their way to the scene of the accident with wire basket [and] litters; three ranger ambulances stood by, and communication was established by walk[ie]-talk[ie].

[About 10:30 p.m.] The first victim to be brought to the [Rising Sun] Campground area was the boy, about 10:30 p.m. He was conscious, and talked some. He was found to be suffering from [redacted]. He also had a fracture of the distal end of the right humerus [and] severe lacerations and [a] crushing injury to the right chest. His right arm was splinted and placed in a sling. His head was bandaged and an intravenous solution of normal saline was started. He was placed in the ranger ambulance with an attendant to hold the IV solution, and two people (campers) were sent along—type O universal blood donors for possible transfusion.

About 11:20 p.m., the second victim brought down was Mrs. [Swedish visitor]. She was conscious but in considerable pain. She was said to be suffering from [redacted]. Pressure bandages were applied, and she was given one-quarter grain of morphine and sent on to the Cardston Hospital.

About 1:00 a.m., the third victim, Ranger Nelson, was brought down. He was conscious, and had considerable pain. He was suffering from [redacted]. Pressure bandages were applied. He was given one-quarter grain of morphine and sent on to the Cardston Hospital.

What happened to the most seriously injured, the ten-year-old child, Smitty Parratt?

Albert Ruffin of *Life* magazine wrote, "The surgeons' guess: He will not live," at five minutes before midnight, when Smitty arrived at Canada's Cardston Hospital, forty-two miles to the north.

"His pain was excruciating," Ruffin wrote. "Infection brought on fever. Only a sunken socket remained of his left eye, and his right eye, when the bandages were removed, was so swollen that months would pass before partial vision returned. He lived in a world of soft darkness and raw suffering. And yet, amazingly, he continued to live. Then, finally, after long weeks, his condition began to improve."

What happened to the female grizzly bear, which was sighted by Ranger Mazzer with two cubs, and was later determined to be nursing two to three cubs?

A bear disposition report was written by ranger Don Dayton, detailing the last thing any Park Service ranger chooses to do in their career. "Steps were immediately taken to locate and destroy the offending bear," Dayton wrote. This is never a quick and easy process. Dayton's report continues below, emphasizing the long and exhaustive nature of the bear hunt, undertaken to protect other park visitors from injury.

On July 19, a hunting party composed of [three rangers, names redacted] and Don Dayton was organized, and proceeded into the Rose Creek valley on horseback. The horses were left below the attack site, and the hunters proceeded on foot up through the valley bottom and on to Otokomi Lake, at the head of the valley.

The vegetation in most parts of the valley bottom was found to be so dense that vision was limited to about 75 feet or less in places. Hunting a bear in this type of terrain, without bear dogs, was deemed almost impossible unless one happened to run into the bear by chance. No tracks were visible anywhere.

The search proved fruitless and the party returned to St. Mary, reaching there about 8:00 p.m. . . . It was concluded by the hunting party that additional measures would have to be taken in order to get the bear. Bear traps were recommended.

On July 20, the hunt was resumed. The party proceeded up the valley bottom to the head of the valley, and then climbed up high on the northeast slope. The party proceeded back down the valley, keeping high above timberline on the scree slopes. This afforded a view of the entire valley, and frequent checks were made with binoculars. The only bear sighted was a huge black grizzly, apparently a male, on the opposite side of the valley. Again the party returned to St. Mary, arriving about 7:30 p.m.

On July 21, the hunting party . . . proceeded to the upper end of the valley and climbed up high on the scree slopes above the lake, where the whole upper end of the valley could be kept under observation with field glasses. Still no evidence was seen of the grizzly. There were no tracks along the valley bottom, or around Otokomi Lake. . . .

[After an unsuccessful spotting effort by airplane], on Saturday, July 23, [a professional bear trapper] accompanied a ranger and Dayton to Rose Creek. Two large bear traps were packed to the area. One was set at each attack site.

After the traps were set, a sighting was made of a grizzly bear with three cubs on the mountainside, high above Otokomi Lake. Only fleeting glimpses of the bears were seen as they passed in and out of heavy brush at a considerable distance from us. The distance was much too great to try a rifle shot. Due to the steepness of the slope and the denseness of the vegetation, it was not possible to move closer, and the bears disappeared into the heavy growth.

On Sunday, July 24, the traps were checked and hunting continued without success. . . . The traps were checked and hunting continued on July 25, 26, 27, and 28. Although a grizzly was trapped in the lower trap, it did not prove to be the right bear. . . .

On August 2, rangers [redacted] and Dayton hiked on foot via an abandoned trail to the top of Goat Mountain, at an elevation of 8,300 feet. From here it was possible, with difficulty, to move across the mountaintop and view a large portion of the Rose Creek valley and the adjoining Goat Lake valley. These areas were scanned with binoculars, but no evidence of a bear was sighted. On returning down the mountain, a large portion of the Baring Creek drainage and Siyeh Pass were scanned with glasses, but to no avail. . . .

On August 3, a grizzly bear was found to be caught in the trap located near the last attack site. As the bear did not appear to be securely caught, it was immediately shot. Investigation disclosed that it was a nursing female. Milk in each teat indicated it had been nursing at least two cubs. The color, size, and other characteristics corresponded to the description given by the attack victims. Cub feces [were] observed near the trap. A noise was also heard in the shale at some distance from the area. A search was conducted for the cubs, but the heavy brush and undergrowth limited the search. . . .

Mr. [redacted] requested permission to set smaller traps in order to live-trap the cubs to give to a scientific organization. This permission was granted. These traps were set, but due to the press of other work it was necessary for him to remove the traps on August 6, and terminate trapping operations in the area before sufficient time had elapsed to catch the cubs.

The hunting party covered about 12 miles each day that the hunting and trapping was conducted.

Approximately 263 man-hours were expended by Park Service employees. Part of this was contributed time. Approximately 57 horse-days were expended. Fish and Wildlife men have expended approximately 103 man-hours.

Signed, Donald A. Dayton

Acting Assistant District Ranger

Did Smitty Parratt fully recover from this bear mauling?

Five years later, in 1965, Smitty Parratt was still healing from his reconstructive surgeries and struggling to return to a normal life. Often we, the public, have little idea how long and torturous the journey to recovery can be.

"But for Smitty Parratt, an inexorable pattern lay ahead: operation, a few months of recovery, another operation, another healing period, and then another operation," continued reporter Ruffin for *Life* magazine. "The surgeons required many months between [surgeries], not only to give living tissue a chance to heal before beginning again, but also to give Smitty a period in which to recover from the shocks to his nervous system."

Although still facing more surgery five years after the attack, *Life* magazine reported that "Smitty feels life is almost normal, 'as if I hadn't had the accident. I don't think about it until people stare at my face—then I remember it. This is the hardest part, people staring at me and asking questions.'"

"His love of nature is as strong as ever," *Life* magazine reported, "and especially his love of Glacier National Park. First taken there as a baby of seven months, he continued to return every summer, even after the accident."[34]

In the next chapter, a predatory attack on a hiker in 1959 may have proven early on that the once-trusted maxim, "Bears don't consume people," might be incorrect.

22

FINDING JOE

1959: THE ALTYN PEAK GRIZZLY

Of course, very few people have actually been eaten by a bear, and even fewer have lived to tell about it. My big brother is one of the few. Fifty years ago, on June 18, 1959, he battled a grizzly for close to an hour, as a hungry bear consumed a good part of him.
> —"KIWIHEART," POSTED ON KOS MEDIA, JUNE 20, 2009

National Park Service–Glacier Park
Report of Grizzly Bear Attack on Joe Williams: Joe Williams
Location: Just below the saddle on Altyn Peak, at Many Glacier
Date/Time: June 18, 1959, 8:00 p.m.

As long ago as 1959, a predatory attack by a bear (meaning, the bear is exploring you as food) occurred in the Park's front country, on Altyn Peak, across from the many-windowed Many Glacier Hotel.

But was this predatory behavior by a grizzly a fact widely known, or even acknowledged?

"There are bears in the woods, but not in such numbers nor of such unspeakable ferocity as town-dwellers imagine, nor do bears spend their lives in going about the country like the devil, seeking whom they may devour," John Muir wrote in his book *Steep Trails*. "Oregon bears, like most others, have no liking for man either as meat or as society."[35]

Fellow naturalist Enos A. Mills agreed. "I have not heard of an authentic instance of a grizzly eating human flesh," he wrote in his book, *The Grizzly: Our Greatest Wild Animal*, published in 1919. "Numbers of hunters have been killed by grizzlies; but their bodies were not eaten; they were not killed for food. . . . A prospector, his horse, and his burro were killed by a falling tree. Grizzlies devoured the bodies of the animals, but that of the prospector was not disturbed. Human flesh appears to be the only thing a grizzly does not eat."[36]

Sadly, both John Muir and Enos Mills were mistaken, as we know from the following predatory incident involving Joe Williams, from 1959, and from "Night of the Grizzlies," in 1967, when two different bears dragged away two different women as prey. Incidents of grizzlies treating Native Americans as prey also exist. Of all bear attacks, this predatory motivation is the most dangerous. The only human defense is bear spray, a gun, or fighting as if your life depends on it, which it does.

And fighting is what Joe Williams certainly did that early evening of June 18, 1959. Joe arrived in Glacier in search of an adventure with his buddy Ron. They had planned to drive Joe's Ford Fairlane to Alaska on the then-graveled Alcan Highway, but were turned back at the Canadian border for not having sufficient cash (according to a rule at the time).

So they drove to Glacier Park and got summer jobs—Joe, as a waiter at Swiftcurrent Motor Inn, for $1 an hour, plus room and board. Joe's job looked promising, especially as there were so many college students like him working in the park.

The June 18 evening was already advanced, at 6:45 p.m., but Mount Altyn rose directly across Swiftcurrent Lake from the Many Glacier Hotel. Joe had planned to climb alone, but a fellow Swiftcurrent Motor Inn employee named Bob Winter, a seventeen-year-old from Michigan, joined him, and soon they had climbed two-thirds of the way. From the top they would have splendid views of the Many Glacier Valley and its peaks. Having climbed a mile, Joe sat on a rocky ledge to rest.

"I was sitting, resting," Joe later told supervisory park ranger Donald Dayton at Cardston Hospital, Alberta. "Bob was some distance above me." (Joe was interviewed after recovering from six hours on the operating table, during which four doctors placed six hundred to seven hundred stitches.) Dayton's interview of Joe on June 26, 1959, continues, below.

I first saw the bear at a distance of about 30 yards from me. The bear was moving from east to west along the slope and below me. I was not concerned at first. I motioned to Bob and pointed to the bear. The bear started to pass on by and then turned and angled up toward me. The bear came up to me, circled halfway around, and began sniffing at the small of my back.

I told Bob then that I was scared. The bear was making a noise that sounded like soft purring. The bear bit me but did not get anything but cloth the first time.

I tried to run, and Bob threw stones off to the side to try to distract the bear, but without success. The bear then caught me and began mauling me.

This first attack occurred at an elevation of 7,000 feet, in an area patched with snow. "Again," Ranger Dayton noted in his report, "as when I talked to him before, Bob Winter said that they did nothing to provoke the bear's attack." Bob courageously tried to distract the bear away from Joe three times, as he recounts in his signed statement, below:

About 6:45 p.m. we left the Swiftcurrent Motel and Cabins [as it was named then] and started climbing Mount Altyn.

We were about ¾ the way up and I was about 300 yards above Joe when I turned and saw Joe sitting quietly on a rock facing the hotel. Joe motioned [for] me to come down, and at that time I saw a bear approaching from the west.

The bear walked around Joe, sniffing him and looking at him. I started slowly down the hill and the bear again started sniffing and apparently licking Joe. Joe became startled and turned away from the bear, who took hold of Joe's wrist with his jaws. Time was about 8:00 p.m.

The bear then tore Joe's jacket with his claws and Joe became more excited and got up, intending to flee. The bear bit Joe's buttocks and nipped him about the body. Joe was scared and yelling, which seemed to make the bear more angry and excited. The bear jumped and knocked Joe down.

I ran downhill, trying to scare the bear off of Joe. I got to within 15 ft. of the bear and Joe, who was yelling and in panic. The bear was on top of him by this time. I picked up a large piece of slate (size, about 20 by 2 inches) and threw it from close range, hitting the bear on the lower neck and shoulder. The bear was knocked off Joe by the blow.

Joe ran down the slope with the bear chasing him. Joe was about 20 ft. in front of the bear when he tripped, fell, and rolled down the hill. The bear caught him about 500 yards below the first mauling spot.

Again the bear got on top of Joe, clawing and biting him about the neck and face. I caught up to them and picked up another rock (12 inches) and hit the bear on the head. The bear fell away and Joe got up and ran, tripping and stumbling downslope for about 150 yards, where he again fell. The bear again got on Joe and began mauling him.

I ran down and began throwing stones at the bear, but the bear paid no attention to the rocks, only looking up from his mauling. He would not leave Joe. The bear took Joe's head between his jaws.

I ran down the hill for help, yelling as I went. On the trail above the cabins [at 5,000 feet elevation] I met the rangers climbing up to investigate. I briefly gave them a description of what happened, and where. The rangers continued up the hill and I returned to the cabins.

I did not see the bear approach and did not know if Joe was aware of the bear at first. Joe was yelling and trying to fight the bear off all during the bear's attack.

Signed, Bob Winter

Up on Mount Altyn, the bear continued attacking Joe for more than forty-five minutes, tearing off his jacket, shirt, and pants. In 2009, Joe Williams's sister (as "Kiwiheart," on Kos Media) posted a blog entry detailing Joe's description of the attack:

At first, the bear put Joe's entire head in her mouth and ground her teeth against his skull, like a dog with a large bone. This resulted in the removal of his scalp. Joe knew he had to do something, so he pulled away and faced the bear. He was able to keep her occupied for several minutes by punching her in the snout, which is quite sensitive—actually boxing the bear. This worked for a while, until she blocked his punch with one paw and brought the other around, hooked her claws in his mouth, and ripped his chin off. At this point, he knew the boxing idea had run its course.

He lay on his stomach, as she bit and clawed at his back. When she reached his buttocks, she found what she was looking for—something to sink her teeth into. . . . As she tore into his buttocks, chewing and swallowing, Joe realized that she was literally eating him alive. His next tactic was to stick his heavy leather boot in her mouth. She chewed on the boot but was not able to penetrate it. This worked for maybe 10 minutes, but then she gave up and ripped the right side of Joe's face off. Eventually, they found several pounds of Joe in the bear's stomach.[37]

But help was on the way. Don Dayton, a thirty-year-old ranger, along with a second ranger (name redacted), answered the call saying that "a bear had a boy up on Mount Altyn." Dayton's "Report of Grizzly Bear Attack on Joe Williams," dated June 19, 1959, and addressed to Glacier's chief ranger, describes what the two rangers saw, and what they did to help Joe.

Ranger [redacted] and I proceeded immediately to the ranger station, where I picked up my .30-06 Springfield rifle. We then rushed to the rear of the Swiftcurrent cabin area. Motel employees pointed out the general direction in which screams and shouts had been heard to the effect that a bear had a boy. Ranger [redacted] and I then climbed the mountain as fast as possible. A short way up, we met Bob Winter, a Swiftcurrent Motel [as named then] employee. He stated that a bear had his friend, Joe Williams, up on the mountain. He stated that he had tried to drive the bear off but was unsuccessful. He pointed out the vicinity in which Joe and the bear were located. Bob Winter proceeded on down to the motel area and ranger [redacted] and I headed on up the mountain.

Presently, we spotted the bear high up on a grassy slope about ⅔ the way up the mountain. A long drag or skid mark was visible above the bear even at this distance. We moved on up the mountain and slightly to the right of the bear. Approaching the area, we were able to see a body under the bear.

Occasional screams were heard. We tried to drive the bear off the victim by shouting and running but without success. It was then apparent that I would have to shoot over the victim to hit the bear. The bear was sitting on the opposite side of the victim, facing downhill and slightly toward me. He was continually biting Joe and appeared to be [redacted]. During all of this, the victim was conscious and screaming for help.

I arrived at a position about 50 yards to the right of the bear and at approximately the same elevation. The time was about 9 p.m. I had four shells for my rifle and decided to fire from a location where I would have a chance to use all four shells if the bear charged.

I flattened out on the ground and aimed as high as possible to avoid hitting Joe. The bear had his head down and was chewing on the victim when I fired the first shot. The bear then raised his head and looked at me. I fired the second shot and the bear still looked at me. At the third shot, the bear immediately fell off the victim and rolled approximately 200 yards down the slope. I fired my last shot at his body lying below. Later examination of the bear revealed a bullet hole in the front shoulder and one in the spine, about halfway back.

Ranger [redacted] and I then moved over to the victim. The boy was conscious and in considerable pain. He was lying on his stomach. [Next sentences redacted.]

His neck was badly bitten. There were bites and scratches over most of his face.

We made the victim as comfortable as possible until a stretcher should arrive. We then shouted instructions to others climbing from below and had them relay a message to send up a stretcher, notify the hotel doctor, notify the hospital in Cardston, Alberta, and to try and obtain blood plasma. Shortly afterward, seasonal ranger [redacted] arrived with a blanket and we improvised a stretcher. After moving the victim a short distance, the Stokes litter arrived and we transferred the victim.

Joe had some trouble breathing due to blood in his air passages. We therefore had to stop frequently in order to turn his head and clear his mouth and nose.

About 10 p.m. we got the victim to the Swiftcurrent cabin where Dr. [redacted] was waiting. Mr. and Mrs. [redacted] of the Glacier Park Hotel Co. were also there. The [hotel] doctor gave the victim a hypodermic injection and we loaded him into the patrol car. With the [hotel] doctor attending, we transported the victim to the hospital at Cardston, Alberta, arriving there about 11 p.m. The [ER] doctor immediately placed him on the operating table. Blood was not available at the hospital, but the hospital had been previously notified and blood was on the way from Lethbridge. We waited at the hospital until the doctor examined the victim and said that *he might live* [emphasis added].

Dr. [redacted] arrived at the hospital. He made arrangements with the hospital and also arranged to notify the victim's parents.

Ranger Dayton's report continues, explaining what was discovered about the bear attack, the attempts to recover Joe Williams's belongings, and considering possible causes of the bear attack.

The next day, June 19, we returned to the area of the bear attack. The approximate location of the attack was determined. The billfold of the victim had not been recovered the previous night, and a search was made for this. It was finally found, together with a cigarette lighter, on the edge of a cliff. These were turned over to the Swiftcurrent Motel [as named then] manager for safekeeping until the parents arrived.

The bear carcass was dragged down to the road. The head was removed and sent to the chief naturalist at Park headquarters.

Possible causes of the bear attack are hard to determine. The bear was a "dry" female [not nursing cubs], 4–5 years old, weighing approximately 250 pounds. A band of bighorn sheep was sighted high on the mountain in the vicinity of the attack. The band included a number of lambs. It is possible that the bear was stalking the sheep when the two boys arrived on the scene. The intrusion may have angered the bear. From the witness report—that the bear began licking the boy—it is also possible that the bear was trying to obtain salt from the perspiration on the victim's arms and face. The sudden movement of panic may have angered the bear and caused her to attack.

Signed, Donald A. Dayton

Supervisory Park Ranger

In summary: "As far as we know," wrote acting superintendent Stanley C. Joseph in his June 22, 1959, report, "the boys did not have any lunch nor any food with them that might have attracted the bear." Causes for the attack, if there were any, remained unknown.

Joe Williams faced a very long and torturous road to recovery. In the end, he required more than 1,200 stitches and was hospitalized for five months in total, undergoing many more surgical and reconstructive procedures to repair his scalp, his right ear and face, his mouth, and extensive wounds to his buttocks and legs.

For the fiftieth anniversary of this attack, in 2009, Joe returned to Glacier Park to have dinner with ranger Don Dayton, then eighty, at one of the Glacier Park lodges. "Park officials do not plan an observance," the Associated Press's Susan Gallagher wrote. "But [Joe] Williams, who has survived colon cancer and heart trouble, is scheduled to speak about human resilience during an appearance Friday at Flathead Valley Community College in Kalispell, near the park.

" 'This for me is an opportunity to acknowledge Don Dayton,' Williams said. 'It's a great time to get together in an incredibly gorgeous place with some people who are extremely important to me.' "[38]

The next chapter relates the indescribable feeling of awakening in the open, in your sleeping bag, to a biting bear.

23

FINDING TOBY

1956: THE STONEY INDIAN PASS CAMPSITE GRIZZLY

I was sleeping, then I felt as if someone was grabbing my leg. When I was fully awake the bear had let go of my leg and was just standing there, looking at me.
—Anthony "Toby" K. Johnson, interviewed by Park
PERSONNEL

National Park Service–Glacier Park
Individual Bear Damage or Injury Number 569008: Toby Johnson
Location: Stoney Indian Pass Trail
Date/Time: Sunday, August 25, 1956, 8:00 a.m.

On June 12, 1956, a headline on the *Daily Inter Lake*'s front page read "Ike Issues Urgent Appeal to Restore Aid Fund Cuts," detailing President Eisenhower's campaign to restore foreign aid programs. This issue also includes a photo of a partly reclining grizzly bear on a Glacier Park road, next to a 1956 vintage car. The reporter notes: "The Season Is Here."

This burly brown bear was out to greet early-season Glacier National Park tourists, but his roadside antics were to no avail in getting hand-outs. All Park tourist facilities will be in full operation by Friday. Glacier Park Co. hotels, motels, and cabin units open that day . . . So far, Park travel has been 163 percent higher than last year. Stanley C. Joseph, assistant park superintendent, said season prospects "look good."[39]

On August 25, 1956, the Stoney Indian Pass Trail was moving from dark to first light. Inside their sleeping bags, sixteen-year-old Californian Toby Johnson and a friend were asleep in a lean-to shelter. Rangers later noted that their camp was one mile below Stoney Indian Pass itself (on the Belly River side, just above the falls on the Stoney Indian Pass Trail).

Toby awoke to an assailant, which proved to be a bear, believed to be a grizzly. The Glacier Park report of Individual Bear Damage or Injury Number 569008, dated August 26, 1956, continues in the words of the victim, below.

> I was sleeping, then I felt as if someone was grabbing my leg. When I was fully awake the bear had let go of my leg and was just standing there, looking at me. I yelled at him to get out of there. All he did was to move slowly away. About all he (the bear) did to me was scratch my leg, but he put a large hole in our poncho and a small hole in my sleeping bag (about an inch square), and a few other small tooth holes.
>
> —Anthony ["Toby"] K. Johnson

His friend's witness statement (name redacted) follows.

> I was also sleeping in the makeshift lean-to. I was awakened by Anthony's yell. I went out the other side and saw a small, dark brown cub. The bears weren't after food because we didn't have any.

The Individual Bear Damage or Injury Report stated that "The unprovoked attack [by an adult grizzly bear] occurred while the boy was in his sleeping bag. However, a cub was observed nearby soon after the attack. The superficial wound was treated on the spot. A shelter was completely destroyed."

Based on later Glacier Park experiences, this early-morning attack is believed to have been possibly predatory in nature, meaning the bear was exploring the two young men as prey.

In the following chapter, one hiker in a group of two is attacked by one of three bears, identified as a grizzly, in Glacier Park. Should he play dead, or fight back?

24

FINDING JACK

1939: THE PIEGAN PASS TRAIL GRIZZLY

Daubney thrashed about more or less aimlessly as the bear cuffed and clawed him. He inadvertently got one of his hands into the bear's mouth, but managed to get it out, although he was bitten.
—GLACIER PARK REPORT, AUGUST 13, 1939

National Park Service-Glacier Park
Case Incident Record Number (none known): John "Jack" Daubney
Location: Piegan Pass Trail
Date/Time: Sunday, August 13, 1939, 3:30 p.m.

Jack Daubney was employed for the summer as a "key clerk" at Many Glacier Hotel (registering guests, issuing room keys, and keeping accounts). That Sunday afternoon on August 13, 1939, he and a friend were hiking the Piegan Pass Trail when the friend spotted movement, and then, three grizzly bears.

Jack Daubney's encounter, described below ("Report of Case of John ['Jack'] Daubney Who Was Attacked by a Bear in Glacier Park, August 13, 1939"), demonstrates that at times, fighting back against a grizzly may not be the wrong thing to do. Jack was also fortunate to have an altruistic hiking companion who stayed with the badly mauled Jack and helped him hike three miles to a highway, where they found help. In 1939, wildlife injuries to humans required a combined tetanus-gas bacillus antitoxin, but fortunately, no rabies injections. Treatment followed as below, in the Glacier Park report.

[Victim: John "Jack" Daubney]
Employee of Glacier Park Hotel Company, stationed at Many Glacier Hotel in capacity of key clerk
Home Address: [redacted] St. Paul, Minnesota
Father: [name redacted] Daubney

On August 13, 1939, at about 3:30 p.m., John ["Jack"] Daubney was hiking from Sun Chalets to Many Glacier Hotel with [name redacted], also an employee at Many Glacier Hotel. The boys had crossed Siyeh Pass and were almost up to Piegan when [name redacted], who was walking ahead and rounded a turn, stated that he could see three bears, which ran immediately.

Daubney stated he did not see these three bears. The boys were frightened and moved off the trail toward the left. They wanted to be near taller trees, so that, if attacked, they could climb to safety.

After waiting a few minutes, they resumed the journey slowly, each watching opposite sides of the trail. Then, some 200 yards from the point where the bears were first seen by [name redacted], Daubney saw a bear some thirty or forty feet away among the underbrush, running rapidly in his (John's) general direction. He stated he thought the bear was going to run by him. When the bear got about ten feet away, he suddenly swerved in and knocked Daubney over.

Daubney thrashed about more or less aimlessly as the bear cuffed and clawed him. He inadvertently got one of his hands into the bear's mouth, but managed to get it out, although he was bitten. The bear backed away, and seemed about to attack John again. John arose and ran toward the bear and kicked at him. The bear then turned and ran away.

Meanwhile, [name redacted] did not join in the encounter. The boys were not clear as to what type of bear attacked Daubney. Daubney stated that he thought it was a grizzly, but was not sure. [Name redacted], according to immediate statement, thought the bear was brownish in color.

Immediately after the attack, [redacted] came to the rescue of Daubney, assisting him in walking the route to the highway. Daubney had great difficulty in negotiating this route. When they arrived on the highway, they hailed a passing automobile driven by some Indians and were taken to Sun Chalets. They arrived at Sun Chalets about 5:30 p.m., and were at once attended by Miss [redacted], the Chalet nurse.

The nurse stated that the boy's clothes were saturated with blood when he came in. She believes that the heavy clothes worn by the boy were a great protection to him. She also said that the boy was in a state of great shock. A telephone call was at once made to me to come to Sun Chalets, and I left immediately, arriving there about 7 p.m. by special bus supplied by the transport company.

Daubney was in bed and temporary dressings had been applied by Miss Hoach. Heat had been applied to the boy by hot water bottles. The boy appeared very pale, although apparently he had at no time lost consciousness. He complained of no head or back injury. The blood pressure was [redacted] and the pulse was [redacted].

[Two more paragraphs redacted.]

[The doctor's report]: The treatment: The patient was given a [redacted], then the wounds were washed thoroughly with a solution of tincture of green soap. Foreign material in the wounds was washed out. Mercurochrome, and in some places, iodine, was applied to the wounds and wound edges, and novocaine anesthesia was introduced locally into some of the areas. Plain chromic catgut sutures were used in the [redacted], and various wounds were closed loosely with dermal sutures. In general, the wounds were left only loosely closed. Boric packs were immediately applied and continued thereafter for considerable periods daily. Combined tetanus-gas bacillus antitoxin was ordered from Kalispell. The treatment of the patient by me commenced at 7:20 p.m. and was completed at 11:00 p.m. The patient was in good condition when this work was completed.

After consulting the Park naturalist and Park authorities at Belton, it was decided not to give Daubney the twenty-one injections for rabies immunization.

On August 19, Daubney got [redacted], apparently from [redacted].

At the present time, August 20, Daubney has a normal temperature and appears to be doing reasonably well.

The above record and account was checked by John ["Jack"] Daubney, August 21, 1939.

What did Jack and his friend experience at the time of the bear attack? Jack's hiking companion wrote the following letter, explaining the harrowing details to Glacier Park personnel:

August 17, 1939
To Elmer Ness, District Park Ranger, St. Mary
Mr. Howell, Glacier Park, Montana

Dear Sir,

On request by you [to recount exactly] what happened last Sunday regarding Jack Daubney's accident, I will try to give the most accurate information I am able.

We started out from Sun Camp with the intention of hiking over Siyeh and Piegan Passes.

We started out from the Sun Camp Chalets about 11:15 [a.m.]. We ate our lunch by the time we got to the hill on top of Siyeh Pass. After this, we had no food on us at all. We then went on to Preston Park, arriving there about 3:15 [p.m.].

About a quarter of a mile from here I saw three brown bears coming up the trail toward us, and when they saw us they turned around and ran up the trail and around a bend, out of sight. I told Jack what I saw and we stopped a few minutes and then started up the trail again. We walked about 40 to 50 ft. out of a little bunch of trees into a clearing. In the clearing about 40 ft. up an embankment, on our right, there was a bunch of brush and trees.

When we got here, the bear ran down the bank from this brush toward us. I was in the lead, about 10 ft. ahead of Jack. The bear seemed to be running toward me but changed its course and ran between us, and both of us stopped dead for a few minutes.

About the same time as the bear was between us, I started to run up the trail and the bear jumped on Jack, knocking him down and mauling him. To my knowledge the bear was attacking Jack for about 20 to 30 sec.

I had run about 30 yds.and stopped, and Jack was walking toward me. We then walked a little ways in order to be [a] safe distance from the bear. We spotted a little curve of the highway down in the valley, and as Jack was able to walk, I was able to get him to the highway, which must have been at least 3 [miles] from the scene of the accident. We hailed a car from the highway to Sun Camp.

—◦—

Park ranger Elmer Ness interviewed the victim and investigated the attack circumstances, detailed in the report below.

August 24, 1939
From: Elmer N. Ness, District Park Ranger

On the evening of August 13, 1939, about 9 p.m., I went up to Sun Chalets to see John ["Jack"] Daubney, who was attacked by a bear on the Piegan [Pass Trail]. The doctor and nurse were still treating him. He was in no condition to be questioned.

I went up to visit him again on the evening of August 14, and spent about one hour with him. The account he gave me is the same as the statement made by [name redacted] to George Hetherington, and the statements written by doctor and nurse [names redacted].

On August 15, I sent ranger Burton Edwards up to the scene of the accident. He could find no bear tracks near the scene of the accident because of the dry and hard condition of the ground; but the tracks of a grizzly bear were found around a small water hole a short distance from there.

Daubney's camera was lost when the bear attacked him. This could not be found.

This 1939 attack is notable for the fact that it recorded the bear species involved as a grizzly.

Other than 1905's fatal attack by a grizzly on Slim Links, detailed in the next chapter, other attacks recorded as by a grizzly include September 2, 1907, when a visitor, "Dr. [redacted], was badly mauled by a grizzly," and which occurred at Great Bear Mountain in the Flathead National Forest. Also on August 23, 1918, without injury to people, a grizzly "[t]ore down a meat safe and ate contents at Upper Lake McDonald."

In later years, from 1935 through 1939, bear attacks are listed as perpetrated by "black" bears, or by "species unknown." The information in the above paragraphs is taken from "Summary of Bear Attacks, Glacier National Park," a report which includes dates from 1905 to 1993.

⬝⬝⬝

The next brief chapter, "Finding Slim," relates how in 1905, a grizzly consumed an unlucky landowner who had tried to get rid of the grizzly. Although Glacier Park was not founded until 1910, the death of Slim Links is listed in Glacier Park records as the first recorded death in Glacier's history. The chapter also describes bear incidents dating back to 1864.

25

FINDING SLIM

1905: THE KISHINA CREEK CABIN GRIZZLY

Shot himself. Bear ate him.
> —SUMMARY OF BEAR ATTACKS, GLACIER
> NATIONAL PARK, 1905–1993

Before establishment of Glacier Park
No Case Incident Record: Slim Links
Location: Kishina Creek Cabin
Date: 1905

Glacier Park's first recorded grizzly-caused death is listed in the archives as "in the Park," although it occurred in 1905, five years before Glacier Park's establishment in 1910 (and its first full year of operation, in 1911).

Slim Links was a landowner who built a cabin near Kishina Creek, in the North Fork, Flathead Valley. His death is listed as a bear attack in Glacier National Park in the archival report titled "Summary of Bear Attacks, Glacier National Park," which covers the years 1905–1993.

Slim set up what was called a "trip-trap" for a troublesome grizzly, in which a gun would fire and kill the grizzly upon triggering of the trap. It is believed from the evidence at hand that Slim must have fallen over his gun and shot himself accidentally. A bear identified as a grizzly then ate the unfortunately trapped trapper.

Slim was buried by neighbors at his cabin near Kishina Creek, in what is described as "just north of the Park in Canada." His remains were later moved and reburied in Columbia Falls, Montana.

In a "Revised 7/98" report, "Grizzly Bear–Related Fatalities at Glacier National Park," Slim Links is again identified as a "Grizzly Bear–Related Fatality at Glacier National Park," with an asterisked note explaining that his death occurred "prior to Park establishment."

According to the "Revised 7/98" report, "Death occurred by accidental gunshot; subsequent opportunistic feeding by grizzly bear." The report also states under "Action Taken" that the grizzly bear received no retribution for his actions.

———

There are even earlier reports of grizzly bear activity, including this report from the Park's wildlife biologist C. J. Martinka, in 1971:

> Significant developments in the relationship between modern man and grizzly bears are reflected in the history of Glacier National Park. Grizzlies were encountered and shot when railroad survey parties first entered the area in the mid-1800s (Stevens 1860; Pumpelley 1918). Faunal richness attracted sport hunters during the late 1800s (Schultz 1962), and by 1890, commercial trapping of the bears for hides was a common activity (Bailey and Bailey 1918). These activities undoubtedly influenced grizzly populations until establishment of the Park in 1910 provided protection. Limited control continued thereafter, but of insufficient magnitude to prevent restoration of a natural grizzly bear population (Martinka 1971; 1974a).[40]

1895: THE ST. MARY GRIZZLIES

In what is now Glacier Park, naturalist Vernon Bailey reported in the early twentieth century that grizzlies were the most common bears of the St. Mary area. "Throughout the forest in this region bear tracks, beds, and signs were abundant at lower levels," he wrote, quoted in *The Grizzlies of Glacier*. "From the earliest 1880s to the time when Glacier Park was created, in 1910, this was one of the most popular regions for hunting bears in the whole United States, and many were killed each year by sportsmen, and others were caught by the numerous trappers of the region. In 1895 I found lines of bear traps between Summit and Belton up to late in June.

"Even then some of the trappers who were thoroughly familiar with the methods of killing large game for bear bait considered bear trapping the greatest menace to the game of the region. Traps were baited with mountain sheep, goats and deer, and I was told that at least 500 elk and moose were killed every year for bear bait. Most of the trapping was done in spring, when the bears first came out of hibernation and the fur was at its longest and best."[41]

1864: THE TWO MEDICINE LAKE GRIZZLY

The place is Glacier Park, before it was established in 1910, and the injury is by grizzly. Glacier Park archives and the biography of William Jackson, Indian scout, reveal an eventual connection here with General Custer in the Black Hills.

Robert and William Jackson, ages ten and eight, "saw the thick brush at the lower end of a small, grassy park quiver as if some animal were passing through. Because of its dark body they thought it was a buffalo, and Robert fired at it. With the report, they heard a frightful, hoarse cry of pain, and out of the brush leaped a monstrous bear, obviously a grizzly. William also fired, and saw the bear flinch as it came bounding toward them.

"The two frightened youngsters fled back up the trail, yelling for help from their grandfather. William leaped for the low-hanging limb of a tree, and pulled himself up, but not before the bear had ripped his trouser leg with its claws. Just as the animal was about to spring at him again, it suddenly sank quivering to the ground as their grandfather's rifle gave a thunderous boom.

"Ten years later, this same William Jackson and his brother were serving as scouts with General Custer in the Black Hills."[42]

The next chapter relates the stories, in brief, of Glacier Park visitors and staff who sustained injuries—both major and minor—inflicted by grizzly, black, and unidentified bears.

MAJOR AND MINOR INJURIES IN BRIEF BY GRIZZLY, BLACK, AND UNIDENTIFIED BEARS

Is it just grizzly bears that injure people in Glacier Park?

The facts below are from an untitled Glacier Park report detailing attacks that occurred between the years 2000 and 1960 (obtained by a Freedom of Information Act request). This summary of bear-caused injuries to people helps humans understand the role that all bears play in our efforts to peacefully coexist with these creatures.

How do we define what is a major injury versus a minor one?

"There is no formal definition of minor versus major injury," Glacier Park supervisory wildlife biologist John Waller stated on June 13, 2019. "It's somewhat subjective, due to the wide variety of possible wounds. In general, wounds that require hospitalization and that are potentially life-threatening are considered major. Wounds that do not require hospitalization (e.g., [being] treated and released), or that require first aid only, are considered minor. To my knowledge, this has been the case since record keeping began."

As of late 2019, what have we learned about bear-caused injuries?

"Bears attack people in northwest Montana [which includes Glacier Park] a few times a year," writes Nicky Gullet of Montana Public Radio (quoted in the *Missoulian*, February 24, 2019). "That's enough for medical professionals and wildlife managers to have developed a special protocol that's part treatment, part forensics, to ensure [that] both parties recover." In the Montana Public Radio report, Dr. Joe Bergman, emergency room physician at Kalispell Hospital, describes his experiences with bear attack victims:

> A grizzly bear's bite—basically they'll bite into your tissue and kind of lift up and then let go—so the wound superficially looks like puncture wounds. So it doesn't look like a very big deal, when in reality they've separated a large area of tissue, deep, that is now contaminated with all that bacteria. . . .
>
> Gas gangrene—or clostridium, for example—is one of the bacteria in bears' mouths. [It's] one of [the] more-aggressive infections, [and] can be life- and limb-threatening.

When a bear attack victim comes into the emergency room, Montana Public Radio's Nicky Gullet reports, "Bergman sets up an IV drip of the antibiotic cocktail right away. As a trauma team stabilizes the patient, Bergman swabs their wounds to ferret out any bacteria the cocktail doesn't cover, and surgically washes cuts and gashes."

Dr. Bergman adds, "We take a lot of measurements, a lot of photographs, just to see how many bites they have, measure how wide the teeth are, so the Fish, Wildlife and Parks guys can correlate that to any grizzly bear they catch or think may be involved in the attack."[43]

MAJOR AND MINOR BEAR-CAUSED INJURIES: 2000 TO 1960

(From an untitled Glacier Park report obtained by a Freedom of Information Act request)

2000—Minor injuries. Punctures/lacerations.
August 14, 2000. Case Incident Record Number 000625.
Unidentified species of bear injured one visitor in a party of two in the Swiftcurrent Pass Trail near Bullhead Lake.

2000—Minor injuries. Punctures.
June 26, 2000. Case Incident Record Number 000202.

One black bear injured one visitor in a party of two near the junction of Two Medicine Lake S. Shore Trail.

1999—Minor injuries. Punctures/lacerations.
August 13, 1999. Case Incident Record Number 990550.
Two grizzly bears injured one visitor in a party of two, 3 to 3.5 miles up Scalplock Lookout Trail.

1999—Minor injuries. Punctures/lacerations.
August 13, 1999. Case Incident Record Number 990550.
Two grizzly bears injured two visitors in a party of two, 2.5 to 3 miles up Scalplock Lookout Trail.

1998—Major injuries. Punctures/lacerations/bites.
October 24, 1998. Case Incident Record Number 981104.
Three grizzly bears injured two visitors in a party of two, 5 miles up Cracker Lake Trail.

1998—FATALITY, Craig Dahl.
May 17, 1998. Case Incident Record Number 980106.
(See chapter 9, "Finding Craig.")

1997—Minor injuries. Lacerations.
September 19, 1997. Case Incident Record Number 971153.
One grizzly bear injured lone visitor at St. Mary Campground, Site Number 874.

1996—Minor injuries. Punctures.
July 24, 1996. Case Incident Record Number 960531.
One grizzly bear injured one visitor in a party of two at Piegan Pass Trail, ⅓ mile beyond Preston Park Junction.

1996—Major injuries. Punctures/lacerations.
June 5, 1996. Case Incident Record Number 960124.
One grizzly bear injured lone visitor 700 yards south of Avalanche Lake Trail and Trail of Cedars Junction.

1995—Minor injuries. Punctures/lacerations.
August 16, 1995. Case Incident Record Number 951549.
Two grizzly bears injured one visitor in a party of three at Preston Park–
Siyeh Pass Trail.

1995—Minor injuries. Punctures.
September 12, 1995. Case Incident Record Number 951521.
Two grizzly bears injured lone National Park Service staff person at
Highline Trail, 1 mile north of 50 Mountain Campground.

1995—Minor injuries. Punctures.
June 19, 1995. Case Incident Record Number 950259.
One grizzly bear injured one concession employee in a party of four at
Cracker Lake Trail, 200 yards beyond uppermost switch.

1995—Minor injuries. Punctures.
June 10, 1995. Case Incident Record Number 950186.
One unidentified bear injured one concession employee of a party of
two at St. Mark Lakeshore near Roes Creek Outlet.

1994—Major injuries. Multiple injuries.
August 28, 1994. Case Incident Record Number 941390.
One grizzly bear injured lone visitor at Iceberg Trail, ¼ to ½ mile east
of Ptarmigan Falls.

1993—Minor injuries. Punctures.
September 29, 1993. Case Incident Record Number 931476.
One grizzly bear injured Jim Cole, visitor in a party of two at Flattop
Trail, near 50 Mountain Campground.
(See chapter 13, "Finding Jim.")

1993—Minor injuries. Punctures/lacerations.
September 23, 1993. Case Incident Record Number 931440.
One grizzly bear injured one visitor in a party of four at Firebrand Pass
Trail, approximately 0.6 mile from Firebrand.

1993—Major injuries. Punctures/bites/lacerations.
August 1, 1993. Case Incident Record Number 930785.
Three grizzly bears injured two visitors in a party of two at Cracker Lake Trail.

1992—Major injuries. Punctures.
August 21, 1992. Case Incident Record Number 921274.
One grizzly bear injured one visitor in a party of two at the head of Swiftcurrent Valley, "Devil's Elbow."

1992—FATALITY, John Petranyi.
October 3, 1992. Case Incident Record Number 92158.
(See chapter 8, "Finding John.")

1991—Minor injuries. Punctures.
June 3, 1991. Case Incident Record Number 910122.
One black bear injured lone visitor at Bowman Lake Campground.

1991—Major injuries. Punctures, bites, fractured elbow.
October 5, 1991. Case Incident Record Number 911212.
Two grizzlies injured two visitors in a party of two at Trout Lake near Howe Ridge Trail Junction.

Additional information about this attack appeared in an article published in the *Hungry Horse News* on October 15, 1992:

> Dale Johnson, 31, of Kalispell, and Rhonda Anderson, 27, of Whitefish, surprised two grizzlies October 5, 1991, on the Trout Lake Trail near the top of Howe Ridge that separates the Lake McDonald valley from the Camas Creek drainage.
>
> In the 1991 attack, Johnson and Anderson were hiking up a steep hill when they saw the bears 35 feet away. The larger bear attacked Johnson first, and Anderson took off her pack and used it as a shield as she tried to chase the bruin off.
>
> The bear attacked her, bit through the pack and her arms, and bit her once in the neck. Johnson tried to help Anderson

and the bear turned on him again, then to Anderson, then to him once more.

After the bears left, the pair walked three miles to their car at the trailhead near the vacant Lake McDonald Ranger Station, then drove to Lake McDonald Lodge, also closed for the season where they dialed a pay phone and waited for help.

Park officials decided the bears had acted defensively in the surprise encounter and no action was taken.[44]

1991—Minor injuries. Lacerations/punctures.
August 30, 1991. Case Incident Record Number 911002.
Three grizzlies injured one visitor in a party of two, ½ mile down trail from Iceberg Lake.

1991—Minor injuries. Lacerations/punctures.
July 17, 1991. Case Incident Record Number 910494.
Two grizzly bears injured two visitors in a party of two, ½ mile up Avalanche Lake Trail.

1990—Major injuries. Bites/punctures/lacerations.
July 31, 1990. Case Incident Record Number 900568.
One grizzly bear injured two visitors in a party of two at Iceberg Trail, 1 mile from trailhead at Many Glacier.

1990—Minor injuries. Lacerations.
July 1, 1990. Case Incident Record Number 900285.
Three black bears injured one visitor in a party of two at Elizabeth Lake Campground.

1989—Minor injuries. Punctures.
August 18, 1989. Case Incident Record Number 890808.
Three grizzly bears injured one visitor in a party of two at Loop Trail, ¼ mile above Loop/Packers Roost Junction.

1989—Major injuries. Punctures/broken bones.

July 17, 1989. Case Incident Record Number 890397.
Three grizzly bears injured two visitors in a party of two at Cracker Lake Trail.

1988—Minor injuries. Punctures/lacerations.
July 3, 1988. Case Incident Record Number 880316.
Three unidentified bears injured lone concession employee at Mount Brown Trail.

1987—Minor injuries. Punctures.
September 17, 1987. Case Incident Record Number 871067.
One grizzly bear injured one visitor in a party of two at Piegan Pass Trail.

1987—FATALITY, Gary Goeden.
July 23, 1987. Case Incident Record Number 870092.
(See chapter 7, "Finding Gary.")

1987—Minor injuries. Punctures.
July 2, 1987. Case Incident Record Number 870304.
Three grizzly bears injured lone visitor at Little Dog Mountain.

1987—FATALITY, Chuck Gibbs.
April 25, 1987. Case Incident Record Number 870092.
(See chapter 6, "Finding Chuck.")

1987—Injuries not rated.
Month and day not known. "Grizzly mauls lone hiker at Summit Mountain" (Appendix 3, 1939–1990, "Recorded Injuries to Hikers and Campers by Grizzly Bears in Glacier National Park").

1987—Injuries not rated.
Month and day not known. "Grizzly mauls one of two hikers at Preston Park" (Appendix 3, 1939–1990, "Recorded Injuries to Hikers and Campers by Grizzly Bears in Glacier National Park").

1986—Major injuries. Punctures/bites.
September 11, 1986. Case Incident Record Number 860836.
One grizzly bear injured two visitors in a party of two at Loop Trail at Granite Park.

1986—Major injuries. Lacerations.
July 7, 1986. Case Incident Record Number 860345.
One grizzly bear injured one visitor in a party of three near Preston Park.

1984—Minor injuries. Lacerations.
September 6, 1984. Case Incident Record Number 841017.
Three black bears injured one visitor in a party of two at Red Rock Point Area.

1984—Minor injuries. Punctures/lacerations.
September 4, 1984. Case Incident Record Number 841013.
One grizzly bear injured two visitors in a party of four at 50 Mountain Campground, 1 mile NW of campground.

1984—Major injuries. Punctures/lacerations.
July 26, 1984. Case Incident Record Number 840595.
One grizzly bear injured one visitor in a party of two at Iceberg-Ptarmigan Trail.

1984—Minor injuries. Punctures.
June 26, 1984. Case Incident Record Number 840295.
One grizzly injured one National Park Service staff person in a party of four at Boulder Pass Trail.

1984—Injuries not rated.
Month and day not known. "Grizzly injures one hiker at Goat Haunt" (Appendix 3, 1939–1990, "Recorded Injuries to Hikers and Campers by Grizzly Bears in Glacier National Park").

1983—Minor injuries. Punctures.
July 22, 1983. Case Incident Record Number 830547.
Three grizzly bears injured one visitor in a party of two at Elk Mountain Trail.

1983—Major injuries. Punctures/lacerations.
June 10, 1983. Case Incident Record Number 830165.
Three grizzly bears injured lone National Park Service staff person at trail between Kintla and Upper Kintla Lake.

1982—Minor injuries. Punctures.
Month and day not known. Case Incident Record Number 820406.
One grizzly bear injured one visitor in a party of two, 150 yards East of Long Knife Creek.

1982—Injuries not rated.
July 18, 1982. "One man and one woman hiking upper portion of Kintla Lake. A lone adult bear jumped from brush 10 yards away. Played dead. Woman behind tree. Bear didn't see. Bit shoulder of man, batted him around. Bit into boot, dragged him 15 feet, then ran off" (Appendix 3, 1939–1990, "Recorded Injuries to Hikers and Campers by Grizzly Bears in Glacier National Park").

1981—Minor injuries. Punctures.
September 6, 1981. Case Incident Record Number 811470.
One grizzly bear injured one visitor in a party of two at North Slope of Heavens Peak.

"Two men hiking off trail on Heavens Peak ran when they encountered a lone adult grizzly bear. One person succeeded in climbing a tree, but the bear caught and injured the other person" (Appendix 3, 1939–1990, "Recorded Injuries to Hikers and Campers by Grizzly Bears in Glacier National Park").

1981—Major injuries. Punctures/lacerations.
July 31, 1981. Case Incident Record Number 811000.

One grizzly bear injured lone visitor at Camas Trail Head inside North Fork Road.

"A hiker nearing the Camas Creek Trailhead was injured by a lone bear. The hiker was wearing bear bells attached to the back of his daypack, but the sound of a nearby creek may have made them less noticeable for the bear" (Appendix 3, 1939–1990, "Recorded Injuries to Hikers and Campers by Grizzly Bears in Glacier National Park").

1981—Minor injuries. Punctures.
July 21, 1981. Case Incident Record Number 810838.
One grizzly bear injured lone visitor at North Fork Flathead River near Kintla Well Road.

"A lone adult grizzly bear injured a fisherman, who surprised it in downed timber off trail, in the North Fork Flathead River drainage. The bear knocked him down, bit his ear, and then sniffed his fishing gear, catching a fishhook in its nose" (Appendix 3, 1939–1990, "Recorded Injuries to Hikers and Campers by Grizzly Bears in Glacier National Park").

1980—TWO FATALITIES, Jane Ammerman and Kim Eberly.
July 24, 1980. Case Incident Record Number 801073.
(See chapter 4, "Finding Jane and Kim.")

1980—FATALITY, Larry Gordon.
September 27, 1980. Case Incident Record Number 801998.
(See chapter 5, "Finding Larry.")

1979—Minor injuries. Punctures.
September 12, 1979. Case Incident Record Number 792093.
Three grizzlies injured one visitor in a party of two at Ole Creek Trail, east of Debris Creek.

"A female bear with two yearlings near Firebrand Pass injured one of two men, who ran to climb trees. The hikers had been playing music on a portable music deck" (Appendix 3, 1939–1990, "Recorded Injuries to Hikers and Campers by Grizzly Bears in Glacier National Park").

1978—Minor injuries. Puncture wounds.
July 22, 1978. Case Incident Record Number 78116[?].
One black bear injured lone visitor at Trout Lake.

1978—Minor injuries. Scrapes.
August 18, 1978. Case Incident Record Number 781825.
Two grizzly bears injured one visitor in a party of two at Cracker Lake
Trail.

"A man and a woman on the Cracker Lake trail surprised a female
grizzly bear with one yearling feeding next to the trail. The yearling
knocked the woman down and bit her but did not break the skin"
(Appendix 3, 1939–1990, "Recorded Injuries to Hikers and Campers
by Grizzly Bears in Glacier National Park").

1977—Minor injuries. Punctures/lacerations.
July 31, 1977. Case Incident Record Number 771692.
One black bear injured one visitor in a party of seven at Arrow Lake.

1976—FATALITY, Mary Pat Mahoney.
September 23, 1976. Case Incident Record Number 761630.
See chapter 3, "Finding Mary Pat."

1976—Major injuries. Lacerations.
September 9, 1976. Case Incident Record Number 761586.
One grizzly injured Roscoe Black and Teresa Waden, in a party of three,
1½ miles west of Stoney Indian Lake.
See chapter 15, "Finding Roscoe and Teresa."

1976—Minor injuries. Punctures.
July 16, 1976. Case Incident Record Number 760805.
One grizzly injured William Schweighofer, in a party of two, at Midway
Campground, Logging Lake.
See chapter 16, "Finding William."

1975—Minor injuries. Punctures.
August 27, 1975. Case Incident Record Number 750719.
One unidentified bear injured one visitor in a party of two at Upper Kintla Lake Campground.

1975—Major injuries. Fractures, lacerations.
August 7, 1975. Case Incident Record Number 750450.
One grizzly injured three visitors in a party of four at Grinnell Glacier Trail.

1975—Minor injuries. Lacerations.
September 7, 1975. Case Incident Record Number 750763.
Two grizzly bears injured two concession employees in a party of two at Rockwell Falls.

"Two unknown-age grizzly bears feeding in a huckleberry patch along the Rockwell Falls Trail injured two men, pulling them down as they tried to climb trees" (Appendix 3, 1939–1990, "Recorded Injuries to Hikers and Campers by Grizzly Bears in Glacier National Park").

1974—Injuries not rated.
July 25, 1974. Field Report No. 74-36. "A female grizzly bear with cubs injured Gordon Edwards, who was hiking alone off trail near Feather Plume Falls. The man had not been making noise and surprised the bear at close range" (Appendix 3, 1939–1990, "Recorded Injuries to Hikers and Campers by Grizzly Bears in Glacier National Park").
See chapter 19, "Finding Gordon."

1974—Minor injury. Scratch.
July 23, 1974. Case Incident Record Number 740082.
One unidentified bear injured one visitor in a party of three at Brown Pass Campground.

1974—Minor injury. Puncture.
July 13, 1974. Case Incident Record Number 740060.
One black bear injured one visitor in a party of two at Ole Lake Campground.

1973—Minor injury. Lacerations.
July 13, 1973. Case Incident Record Number 739046.
One black bear injured lone visitor at Avalanche Campground.

1972—Minor injury. Punctures.
August 4, 1972. Case Incident Record Number 729023.
One black bear injured lone visitor at Lincoln Lake Campground.

1971—Minor injury. Punctures.
August 14, 1972. Case Incident Record Number 719063.
One black bear injured lone visitor at Quartz Creek Campground.

1971—Minor injury. Lacerations/bruises.
June 9, 1971. Case Incident Record Number 719027.
One black bear injured one visitor in a party of two at Avalanche Campground.

1968—Injuries not rated.
May 20, 1968. Case Incident Record Number 689063.
One grizzly bear injured lone visitor Bob Hahn, just east of the tunnel close to Logan Pass Visitor Center.
See chapter 20, "Finding Bob."

1967—FATALITY, Julie Helgeson.
August 12–13, 1967. Case Incident Record Number 679050 and A7623.
See chapter 1, "Finding Julie."

1967—FATALITY, Michele Koons.
August 12–13, 1967. Case Incident Record Number 679050 and A7623
See chapter 2, "Finding Michele."

1965—Minor injuries. Bites on arm and back.
September 17, 1965. Case Incident Record Number 659092.
Three unidentified bears injured visitor accompanied by ranger Robert Sellers at Mineral Creek Trail, near Packers Roost.

1963—Major injuries. Severe bites and lacerations.

July 23, 1963. Case Incident Record Number 639000.

Two unidentified bears injured two visitors, Mr. and Mrs. Duvall.

"Severe bites and lacerations to Mrs. Duvall. Superficial injuries to Mr. Duvall. 3 and ½ miles up from head of Bowman Lake. Victims requested no action against bears" (Appendix 3, 1939–1990, "Recorded Injuries to Hikers and Campers by Grizzly Bears in Glacier National Park").

1962—Minor injuries. Lacerations. Scratched and bit netting while in sleeping bag.

July 7, 1962. Case Incident Record Number 629054.

One unidentified bear injured one National Park Service staff person sleeping outside near trail crew cabin at Granite Park Chalet.

1960—Major injuries. Severe multiple lacerations and bites, especially to Noring and Parratt.

July 18, 1960. Case Incident Record Number 600045.

Three grizzlies injured three persons in a party of five, including park ranger Alan Nelson, 1 mile from Otokomi Lake–Rose Creek Trail.

See chapter 21, "Finding Five (Including a Ten-Year-Old)."

1960—Minor injuries. Scratches on arms.

July 8, 1960. Case Incident Record Number 600035.

Three grizzlies injured lone visitor walking with dog about 2 miles up Rose Creek Trail.

PART 8

TRENDS

RECENT MAULINGS, 2009–2019

2009: THE LAKE MCDONALD VALLEY TRAIL GRIZZLY

I located a small stick and I hit it in the face with the stick and he backed off again. . . . He immediately came in and got ahold of my thigh, and that was the more severe bite.
        —TOM NERISON IN *DAILY INTER LAKE*, JUNE 10, 2009

Tom Nerison, sixty, heard the sound of his own breathing, practiced and calm, and the early-morning sounds typical of the Lake McDonald Valley as he trail-ran alone that Sunday, June 7, 2009. His plan was to join a group of fellow runners.

Perhaps he had not heard that in 1996, also in June, a seventy-year-old man had been hiking alone on that same backcountry trail when a grizzly bear attacked him, causing him injuries.

Now, at about 9:45 a.m., Nerison was one and a half miles from the Avalanche Lake trailhead when he heard sounds that were not "usual." He described what sounded like a dog barking and a commotion like horses galloping.

"Nerison said he had just enough time to turn around and get off the trail about a foot when he saw what he estimated to be two 250-pound grizzly bears running toward him," reported the Glacier Park media release of June 10.

One of the bears stopped near him, Nerison told Jim Mann of *Daily Inter Lake*, and then came toward him. Nerison decided to fight back.

"He started advancing on me, and I knew he was going to try to bite me, so I kicked at him. He came at me a second time and I kicked again, but fell," Nerison said. "So he came at me again. He got ahold of my shoes and pulled them both off without actually biting my feet." The bear lunged at Nerison again, this time biting his right calf.

"I located a small stick and I hit it in the face with the stick and he backed off again," he said. "He immediately came in and got ahold of my thigh and that was the more severe bite." Nerison found a larger stick, several feet long, and prepared for the attack to resume. But it didn't.[45]

"The bear lost interest in him," the Glacier Park media release noted, "[and] moved back toward the way it had come, then went uphill and away from the trail. [Nerison] stated that he then walked downhill and cross-country to the Going-to-the-Sun Road, where he got a ride from a visitor back to his own car at the Avalanche trailhead. He then drove himself to the Kalispell Regional Medical Center's emergency room for medical treatment."

When Nerison left the hospital, he was in a wheelchair.

"Sunday afternoon, rangers closed the trail between the junction with the Avalanche Trail and the Johns Lake Loop Trail," the Glacier Park release said, "per the park's bear management policies. Park rangers are investigating the incident, and based on their findings, in accordance with Glacier's Bear Management Guidelines, park managers will determine what, if any, further actions will be taken."

"Make no mistake, bears are active," Park superintendent Chas Cartwright commented that June 7. "All Park visitors should be alert while bicycling or simply walking and/or driving along Park roads. Running along trails is discouraged because of the potential of surprising a bear. A runner alone on a trail can inadvertently startle or frighten a bear (or mountain lion), causing it to react in a defensive or aggressive manner."

2010: GLACIER PARK'S CENTENNIAL (100TH YEAR).

No reported attacks.

2011: THE PIEGAN PASS TRAIL GRIZZLY

The animal attacked and bit the hiker on an arm, leg and foot and then shook him before leaving. The man had bear spray but couldn't use it in time.

—PARK SPOKESWOMAN DENISE GERMANN,
QUOTED IN *HUFFPOST GREEN*, 2012

"Grizzly Mauls Hiker" reported the *Missoulian* about the attack that occurred on a backcountry trail around noon on Friday, August 5, 2011. The man's name was withheld.

The newspaper continued. "Park officials say the 50-year-old man—from St. Paul, Minn.—was hiking alone on the trail from Many Glacier to Piegan Pass. He rounded a bend in the trail and encountered a sow grizzly with a sub-adult bear."

The hiker was carrying bear spray, but was unable to deploy it before the bear attacked. The hiker suffered bites to his left thigh and left forearm, then the bear grabbed his foot, shook him, released him and left the area. The man hiked back toward Many Glacier, encountering a naturalist-ranger leading a hike. The ranger notified Dispatch while the man continued to the Many Glacier Ranger Station. There, he was treated for his injuries and eventually taken to the Blackfeet Community Hospital in Browning by the Babb Ambulance. Initial reports indicated the hiker was making noise as he hiked.[46]

"The hiker was hospitalized in Browning," Park spokeswoman Germann's account in *HuffPost Green* continued, "but his condition was not immediately available. Germann says the trail from Piegan Pass to Feather Plume Falls has been closed as rangers investigate. Park officials say cases of grizzly or black bears injuring people at Glacier occur less than once a year."[47]

2014: HIKER USES BEAR SPRAY AND GUN ON BEAR

The bear was wounded and the hiker was not.

—Anonymous

From the Glacier Park media release: "At approximately 9:30 a.m., Saturday, July 26, Park Dispatch received notification from a Park volunteer backcountry ranger of a hiker–bear incident on the Mount Brown Lookout Trail, on the west side of the park."

Initial investigation indicates that a 57-year-old hiker [name redacted] from Texas was hiking alone on the Mount Brown Lookout Trail when a bear charged him from an area below the trail. The hiker deployed his canister of bear spray and then discharged one round of his handgun. It is believed the bear was wounded, and ran away.

The hiker then turned around and quickly hiked back to the trailhead, warning other hikers on the trail of the incident. The hiker met a Park volunteer backcountry ranger on the trail, and the ranger notified Park Dispatch of the situation. The hiker received no physical injuries.

Park rangers immediately closed the trail and initiated an investigation. They staffed the trailhead to communicate the situation to other Park visitors and began a search for the bear. Park rangers and bear specialists hiked from the trailhead, and were transported via helicopter to the summit of Mount Brown to investigate and search for the bear. It is unknown if the bear was a grizzly or black bear, but evidence indicates the bear was wounded. The investigation and search for the bear will continue, and the trail will remain closed until further notice.

2015: THE MOUNT HENKEL GRIZZLY

The man received puncture wounds to his lower leg and injuries to a hand during the attack. He hiked back to his vehicle at Many Glacier and drove himself to the emergency room.

—The *Missoulian*, October 1, 2015

"Surprised Grizzly Shakes Hiker" reported the *Missoulian*, initially on September 29, 2015. The man's name was redacted. "A hiker from Wisconsin was 'grabbed and shaken' by a grizzly bear in Glacier National Park early Tuesday evening, park officials reported Wednesday."

The article continues:

> The 65-year-old man was hiking alone, off trail, near Mount Henkel in the Many Glacier Valley when he surprised a sow grizzly and her two sub-adult cubs at approximately 5 p.m., Glacier spokeswoman Katelynn Liming said. The hiker successfully deployed his bear spray, causing the grizzly to release him and leave. Liming said the man received puncture wounds to his lower leg and injuries to a hand during the attack. He hiked back to his vehicle at Many Glacier and drove himself to the emergency room at the Northern Rockies Medical Center in Cut Bank, approximately 55 miles away. He was treated and released, and called Glacier Park Dispatch to report the incident.[48]

2016: THE HUCKLEBERRY GRIZZLY

A Park employee, while off duty picking huckleberries in the Swiftcurrent Valley, surprised what is believed to be a grizzly bear.
—GLACIER PARK MEDIA RELEASE, AUGUST 29, 2016

"Berry Picker Surprises Bear," announced the Glacier Park media release of August 29.

In Montana, picking and eating huckleberries is a popular pursuit among both people and bears. When they burst to ripeness in August, the delicious red-blue berries are used for many iconic Montana treats, including huckleberry shakes, huckleberry fudge, and T-shirts that proclaim "I Want to Be Your Huckle Bear-y."

"A park employee, while off duty picking huckleberries in the Swiftcurrent Valley, surprised what is believed to be a grizzly bear," said the Glacier Park media release of August 29, 2016. The release continued:

> She sustained non-life-threatening injuries to the leg and hands. The surprise encounter which led to a non-predatory attack occurred on

Saturday, August 27, in the early evening hours, a quarter-mile off the Swiftcurrent Pass Trail near Red Rock Falls, and reported to Dispatch at 7:15 p.m. The park employee walked most of the Swiftcurrent Pass Trail back before she was met by park rangers. She was then transported by Glacier county EMS to Browning for further treatment and evaluation. She was carrying bear spray but it was not deployed. Hikers reported a grizzly bear sow and two cubs leaving the area shortly after the incident.

2017: FIFTY YEARS AFTER "NIGHT OF THE GRIZZLIES"

Patrol ranger Bert Gildart was driving down the highest pass in Glacier National Park just after midnight on August 13, 1967, when a woman's voice suddenly crackled over his two-way radio. . . . A grizzly bear had mauled someone at the popular Granite Park guest chalet.
—*Washington Post*, August 3, 2017

A half-century has passed since the nation awoke to news of the "Night of the Grizzlies." Two fatal grizzly bear attacks occurred in Glacier Park on the same night, one near the Granite Park Chalet, and another nine and a half miles away, at Trout Lake. Julie Helgeson and Michele Koons were both killed.

"Those attacks, which took place 50 years ago this summer," wrote Karin Brulliard in the *Washington Post* on August 3, 2017, "set off an immediate quest at Glacier to understand how a tragedy of such infinitesimal odds could have happened."

> But they also marked a turning point in relations between North Americans and the continent's largest predators, revolutionizing how public agencies deal with bears and inspiring new paths of research on grizzly behavior. The impact of the deaths still echoed in federal officials' recent decision to remove Yellowstone-area grizzlies from the endangered species list. . . .
>
> The big idea is conflict prevention, Waller said [John Waller, Glacier Park supervisory wildlife biologist]. These days, Glacier regularly

closes trails so grizzlies can access berry patches or carcasses without running into people. And all those bear-proof garbage cans in national parks and elsewhere bears live? They're produced by an industry that grew out of the Glacier attacks, Herrero said [Stephen Herrero, a leading authority on bear attacks and behavior]. "Tremendous progress has been made to keep bears away from these attractants," Herrero said. "It's really been quite successful—not only saving people's lives, but also saving bears' lives."[49]

2017: NO REPORTED BEAR ATTACKS IN GLACIER

[No attacks, but] the Park Service received multiple reports of grizzly bears approaching people.
—ASSOCIATED PRESS, QUOTED IN THE *FLATHEAD BEACON*

While there were no reported bear attacks in Glacier Park in 2017, the Avalanche Lake Trail had to be closed "due to grizzly bear activity."

"The *Flathead Beacon* reports the trail on the west side of Glacier National Park reopened Wednesday afternoon," according to an Associated Press report on June 23, 2017. "The trail was closed earlier this week after the Park Service received multiple reports of grizzly bears approaching people."[50]

Meanwhile, the Park Service itself noted that "Vehicles can drive to Avalanche Lake Trail on Going-to-the-Sun Road on the west side of Glacier. Crews are finishing clearing efforts along the upper stretches of the road before fully opening the thoroughfare for summer."

2018: NO REPORTED BEAR ATTACKS IN GLACIER

[But in the Cabinet Mountains of northwestern Montana:] Bear researcher attacked by grizzly to stay on career path.
—MATT VOLZ, ASSOCIATED PRESS, JUNE 21, 2018

That a grizzly bear researcher should stay on her career path after being attacked herself makes the following story significant. Amber Kornak, twenty-eight, is a grizzly bear researcher for the US Fish and Wildlife

Service (not working in Glacier Park). Despite being attacked by a grizzly in the Cabinet Mountains of northwestern Montana, she says that she will keep on doing her job. In fact, she plans to become a grizzly bear wildlife manager.

On May 17, 2018, she was working alone in the backcountry. Her job was to collect grizzly bear hair samples which would then be analyzed for their DNA, to provide information about each individual bear, and also provide a census report for how many grizzlies remain in the Cabinet Mountains. The number is estimated at fifty grizzlies, and the bears are protected as a threatened species.

Because Amber was alone, she regularly blew a whistle and clapped her hands as she worked, to alert any nearby bears to her presence. But her warning sounds, according to an investigation by Montana Fish, Wildlife and Parks, were eclipsed by the sounds of rain, wind, and a rushing creek. When she saw the grizzly, it was just twelve feet away.

"We spooked each other," Kornak told the Associated Press (quoted in the June 21, 2018, *Spokesman Review* in Spokane, Washington). "I got down on the ground and pulled out my bear spray. He bit down on my skull, and I just reached over with my left arm and sprayed him and he was gone."

> But her skull was cracked open, her back and arm had been clawed, and she was two miles from her truck. She sent out an emergency notification using her Garmin inReach Global Satellite device, then she washed the Mace-like bear spray out of her eyes with water. . . . Kornak made it to her car, then drove about 3 miles along a dirt road until she came across a pickup truck. She flagged down the driver, and he gave her a ride until they came across an ambulance winding up the mountain road in response to her emergency call. . . . Kornak spent a week in the hospital and has since been recovering at home. . . . She said her recovery is going well, though it's a long process, and she misses being in the field.[51]

The future wildlife manager—again, who was *not* attacked in a national park—said that "The bear spray saved my life."

Since 2010, it has been legal to carry guns in national parks, but firing one remains illegal.

— ◦ —

2019: NO REPORTED BEAR ATTACKS IN GLACIER

As of October 28, 2019, there have been no reported bear attacks in Glacier Park for this calendar year. There have, however, been a number of incidents and close encounters between bears and humans.

Fifty-two years have passed since "Night of the Grizzlies"—the night in 1967 during which two young women died in two separate attacks, by two different grizzlies. "Night of the Grizzlies" is the night that does not end. It should be noted that hard lessons have been learned, and all those who have lost their lives or been injured in Glacier Park due to grizzly bear attacks are remembered.

— ◦ —

But within the park, some people remain missing to this day. In the following chapter, "Still Missing and Presumed Dead," we remember these people, as well. The hope is that one day they will be found.

28

STILL MISSING AND PRESUMED DEAD

1924–2019

For the friends and families of those missing, not knowing what happened to the person has been said to be more unbearable than learning of a tragic end for their loved one.

Here is a story from 2008 of one person who went missing in Glacier National Park, and was found.

That August of 2008, Yi-Jien Hwa, a twenty-seven-year-old native Malaysian attending a seminary in Kentucky, planned to hike ninety-seven miles in Glacier. He registered for (and received) a backcountry permit detailing his itinerary, beginning August 11 and ending August 18. He planned to camp at Sperry, Reynolds Creek, Granite Park, Fifty Mountain, Kootenai Lake, Hole-in-the-Wall, and Upper Kintla Lake. Hwa would climb a total elevation of 15,000 feet and descend a total of 14,000 feet.

Point last seen: On August 2, Hwa left the St. Mary Visitor Center carrying a dark blue Kelty backpack, hiking poles, and other equipment. Only his car, parked at the Glacier Park high point of Logan Pass Visitor Center, was found. Untouched: The car was his midway restocking depot, holding his food and supplies for the second half of his trip.

His wife was meant to accompany him on this adventure, but a family emergency intervened, and she did not go. Now there was another emergency: She reported him missing on August 19.

Then-superintendent Chas Cartwright details the tremendous efforts made by Park search teams, as well as those from other search-and-rescue entities, and even the FBI, to find Mr. Hwa. Thirty to sixty searchers per day combed the backcountry. The Park media release dated September 2, 2008, follows:

Officials at Glacier National Park said today that no clues about the whereabouts or condition of a hiker reported missing in the Park's backcountry last month had turned up in searches that continued over the weekend. They said that pending the emergence or discovery of information that might explain the hiker's disappearance, the search and rescue operation launched nearly two weeks ago would be significantly reduced.

"Reluctantly, after more than 2,500 hours of searching in difficult terrain and challenging conditions, the time has come to acknowledge that we are unlikely to solve this mystery without additional information," the Park's superintendent, Chas Cartwright, said. "We are disappointed that our efforts have not succeeded in explaining what has become of this enthusiastic young outdoorsman, especially for the sake of his family."

Beginning on August 20th, the day after Yi-Jien Hwa, 27, was reported missing by his family, the Park sent teams of hikers and professional alpine searchers into the most forbidding areas of its backcountry to look for him, or for evidence that he had passed through areas he planned to hike. Mr. Hwa, a native of Malaysia, had drawn up an itinerary for himself and his wife that encompassed nearly 100 miles of hikes, as well as climbs and descents of more than 14,000 feet. His wife did not accompany him because of a family emergency.

Each day, between 30 and 60 searchers were shuttled in and out of remote areas by helicopter. The searches included use of human-scent dog teams and of horse-mounted patrols. The search operation also had access to aerial heat-sensing equipment.

Hikers and mountaineers searched through some of northwestern Montana's most forbidding terrain as fall weather arrived early. The search area encompasses lakes, extensive cliff bands, glaciers, glacial melt ponds, crevasses, ice and snow bridges, forests, and shaded areas near ridges. Fresh snowfall, rain, fog, and high winds made search operations and footing especially difficult in this diverse terrain.

Agencies that helped to plan the searches or contributed search personnel included the Flathead County and Glacier County sheriff's departments, the US Border Patrol, and the US Forest Service. The Federal Bureau of Investigation helped to follow up on information received from the public by the National Park Service.

"We have not ceased to hope that we will receive or discover information that will help us to find Mr. Hwa or to find out what happened to him," the operation's incident commander, Patrick Suddath, said today. "We simply had to make the decision that committing the resources at the level we have committed them over the past two weeks could not continue based on the information we had to go on."

Over the weekend, one or two teams of searchers continued to scour locations adjacent to areas that were identified as most likely to have been hiked by Mr. Hwa, assuming that he had followed his plan as outlined in his backcountry permit. Human-scent dog teams also were used. No new clues turned up in those efforts. In a meeting today, the search's managers decided to discontinue regular searches.

Suddath described a continuing operation that represents a vastly reduced effort compared to searches that have been mounted to date. He said he would retain overall responsibility for analyzing any new information and determining how to respond, including whether to send out searchers. He said he would not hesitate to order searches when warranted by such information.

Suddath asks that anyone who has seen Mr. Hwa or who has information that might help to locate him, notify Glacier National Park. He said investigators will follow up on information they receive from Park personnel who regularly hike areas in Mr. Hwa's itinerary.

In addition, fresh posters with Mr. Hwa's picture and description seeking information will be put up in campgrounds and visitor centers, at trailheads, and elsewhere in the Park this week.

Hope to find the missing never ends. Occasionally the opaque curtain parts, but still the news is not good. "On July 3, [2011], a hiker found portions of two clothing items that match the description of what Hwa was wearing and carrying," wrote Tristan Scott in the *Missoulian* on August 2, 2011. "The hiker was able to pinpoint the location of the items, and rangers returned to the site twice for further investigation, with assistance from members of the Flathead County Sheriff's Department and the Search and Rescue Team. Other pieces of evidence were discovered as well, several of which closely match the items identified in Hwa's equipment list. The evidence includes human bone fragments that are being analyzed for DNA identification by the Montana Department of Justice's Crime Laboratory in Missoula. . . .

"Rangers believe the evidence was moved downslope from the cliffs above by water and avalanches."[52]

DNA subsequently confirmed that the remains were those of Mr. Hwa.

What follows is a list of those reported to be "Still Missing" in Glacier Park (and presumed dead). (***Note:*** Among possible fatal events that happen in the Park and cause persons to go missing, the loss of life due to a grizzly bear attack cannot be ruled out.) The names of persons *not* reported to be missing cannot be given here. This list of missing persons was updated on October 29, 2019, via an e-mail from Gina Kerzman, Glacier Park acting public affairs officer.

1924: Joseph Whitehead, visitor, age 29
Last seen near Granite Park Chalet, August 24, 1924, and

1924: Brother of above, William A. Whitehead, visitor, age 22
Last seen near Granite Park Chalet, August 24, 1924.

"A haunting postcard was the last message from Bill and Joe Whitehead, who wrote to their mother on August 23, 1924," reports Montana's *Daily Inter Lake* on May 3, 2010. "[The postcard] read: 'Dear Mom, We've seen beargrass on our trips. These postal cards are on top of the menus. We are just leaving Many Glacier for Granite Park. We are both O.K.' The two young Chicago brothers disappeared the next day.

"After a night at Granite Park Chalet, the two headed down the Garden Wall toward the Lewis Hotel, now Lake McDonald Lodge. They mentioned plans to do some fishing. They never made it to the lodge. Rangers searched every lake within 20 miles. A $1,700 reward was offered by their family and the case received national attention, but they simply vanished."[53]

On September 16 of 1924, Interior Secretary F. M. Goodwin wrote that "Thirteen rangers, two famous Indian Guides and seven tried mountaineers were out for more than two weeks. There never has been a search in the national parks conducted with more vigor and effort." To this day the Whitehead brothers remain missing.

1933: Dr. D. W. Cosby Bell, visitor, age unknown
Mount Brown, summer 1933.

Dr. Bell "hiked up Mount Brown in the summer of 1933, and never hiked down," reports the Flathead *Beacon* on August 6, 2014.[54]

1934: Dr. F. H. Lumley, visitor, age 27
Goat Haunt Camp, August 13, 1934.

"One of the most mysterious disappearances took place in 1934 when Dr. Lumley took off, supposedly to walk to Waterton, and simply vanished," wrote Montana's *Daily Inter Lake* on May 3, 2010. Lumley was an Ohio State University professor. "A postcard of Gunsight Lake written the day before he disappeared read 'Dear Kay, Here is the drink that satisfies. I have been having early morning, afternoon and evening cocktails of the one and only *aqua pura a la* Many Glacier. But swimming is out. Two cold baths have sufficed to prove to me that uncleanliness is preferable to uncomfortableness anytime. [signed] Hillis."[55]

1963: David Paul Wilson, NPS employee, age 21
Going-to-the-Sun Mountain, August 2, 1963.

"David Wilson decided to squeeze in two more mountain climbs that weekend after returning from Chief Mountain with friends," reported the *Daily Inter Lake* on May 3, 2010. "He left them a note saying he was going to tackle Going-to-the-Sun Mountain alone. Wilson, 21, was a summer park crew employee, a senior in pre-medicine at Ohio Wesleyan University. He was never heard from again. The incident raised some eyebrows, considering the story behind Going-to-the-Sun Mountain. According to Blackfeet legend, after the God Napa created the world, he climbed back to heaven via the Going-to-the-Sun peak."[56]

1974: Name unknown.
Backcountry, June 1974.

An abandoned backcountry camp with expensive fishing equipment was reported by J. Gordon Edwards (author of *A Climber's Guide to Glacier National Park*) in June 1974, and one year later, the camp's occupant was said to remain unidentified and missing.

This example is included because other abandoned camps with unknown owners have been found in Glacier Park over the years.

1997: Matthew Truszkowski, concession employee, age 25
Mount Sinopah area, July 7, 1997.

"The search being conducted was for a missing employee who was a computer operator at Glacier Park Lodge," wrote the Glacier Park Foundation in its Winter 1998 newsletter. "Matthew Truszkowski, 25, of Lexington, Michigan, left the lodge on July 5 [1997] to do a solo climb of Sinopah Mountain. When he did not meet his friends at the end of the day, the Park Service was notified and a search was begun. His disappearance remains a mystery. . . . An extensive ground and aerial search was conducted and another was planned for the fall, after the leaves had fallen. Truszkowski is presumed dead."[57]

2000: Patrick T. Whalen, visitor, age 33
Cut Bank Creek Drainage, November 2, 2000

Whalen "was originally from Cleveland, Ohio, but lived in Portland, Oregon, at the time of his disappearance," reported the "Charley Project," a missing persons clearinghouse, on October 12, 2016. "He was a registered nurse and planned to become a doctor in the field of naturopathy. Described as a survivalist who had hiked for thousands of miles on the Pacific Crest Trail and in national parks, Whalen frequented Glacier National Park, the Blackfeet tribal lands and the Columbia Falls area of Montana for several weeks during September and October 2000. . . . On May 27, almost seven months after Whalen's disappearance, a park ranger found an abandoned camp at the Atlantic Creek Backcountry Campground, along the north fork of Cut Bank Creek near Bad Marriage Mountain and Medicine Grizzly Peak. Personal belongings of Whalen's were identified at the campsite, but there was no indication of his whereabouts at the scene, and it appeared the campsite had been abandoned since the previous autumn."[58]

2003: Larry Kimble, visitor, age 40
Fish Creek, Rocky Point area, May 29, 2003.

In an Associated Press report dated July 1, 2003, Park spokeswoman Amy Vanderbilt stated that "Larry Thomas Kimble, 40, of Dorr, Michigan, was listed as missing after park rangers contacted the sheriff's office in Allegan County. Rangers found his 1998 GMC truck at the Rocky Point trailhead on the west shore of Lake McDonald in the third week of June. They began watching it daily after it remained unattended overnight, and impounded it June 23. Park officials contacted Kimble's relatives and authorities in Michigan for information after establishing that he was the owner. The truck had a Glacier National Park entrance receipt dated May 29. Rangers called in tracking dog teams [to search both land and water] last weekend after finding no trace of Kimble in the immediate area or on nearby trails. . . . Rangers have found no indication of Kimble's activities between May 29 and mid-June. He did not have a backcountry permit, and no camping equipment was in the truck. Rangers found no records of recent lodging in or near the park."[59]

Larry Kimble's disappearance is also discussed in "Lost, Never Found," an article in the *Flathead Beacon*, August 6, 2014.[60]

2019: Mark Sinclair, Glacier Park worker (earlier in summer), age 66
Seen on Highline Trail at Rimrocks headed west, July 8, 2019.

A Glacier National Park media release was issued on July 10, 2019, titled "Information Sought on Missing Person in Glacier National Park":

West Glacier, Montana—Glacier National Park is asking for the public's help to locate a missing person.

Mark Sinclair, 66, was last seen at approximately 2:30 p.m. on Monday, July 8, 2019, on the Highline Trail at Rimrocks, headed west.

Park staff working in the Logan Pass Visitor Center observed him leaving an unsecured vehicle, keys, and dog in the Logan Pass parking lot.

Sinclair was wearing all gray or nondescript clothing (possibly in shorts), a yellow bandanna around his neck, a gray waist fanny backpack, and no hat. His hair is completely white, and he may have a beard that is white as well. He is 5-foot-8 and approximately 155 lbs.

If you have information about the missing person, please notify the Park.

Sinclair is a recent resident of Whitefish, Montana, and worked for a period of time earlier this summer at Glacier National Park.

Search efforts began on Tuesday morning, July 9, and are continuing by ground and air.

An Associated Press article was published on July 16, 2019, titled "Trail Still Cold in Search for Missing Man in Glacier National Park":

Glacier National Park officials say there has been no sign of a 66-year-old man who's been missing for over a week. The trail where he was last seen is closed because of grizzly bear activity.

Mark Sinclair of Whitefish was last seen on the Highline Trail on July 8 after leaving a vehicle with a dog inside at the Logan Pass parking lot.

Searchers on the ground and in the air have turned up no clues about his disappearance.

Park officials said in a statement Tuesday that searchers plan to suspend ground-search efforts this week unless something substantive is discovered.

The Highline Trail has been temporarily closed after a young grizzly bear charged visitors and wandered close to search teams last weekend.

Park spokeswoman Lauren Alley says there is no evidence Sinclair was attacked by a bear.[61]

Another Glacier National Park news release was issued on July 18, 2019, titled "Search Efforts for Mark Sinclair Will Continue in Limited Capacity":

West Glacier, Montana—Glacier National Park has scaled back a large search effort for the man who went missing early last week.

Search efforts began the morning of July 9 in the Logan Pass area of Glacier National Park for Mark Sinclair, 66, recently of Whitefish, Montana.

Active search efforts took place between July 9 and July 18. The overall search area encompassed numerous drainages east and west of the Continental Divide, including Upper McDonald Creek, Mineral Creek, Swiftcurrent, and Belly River drainages. Trails and off-trail search areas included Flattop Mountain, the Highline from Logan Pass to Goat Haunt, Swiftcurrent Pass, the Loop, and Hidden Lake. Other associated trail areas attached to the Highline were also searched. Aerial searches included the entire spine of the Continental Divide on both sides, from Logan Pass to 50 Mountain.

The search area is characterized by steep slopes with cliff faces frequently over 100 feet high, gray rocks that act as camouflage, and dense shrubs that conceal the ground. Searchers also encountered high winds and heavy rain and hail.

Flathead County Sheriff's Department—including ground patrols, canine units, a search drone, and a volunteer search-and-rescue division—assisted Glacier National Park search-and-rescue team members. Two Bear Air and the US Forest Service provided daytime aerial search capacity and nighttime infrared flights. The US Geological Survey also assisted with search drone support.

Mark Sinclair is still considered a missing person. The search effort has been moved to a "limited continuous mode," meaning that active searching will not occur every day, but will continue in a reduced capacity with patrols. The park's investigation will actively continue in hopes of gaining further information about his whereabouts. If a clue or witness report provides new information about Sinclair's possible whereabouts or belongings, additional search efforts will follow up.

Updated missing-person posters with Sinclair's picture and description will be posted throughout the park for the duration of the summer.

Park rangers would like to continue hearing from anyone who was in the Logan Pass and Granite Park vicinity on or after July 8 who may have had contact with Sinclair or seen him on a trail, including guests at Granite Park Chalet and backcountry overnight campers.

The park has not ruled out the possibility that he may have traveled further from the Logan Pass vicinity, given the number of trails that connect directly from this area and extend in every direction across Glacier's one million acres.

"We continue to ask the public to think back to their visits to the park last week. Additional sightings or the discovery of Mark's belongings could help investigators identify new search tactics," said search team commander Ed Visnovske. "The park deeply appreciates the efforts of our county and federal partners; we could not have covered such a significant area or conducted such an in-depth search without that support."

After the search began, two visitors called the tip line and reported seeing him between Haystack Butte and Granite Park Chalet on the Highline Trail in the early evening on July 8. No other verified sightings have been received beyond July 8.

Members of the public who have information about Sinclair's last-seen whereabouts are urged to notify Glacier Park.

The park does not expect to issue another press release unless something significant changes with this case.

If any reader has information about any of these missing persons, please contact Glacier Park Dispatch.

If interested, donations may be made to National Park Service, Emergency Services, Search and Rescue Donation, PO Box 128, West Glacier, MT 59936.

The next chapter answers the question "What about the black bears?"

29

WHAT ABOUT THE BLACK BEARS?

Yes, there are black bears in Glacier National Park. How many? On the Glacier Park website, www.nps.gov/glac, under "naturescience/bears .htm," DNA sampling of bear hairs and scats show that in Glacier, "the latest estimates hover around 300 grizzly bears and 600 black bears, but refinements are constantly improving the accuracy of the estimate."

The good news is that in Glacier Park to date, no fatal attacks by black bears on humans have been reported. May it remain so. There have been injuries to humans, but generally much less serious than those inflicted by grizzlies.

Below is a sampling of injuries caused by black (or unknown species) of bears, according to a Park report.

SUMMARY OF BEAR ATTACKS, GLACIER NATIONAL PARK (1905–1993)

Encounters with Unknown Bear Species

In 1939, unknown bear species caused injuries throughout Glacier Park, with a tally of the probable causes: "3 persons injured due to feeding, 3 injuries to persons who watched other people feed bears, 1 injury due to person stepping between sow and cubs, 5 injuries due to persons photographing bears, 4 injuries due to persons neither feeding, photographing, nor in the vicinity of other people doing so."

Unknown species of bear in July of 1953 inflicted the following: "Visitor received a 2- to 3-inch gash in left leg while in sleeping bag." The area was the West Lakes District.

Encounters with Black Bears

On July 12, 1935, a black bear "bit a person on the finger of the left hand" at Lake McDonald Lodge. Also on July 12, a black bear "tore a tent at Avalanche Campground." On July 13, 1935, a black bear caused a "superficial cut on left shoulder," and a second black bear caused a "slight abrasion on left wrist"—both near Lake McDonald Lodge.

Black bears continued their depredations in the Park. In June of 1948, on Going-to-the-Sun Road, black bears injured "2 people feeding chocolate to bears. Woman received scratch below eye, and man had a scratch on lip." In September of 1948, on Going-to-the-Sun Road, "3 visitors injured by [black] bears."

A Park naturalist was luckier in July of 1949, near Lake McDonald Lodge. "Chief Naturalist Beatty, conducting Naturalist Program, was approached by a [black] bear that chased him. There were no injuries."

A Glacier Park media release of June 28, 2000, reports on another attack by a black bear that injured a hiker:

> West Glacier, Montana—Glacier National Park rangers continue to search for the black bear that attacked and injured a hiker in the Two Medicine Valley on Monday, June 26, 2000. Because of the bear's aggressive behavior toward humans, it will be destroyed when located, in accordance with the guidelines of the park's Bear Management Plan.
>
> Jason Sansom, 24, of Malstrom Air Force Base in Great Falls, Montana, suffered puncture wounds to both arms after an unprovoked attack by a brown-colored black bear on the south shore trail of Two Medicine Lake on Monday afternoon. Sansom and his wife had been on a day hike when the incident occurred. His wife was not injured.

The information above relates to incidents involving unknown bear species and black bears. Since grizzly bears have fatally injured humans in Glacier Park, this question can be asked: Do black bears occasionally kill humans?

"Study of Black Bears Finds It's Not the Mamas that Should Be Feared the Most," according to the *New York Times* in May of 2011. " 'The kind of bear you need to be afraid of is not feeling threatened by you—it's testing you out as a possible prey item,' said Dr. [Stephen] Herrero, a professor emeritus at the University of Calgary. 'It's quiet. It stalks you just like a lion might stalk you.'"

The *Times* article further reports that "the black bears most likely to kill are not mothers protecting cubs. Most attacks, 88 percent, involved a bear on the prowl, likely hunting for food. And most of those predators, 92 percent, were male."[62]

These results are included in a research article, "Fatal Attacks by American Black Bear on People: 1900–2009." Published in the *Journal of Wildlife Management* (2011), lead author Stephen Herrero, along with four other bear experts, states that "Black bear numbers and their wide distribution lead to extensive contact with another widely distributed, numerically successful mammal—human beings."

The article continues:

> Most fatal attacks by black bear on people have been judged as predatory (Whitlock 1950; Herrero 1985; Herrero 2002; Herrero and Higgins 1995). Bears did not typically display physical or vocal defensive threat behaviors during predatory attacks (Herrero 1985, 2002; Herrero and Higgins 1995). Behavioral components such as stalking (i.e., searching); full-out attack typically using paws, claws, jaws, and teeth, consuming a person's flesh; and dragging, guarding, and burying a body support the classification of predation (Herrero and Higgins 2003) [p. 597] . . .
>
> Once predatory behavior is initiated, it may persist for hours unless it is deterred [p. 600] . . .
>
> A person should try to aggressively deter or fight off a potentially predatory bear using all possible deterrents, such as bear spray, loud noises, fists, firearms, rocks, knives, or clubs [p. 602].[63]

To summarize, Dr. Herrero indicates that in a non-predatory situation, with a mother bear defending its cubs, "you just back away calmly and give it some space. With a predatory bear, you stand your ground, stomp at it, throw rocks at it, whatever you need to do to convince it you're not easy prey."

For up-to-date information, see the Glacier Park website and the next chapter, "Safer Travel in Glacier Park Bear Country."

30

SAFER TRAVEL IN GLACIER PARK BEAR COUNTRY

Glacier Park personnel—including bear management specialists—are the most informed, experienced resource from whom to learn about safer travel in bear country. While it's important to note that your safety cannot be guaranteed, the Glacier Park website provides tips that will help you better prepare for your trip. You can watch the Glacier Park "Backcountry and Bear Safety" videos (https://www.nps.gov/glac/learn/photos multimedia/backcountry-and-bear-safety-accessible-videos.htm), which provide detailed information for safer travel in bear country, including both backcountry hiking and backcountry camping. The section titled "While in Camp" covers essential steps you can take at your campsite to help make your visit safer. You can watch these videos on the Glacier Park website, and also, when you arrive at the Park. There are both audio and captioned versions available.

When you reach the Park, check for information on campground status, trail closures, and bear activity in the areas where you plan to go. The following Glacier Park media release, "Bear Incidents Prompt Frequent Changes in Campground, Trail Status," dated July 22, 2019, demonstrates the constantly changing status of areas where you may want to go.

West Glacier, Montana—Park staff have had a busy summer responding to bears near campgrounds, trails, roadsides, and other developed areas.

Because of bears frequenting the area, the Hole in the Wall backcountry campground currently is closed temporarily, along with the small spur trail from the main Boulder Pass Trail to the campground.

The park has reopened Many Glacier Campground to tent camping after park rangers confirmed that no bear-related incidents have occurred in the area since July 14, when rangers last hazed [used repellent techniques to drive away] two bears. The campground was first restricted to hard-sided camping on July 6 after incidents involving a black bear that damaged property in the campground. At that time, patrols were increased; [although park rangers] attempted to trap and tag the suspected black bear, [they] were unsuccessful.

"These events demonstrate the critical role that campers play in wildlife conservation," said Park superintendent Jeff Mow. "While bears can wander or even live in developed areas, if we are diligent about keeping food rewards away from them, they can sometimes be relocated rather than euthanized."

Glacier National Park is home to both black and grizzly bears. Hikers are highly encouraged to hike in groups, make noise when hiking, and have bear spray accessible and know how to use it. Visitors are encouraged to check the park's Trail and Area Closings and Postings web page before heading into the park, and to learn more about bears and safety while recreating in bear country.

When you arrive at Glacier, consult a ranger about these issues; Park staff members will be glad to help you.

Glacier Park supervisory wildlife biologist John Waller gives information about safer travel in grizzly country on many platforms, including the Glacier Park website (nps.gov/glac/naturescience/bears.htm), where you can watch a video online. In addition, you can check out "Bear Safety with John Waller" (on Apple Podcast's "Safety Tips for Hikers" and www.facebook.com/GlacierNPS/posts/dr-john-waller-is-a-wildlife-biologist-with-expertise-in-bears-and-hes-going-to-/10155703499694912/).

For your information, the following is reproduced from the Glacier Park website, "Bear Safety—Glacier National Park (US National Park Service)," downloaded on October 28, 2019 (see www.nps.gov/glac/planyourvisit/bears.htm). The Glacier Park website information is the most authoritative and clearly stated, as well as the most frequently updated.

BEAR SAFETY

Bear Identification

Waterton-Glacier International Peace Park is home to both black and grizzly bears. Report any bear or unusual animal sightings to the nearest ranger or warden immediately. Size and/or color are not reliable indicators of species.

- Grizzly bears have a shoulder hump, dished face, rounded ears, and large white claws.
- Black bears have no hump, a straight, dog-like muzzle, pointed ears, and dark claws.

Read more about each species on the Bears informational page.

Keeping a Safe Distance

Approaching, viewing, or engaging in any activity within 100 yards (91.4 meters) of bears or wolves, or within 25 yards (23 meters) of any other wildlife, is prohibited. Use binoculars or a telephoto lens to improve your view. Keep the animal's line of travel or escape route clear, and move away if wildlife approaches you.

Never intentionally get close to a bear. Individual bears have their own personal space requirements, which vary depending on their mood. Each will react differently, and its behavior cannot be predicted. All bears are dangerous and should be respected equally.

Roadside Bears

It's exciting to see bears up close, but we must act responsibly to keep them wild and healthy. If you see a bear along the road, please do not stop near it. If you wish to view the bear, travel at least 100 yards (91.4 meters) and pull over in a safe location. Roadside bears quickly become habituated to traffic and people, increasing their chances of being hit by vehicles. Habituated bears may also learn to frequent campgrounds and picnic areas, where they may gain access to human food. To protect human life and property, bears that seek human food must be removed from the park. Resist the temptation to stop and get close to roadside bears—put bears first at Glacier.

Hiking in Bear Country

Hike in Groups

Hiking in groups significantly decreases your chances of having a bear encounter. There have not been any reported attacks on groups of four or more in Glacier. If you are a solo hiker looking for company, check the Ranger-Led Activity Guide for guided hikes.

Trail Running

While taking a jog or a run may be good exercise, joggers and runners run the risk of surprising a bear on the trail. Trail running is highly discouraged.

Carry Bear Spray

Bear spray is an inexpensive way to deter bear attacks and has been shown to be the most effective deterrent. Be sure you know how to use it and that you are carrying it in an accessible place. Check the Ranger-Led Activity Guide for summer demonstrations.

Make Noise

Bears will usually move out of the way if they hear people approaching. Most bear bells are not enough. Calling out and clapping at regular intervals are better ways to make your presence known. Do your best to never surprise a bear.

Secure Your Food and Garbage

Never leave food, garbage, or anything used to prepare, consume, store, or transport food unattended. Store all food and odorous items safely. Other scented items include: toiletries, feminine products, sunscreen, etc.

Be Aware of Your Surroundings

Some trail or environmental conditions make it hard for bears to see, hear, or smell approaching hikers. Be particularly careful by streams, against the wind, or in dense vegetation. A blind corner or a rise in the trail also requires special attention. Look for scat and tracks. Bears spend a lot of time eating, so be extra alert hiking in obvious feeding areas like berry patches, cow parsnip thickets, or fields of glacier lilies. Keep children close by. Avoid hiking early in the morning, late in the day, or after dark.

While in Camp

Our campgrounds and developed areas can remain unattractive to bears if each visitor manages food and trash properly. Following park regulations will help keep the "wild" in wildlife, and ensure your safety as well.

- Keep a clean camp! Never improperly store or leave food unattended.
- All edibles, food containers (empty or not), cookware (clean or not), and trash (including feminine hygiene products) must be stored in a food locker or hung when not in use, day or night.
- Do not throw any food or garbage into the pit toilets.
- Inspect your campsite for bear sign and for careless campers nearby. Notify a park ranger of any potential problems.

Bear Encounters

If you encounter a bear inside the minimum recommended safe distance (100 yards / 91.4 meters), you can decrease your risk by following these guidelines:

- If a bear or other animal is moving in your direction on a trail, get out of its way and let it pass.
- If you can move away, do so. If moving away appears to agitate the bear, stop. In general, bears show agitation by swaying their heads, huffing, and clacking their teeth. Lowered head and laid-back ears also indicate aggression. Bears may stand on their hind legs or approach to get a better view, but these actions are not necessarily signs of aggression. The bear may not have identified you as a person and is unable to smell or hear you from a distance. Help the bear recognize you as a friendly human.
- Talk quietly.

- Do not run! Back away slowly, but stop if it seems to agitate the bear.
- Try to assume a nonthreatening posture. Turn sideways, or bend at the knees to appear smaller.
- Use peripheral vision. Bears may interpret direct eye contact as threatening.
- Continue to move away as the situation allows.

- If a bear appears intent on approaching you, your group, or your campsite in a non-defensive manner (not showing signs of agitation), gather your group together, make noise, and try to discourage the bear from further approaching. Prepare to deploy your bear spray. If you are preparing or consuming food, secure it. *Do not let the bear get your food!*
- If a bear approaches in a defensive manner (appears agitated and/ or charges), stop. Do not run. Talk quietly to the bear. Prepare to deploy your bear spray. If contact appears imminent and you do not have bear spray, protect your chest and abdomen by falling to the ground on your stomach, clasp your hands around the back of your neck, and leave your pack on for protection. If the bear attempts to roll you over, try to stay on your stomach. If the attack is defensive, the bear will leave once it recognizes you are not a threat. If the attack is prolonged, *fight back!*

For more detailed information, watch our Bear Safety video.

Bear Spray

This aerosol pepper spray temporarily incapacitates bears. It is an effective, nontoxic, and nonlethal means of deterring aggressive bears. Under no circumstances should bear spray create a false sense of security or serve as a substitute for practicing standard safety precautions in bear country.

Bear spray is intended to be sprayed into the face of an oncoming bear. Factors influencing effectiveness include distance, wind, rainy weather, temperature extremes, and product shelf life. It is not intended to act as a repellent. Do not spray gear or your camp with bear spray. Pre-sprayed objects may actually attract bears.

Be aware that you may not be able to cross the US–Canada border with some brands of bear spray. Canadian Customs will allow the importation of USEPA-approved bear spray into Canada. Specifications state that the bear spray must have USEPA on the label.

AFTERWORD

When spring comes again to Glacier National Park, the glaciers begin to melt. All beings strive for life, including people and bears. Every bear and every person has a story, which needs to be respected.

We have not forgotten Julie Helgeson and Michele Koons, who died that night in 1967. We honor their loved ones, family, and friends. We also have not forgotten Glacier Park's other known bear-caused fatalities: Mary Pat Mahoney, Jane Ammerman, Kim Eberly, Larry Gordon, Chuck Gibbs, Gary Goeden, John Petranyi, Craig Dahl, and Brad Treat.

We remember those who were injured but survived in the struggle of people and bears to coexist. We remember that bears are mortal too.

Montana Public Radio reported on November 21, 2018, that the year 2018 was the "deadliest year on record for Montana bears since scientists started keeping track. . . . [There were] 51 [now 52] known and probable documented mortalities of grizzly bears in the NCDE [Northern Continental Divide Ecosystem], the huge swath of land in and around Glacier NationalPark."[64] In addition to mortality due to age, injuries, and disease, grizzlies are euthanized for property damage, livestock predation, injuries to humans, and being habituated to humans. Grizzlies also die when hit by vehicles and trains, and in occasional accidents involving grizzly research projects and management operations such as relocation.

Each of us in the public can decide whether to do nothing, to do something to better safeguard people, and/or to preserve the grizzlies of Glacier Park. We can also educate ourselves on these issues, and practice, embody, and show others the Glacier Park guidelines for safer travel in bear country.

When thinking about preservation in general, consider this: "If we take a step back from wherever we sit at this moment in time, we see the Blackfeet and the Kootenais at the edges of Glacier National Park," concludes the book, *People Before the Park.* "But Glacier National Park, like the tribal homelands surrounding it, is also a remnant."[65] A remnant is defined as what remains behind. A Glacier Park media release from April 2019 makes this point: "Glacier National Park was named for the glaciers that carved, sculpted, and formed this landscape millions of years ago. Despite the recession of current glaciers, the Park's name will not change when the glaciers are gone." Meanwhile, visitation numbers to Glacier Park are projected to grow. An article in the June 23, 2019, edition of *Hungry Horse News* makes the point: "Wind, rain, dense fog in spots, and bumper-to-bumper traffic. That's what it was like as the full length of the Going-to-the-Sun Road opened Sunday morning about 6 a.m."[66] At the same time, Glacier Park rangers are busier than ever. Rangers have experienced a 25 percent increase in calls for service to visitors in 2019, over 2018.

"Statistics shared by Glacier National Park for one week in July show they responded to about 100 calls for service each day," the *Missoulian* reports on September 1, 2019, "or 703 total in one week alone." Much of Glacier Park is out of cell-phone range, but " 'If you call 9-1-1 in the Park, you will get a ranger,' says Micah Alley, the ranger operations coordinator for the Park. Rangers retrieve locked keys in vehicles. They help change flat tires. Stranded at a trailhead? They'll get you back to your vehicle. They'll ticket you for leaving food or campsites unattended. They'll adjudicate disputes over parking spots. They'll race into the wild country to search for lost hikers. They'll recover drowning victims, which is one of the leading causes of death in the park. They'll arrest protagonists in domestic violence encounters. They'll haze bears. They'll carry people out of the backcountry on litters. They'll go in search of human-habituated grizzlies."[67]

People from all over the world come to Glacier National Park to experience and enjoy the wildlife and natural beauty. This affection may help to preserve Glacier Park long after the glaciers are gone.

Are grizzly bears a remnant?

"I want to at least hope that when the clock ticks into the next millennium," writes Montana author Roland Cheek, "that the children's children of my children can still find an occasional grizzly bear in Glacier."[68]

Can people and bears coexist?

In Glacier Park, as the arc of the year turns from spring to summer, fall to winter, the question remains.

NOTES

Chapter 1: Finding Julie

1. Becky Lomax, *Glacier National Park Moon Handbook*, 5th ed., New York: Carroll & Graf / Avalon Travel Publishing, 2009.

Chapter 2: Finding Michele

2. "Encounter Bear at Trout Lake," *Hungry Horse News*, Kalispell, Montana, August 4, 1967.
3. Kerry A. Gunther, "Bears and Menstruating Women," Yell 707, Information Paper BMO-7, Yellowstone National Park, Wyoming, May 2002.

Chapter 3: Finding Mary Pat

4. G. George Ostrom, "Where the Girl Died," *Hungry Horse News*, Kalispell, Montana, September 29, 1976, copy included in Glacier Park record.
5. Ibid.

Chapter 4: Finding Jane and Kim

6. Mary Roberts Rinehart, *Through Glacier Park in 1915*, Boulder, CO: Roberts Rinehart Inc., 1916, 1983, pp. 77, 79, 82.
7. Michael Robbins, "Death in the Wild," *Rocky Mountain* magazine (January–February 1981).

Chapter 5: Finding Larry

8. Blake Passmore, with Scott Burry and John VanArendonk, *Climb Glacier National Park*, vol. 3, Kalispell, MT: Montana Outdoor Guidebooks, 2012, p. 82.
9. Jack Holterman, *Place Names of Glacier National Park*, 3rd ed., Helena, MT: Riverbend Publishing, 2006, p. 80.

Chapter 7: Finding Gary

10. Erik Molvar, *Hiking Glacier and Waterton Lakes National Parks*, 3rd ed., Guilford, CT: FalconGuides, 2007, 2012, p. 18.
11. Ibid., p. 156.

Chapter 9: Finding Craig

12. Alan Leftridge, *Glacier Day Hikes,* Helena, MT: Farcountry Press, 2003, pp. 26–27.
13. Ibid., p. 124.

Chapter 10: Finding Brad

14. Rob Chaney, "Bears vs. Bikes: Who's at Risk?," *Missoulian*, Missoula, Montana, July 12, 2016, https://missoulian.com/news/local/bears-vs-bikes-who-s-at-risk/article_86555c7b-8b4e-5829-bcf0-320b666bdc0d.html.
15. Jim Robbins, "Bears versus Bikes," *New York Times*, October 8, 2019.

Chapter 11: Finding Johan and Jenna

16. Johan Otter, *A Grizzly Tale: A Father and Daughter Survival Story*, Oceanside, CA: Indie Books International, 2016, p. 80.
17. Ibid., p. 138.

Chapter 12: Finding Kathryn and Kelsy

18. Molvar, *Hiking Glacier and Waterton Lakes*, pp. 141–42.

Chapter 13: Finding Jim

19. Jim Cole, with Tim Vandehey, *Blindsided: Surviving a Grizzly Attack and Still Loving the Great Bear*, New York: St. Martin's Press, 2010, p. 19.
20. Kathleen Snow, *Taken by Bear in Yellowstone*, Guilford, CT: Lyons Press, 2016, p. 208.
21. Ibid., p. 213
22. Ibid., pp. 210–14.

Chapter 14: Finding Frances and Rob

23. Frances Lordan as told to Brian Kennedy, "Horrible to Watch Animal Eat You Alive: California Couple Recalls Moments of Grizzly Terror," *Hungry Horse News*, Kalispell, Montana, September 13, 1984, pp. 1, 8.

Chapter 15: Finding Roscoe and Teresa

24. Holterman, *Place Names of Glacier National Park.*

Chapter 16: Finding William

25. Leftridge, *Glacier Day Hikes*, p. 115.
26. Molvar, *Hiking Glacier and Waterton Lakes*, pp. 41–42.

Chapter 18: Finding a Family of Four

27. Carolyn Duckworth, ed., *Hiker's Guide to Glacier National Park*, West Glacier, MT: Glacier Natural History Association, 1978, 1996, pp. 40–41.
28. Bob Frauson and David Casteel, as told to Sherry Devlin, "Montana Life," *Missoulian*, Missoula, Montana, September 16, 1990, p. E-1.
29. Sherry Devlin, "Tales of the Grizzly," *Missoulian*, Missoula, Montana, August 21, 2014.
30. George C. Ruhle, *The Ruhle Handbook: Roads and Trails of Waterton-Glacier National Parks*, Minneapolis, MN: John W. Forney, 1976, pp. 123–24.

Chapter 19: Finding Gordon

31. "Remembering J. Gordon Edwards," *The Inside Trail: Voice of the Glacier Park Foundation*, Winter 2005, vol. 19, no. 1, Minneapolis, Minnesota.

Chapter 21: Finding Five (Including a Ten-Year-Old)

32. Duckworth, ed., *Hiker's Guide to Glacier National Park*, p. 77.
33. Alan Nelson, "In Glacier—Naturalist Tells of Bear Attack," United Press International, reproduced in *Daily Inter Lake*, July 20, 1960, p. 2.
34. Albert Ruffin, "Attacked by a Grizzly Bear: The Ordeal of a Boy All But Eaten Alive," *Life* magazine, August 27, 1965, pp. 74–82.

Chapter 22: Finding Joe

35. John Muir in *Steep Trails*, quoted in Enos A. Mills, *The Grizzly: Our Greatest Wild Animal*, New York: Ballantine Books, Inc., 1919, 1973, p. 116.
36. Mills, *The Grizzly: Our Greatest Wild Animal*, p. 46.
37. "A Grizzly Ate My Brother," Kos Media, DailyKos.com, www.dailykos.com/stories/2009/06/20/745033/-A-Grizzly-Ate-My-Brother-Perseverance-in-Tough-Times (posted by Joe Williams's sister, as Kiwiheart, June 20, 2009).
38. Susan Gallagher, "Survivor of '59 Glacier Grizzly Attack to Reunite with His Rescuer," Associated Press, June 16, 2009.

Chapter 23: Finding Toby

39. "Ike Issues Urgent Appeal to Restore Aid Fund Cuts," *Daily Inter Lake*, Kalispell, Montana, June 12, 1956, p. 1.

Chapter 25: Finding Slim

40. C. J. Martinka, Paper 13, "Ecological Role and Management of Grizzly Bears in Glacier National Park, Montana." Published at the Third International Conference on Bears—Their Biology and Management, June, 1974. Binghamton, New York, USA, and Moscow, USSR. International Union for Conservation of Nature and Natural Resources, Morges, Switzerland, 1976.
41. Vernon Bailey, quoted by Warren L. Hanna in *The Grizzlies of Glacier*, Missoula, MT: Mountain Press Publishing Company, 1978, pp. 3–4.
42. James Willard Schultz, *William Jackson, Indian Scout*, reprinted in 1976 by William K. Cavanagh, First National Bank Building, Springfield, Illinois 62701, pp. 13–18.

Chapter 26: Major and Minor Injuries in Brief by Grizzly, Black, and Unidentified Bears

43. Nicky Gullet, "51 Grizzly Mortalities, Deadliest Year on Record for Montana Bears," Montana Public Radio, report quoted in the *Missoulian* on February 24, 2019.
44. "Two Attacked by Griz a Year Ago," *Hungry Horse News*, Columbia Falls, Montana, October 15, 1992.

Chapter 27: Recent Maulings, 2009–2019

45. Tom Nerison as told to Jim Mann, "I Hit Grizzly in the Face," *Daily Inter Lake*, Kalispell, Montana, June 10, 2009.
46. "Grizzly Mauls Hiker," *Missoulian*, Missoula, Montana, August 8, 2011.
47. Denise Germann, "Grizzly Mauls Hiker," *HuffPost Green*, 2012.
48. Vince Devlin, "Surprised Grizzly Shakes Hiker," *Missoulian*, Missoula, Montana, October 1, 2015.
49. Karin Brulliard, "The True Story of Two Fatal Grizzly Bear Attacks," *Washington Post*, August 3, 2017.
50. "Grizzly Bears Approaching People," Associated Press, quoted in the *Flathead Beacon*, Kalispell, Montana, June 23, 2017.
51. Matt Volz, "Bear Researcher Attacked by Grizzly to Stay on Career Path," the Associated Press, quoted in the *Spokesman Review*, Spokane, Washington, June 21, 2018.

Chapter 28: Still Missing and Presumed Dead

52. Tristan Scott, "Bones, Clothing May Belong to Missing Glacier Park Hiker," *Missoulian*, August 2, 2011, p. B6.

53. "Missing Without a Trace," *Daily Inter Lake*, Montana, dailyinterlake.com/archive/article, May 3, 2010.

54. Tristan Scott, "Lost, Never Found," *Flathead Beacon*, Montana, August 6, 2014.

55. "Missing Without a Trace."

56. Ibid.

57. *The Inside Trail* newsletter, Glacier Park Foundation, Winter 1998.

58. "The Charley Project" (a missing persons clearinghouse), charleyproject.org/case/patrick-terrence-whalen, October 12, 2016.

59. "Search Crews Comb Glacier Park for Missing Michigan Man," Associated Press, July 1, 2003.

60. Scott, "Lost, Never Found."

61. "Trail Still Cold in Search for Missing Man in Glacier National Park," Associated Press, July 16, 2019.

Chapter 29: What About the Black Bears?

62. Pam Belluck, "Study of Black Bears Finds It's Not the Mamas that Should Be Feared the Most," *New York Times*, May 11, 2011.

63. Stephen Herrero, Andrew Higgins, James E. Cardoza, Laura I. Hajduk, Tom S. Smith, "Fatal Attacks by American Black Bear on People: 1900–2009." *Journal of Wildlife Management* 75(3): 596–603; 2011; DOI: 10.1002/jwmg.72, pp. 597, 600, 602.

Afterword

64. "51 Grizzly Mortalities," Montana Public Radio, www.mtpr.org/post/51-grizzly-mortalities-deadliest-year-record-montana-bears.

65. Sally Thompson, Kootenai Culture Committee, and Pikunni Traditional Association, *People Before the Park: The Kootenai and Blackfeet before Glacier National Park*, Helena, MT: Montana Historical Society Press, 2015, p. 203.

66. Chris Peterson, "Sun Road Opens to Rain, Fog and Traffic," *Hungry Horse News*, Columbia Falls, Montana, June 23, 2019.

67. Eve Byron, "Calls for Service Keep Glacier Rangers Busy," *Missoulian*, Missoula, Montana, September 1, 2019, pp. A1 and A6.

68. Roland Cheek, *Chocolate Legs: Sweet Mother, Savage Killer?* Columbia Falls, MT: Skyline Publishing, 2001, p. 292.

BIBLIOGRAPHY

Glacier National Park

Ashley, John. Photographs and essays by John Ashley. *Glacier National Park After Dark: Sunset to Sunrise in a Beloved Montana Wilderness.* Helena, MT: Sweetgrass Books, 2015.

Beaumont, Greg. *Many-Storied Mountains: The Life of Glacier National Park.* Washington, DC: Natural History Series, Division of Publications, National Park Service, 1978.

Brooks, Tad, and Sherry Jones. *The Hiker's Guide to Montana's Continental Divide Trail.* Helena, MT, and Billings, MT: Falcon Press Publishing Co., 1990.

Byron, Eve. "Calls for Service Keep Glacier Rangers Busy," *Missoulian*, Missoula, Montana, September 1, 2019.

Cheek, Roland. *Chocolate Legs: Sweet Mother, Savage Killer?* Columbia Falls, MT: Skyline Publishing, 2001.

Duckworth, Carolyn, ed. *Hiker's Guide to Glacier National Park.* West Glacier, MT: Glacier Natural History Association, 1978, 1996.

Guthrie, C. W., and Dan and Ann Fagre. *Death and Survival in Glacier National Park: True Tales of Tragedy, Courage and Misadventure.* Helena, MT: Farcountry Press, 2017.

Hanna, Warren L. *The Grizzlies of Glacier.* Missoula, MT: Mountain Press Publishing Company, 1978.

Holterman, Jack. *Place Names of Glacier National Park*, 3rd ed. Helena, MT: Riverbend Publishing, 2006.

Kimball, Shannon Fitzpatrick, and Peter Lesica. *Wildflowers of Glacier National Park and Surrounding Areas.* Kalispell, MT: Trillium Press, 2005.

Leftridge, Alan. *Glacier Day Hikes*, 3rd ed. (now with GPS-compatible maps). Helena, MT: Farcountry Press, 2003.

Lomax, Becky. *Glacier National Park Moon Handbook*, 5th ed., New York: Carroll & Graf / Avalon Travel Publishing, 2009.

Martinka, C. J. Paper 13, "Ecological Role and Management of Grizzly Bears in Glacier National Park, Montana." Published at the Third International Conference on Bears—Their Biology and Management, June, 1974. Binghamton, New York, USA, and Moscow, USSR. International Union for Conservation of Nature and Natural Resources, Morges, Switzerland, 1976.

McCloskey, Erin. *Bear Attacks in Canada.* Edmonton, Alberta, Canada: Lone Pine Publishing, 2008.

Minetor, Randi. *Death in Glacier National Park: Stories of Accidents and Foolhardiness in the Crown of the Continent*. Guilford, CT: Lyons Press, 2016.

Molvar, Erik. *Best Easy Day Hikes: Glacier and Waterton Lakes National Parks* (Falcon-Guides), 2nd ed. Guilford, CT: Globe Pequot Press, 2007.

———. *Hiking Glacier and Waterton Lakes National Parks* (FalconGuides). Guilford, CT and Helena MT: Globe Pequot Press, 2007, 2012.

Moylan, Bridget E. *Glacier's Grandest: A Pictorial History of the Hotels and Chalets of Glacier National Park*. Missoula, MT: Pictorial Histories Publishing Company, Inc., 1995.

Olsen, Jack. *Night of the Grizzlies*. New York: G. P. Putnam and Sons, 1969.

On, Danny (photographs), and David Sumner (text). *Along the Trail: A Photographic Essay of Glacier National Park and the Northern Rocky Mountains*. Kansas City, MO: Glacier Natural History Association, Inc., in cooperation with The Lowell Press, 1979.

Ostrom, G. George, with the Over-the-Hill Gang. *Glacier's Secrets: Beyond the Roads and Above the Clouds*. Helena, MT: American & World Geographic Publishing, 1997.

Otter, Johan. *A Grizzly Tale: A Father and Daughter Survival Story*. Oceanside, CA: Indie Books International, 2016.

Passmore, Blake, with Scott Burry and John VanArendonk. *Climb Glacier National Park*, Vols. 1, 2, and 3. Kalispell, MT: Montana Outdoor Guidebooks LLC, 2012.

Peterson, Chris. "Sun Road Opens to Rain, Fog and Traffic," *Hungry Horse News*, Columbia Falls, Montana, June 23, 2019.

Reiner, Ralph E. *Introducing the Flowering Beauty of Glacier National Park and the Majestic High Rockies*. West Glacier, MT: Glacier Park, Inc. 1969.

"Remembering J. Gordon Edwards." *The Inside Trail: Voice of the Glacier Park Foundation*, Winter 2005, vol. 19, no. 1, Minneapolis, Minnesota.

Rinehart, Mary Roberts. *Through Glacier Park in 1915*. Boulder, CO: Roberts Rinehart, Inc., 1916, 1983.

Rubbert, Tim. *Hiking with Grizzlies: Lessons Learned*. Helena, MT: Riverbend Publishing, 2006.

Ruhle, George C. *Guide to Glacier National Park: Approved by National Park Service*. Minneapolis, MN: John W. Forney Publisher, 1963.

———. *The Ruhle Handbook: Roads and Trails of Waterton-Glacier National Parks*. Minneapolis, MN: John W. Forney Publisher, 1976.

Thompson, Sally, Kootenai Culture Committee, and Pikunni Traditional Association. *People Before the Park: The Kootenai and Blackfeet before Glacier Park*. Helena, MT: Montana Historical Society Press, 2015.

Urbigkit, Cat. *When Man Becomes Prey: Fatal Encounters with North America's Most Feared Predators*. Guilford, CT: Lyons Press, 2014.

Bears

"Animals." vol. 8, no. 2, *Parabola, Myth and the Quest for Meaning*, 2nd ed. New York: The Society for the Study of Myth and Tradition, 1989.

Auerbach, Paul S. *Wilderness Medicine: Management of Wilderness and Environmental Emergencies*, St. Louis, MO: C. V. Mosby Company, 1995, 2001.

Baron, David. *The Beast in the Garden: A Modern Parable of Man and Nature.* New York: W. W. Norton, 2004.

Bears: Their Biology and Management. "Abstracts." Ninth International Conference on Bear Research and Management, February 1992, Missoula, Montana. International Association for Bear Research and Management, IBA Publications, c/o Terry D. White, Southern Appalachian Field Laboratory, 274 Ellington Hall, University of Tennessee, Knoxville, TN 37996, USA. 1994.

Bears: Their Biology and Management—A Selection of Papers. Eighth International Conference on Bear Research and Management, February 1989, Victoria, British Columbia. International Association for Bear Research and Management, IBA Publications, c/o Terry D. White, Southern Appalachian Field Laboratory, 274 Ellington Hall, University of Tennessee, Knoxville, TN 37996, USA. 1990.

Belluck, Pam. "Study of Black Bears Finds It's Not the Mamas that Should Be Feared the Most," *New York Times*, May 11, 2011.

Berger, Joel. *The Better to Eat You With: Fear in the Animal World.* Chicago: The University of Chicago Press, 2008.

Blanchard, Bonnie M. *Field Techniques Used in the Study of Grizzly Bears.* Bozeman, MT: Interagency Grizzly Bear Study Team, Forestry Sciences Lab, Montana State University, 1985.

Brown, Gary. *Safe Travel in Bear Country.* New York: Lyons and Burford Publishers, 1996.

Brulliard, Karin. "The True Story of Two Fatal Grizzly Bear Attacks," *Washington Post*, August 3, 2017.

Busch, Robert H. *The Grizzly Almanac.* New York: Lyons Press, 2000.

Calabro, Marian. *Operation Grizzly Bear.* New York: Four Winds Press / Macmillan, 1989.

Caputo, Philip. *In the Shadows of the Morning: Essays on Wild Lands, Wild Waters, and a Few Untamed People.* Guilford, CT: Lyons Press, 2002.

Caras, Roger. *Roger Caras' Treasury of Classic Nature Tales.* New York: Truman Talley Books / Dutton, 1992.

Carey, Alan. *In the Path of the Grizzly.* Flagstaff, AZ: Northland Publishing, 1986.

Chadwick, Douglas H. *True Grizz: Glimpses of Fernie, Stahr, Easy, Dakota, and Other Real Bears in the Modern World.* San Francisco: Sierra Club Books, 2003.

Chaney, Rob. "Bears vs. Bikes: Who's at Risk?," *Missoulian*, Missoula, Montana, July 12, 2016, https://missoulian.com/news/local/bears-vs-bikes-who-s-at-risk/article_86555c7b-8b4e-5829-bcf0-320b666bdc0d.html.

"The Charley Project" (a missing persons clearinghouse), charleyproject.org/case/patrick-terrence-whalen, October 12, 2016.

Cheek, Roland. *Chocolate Legs: Sweet Mother, Savage Killer?* Columbia Falls, MT: Skyline Publishing, 2001.

———. *Learning to Talk Bear, So Bears Can Listen.* Columbia Falls, MT: Skyline Publishing, 1997.

Clark, Ella E. *Indian Legends from the Northern Rockies.* Norman: University of Oklahoma Press, 1966.

Clarke, James. *Man Is the Prey.* New York: Stein and Day Publishers, 1969.

Cole, Jim. *Lives of Grizzlies: Montana and Wyoming.* Helena, MT: Farcountry Press, 2004.

Cole, Jim, with Tim Vandehey. *Blindsided: Surviving a Grizzly Attack and Still Loving the Great Bear.* New York: St. Martin's Press, 2010.

Craighead, Frank C., Jr. *For Everything There Is a Season: The Sequence of Natural Events in the Grand Teton–Yellowstone Area.* Helena, MT: Falcon Press, 1994.

———. *Track of the Grizzly.* San Francisco: Sierra Club Books, 1979, 1982.

Craighead, Frank C., Jr. and John J. Craighead. *Grizzly Bear Prehibernation and Denning Activities as Determined by Radiotracking.* Wildlife Monographs series, Louis A. Krumholz, ed. Louisville, KY: The Wildlife Society, Inc. / University of Louisville, 1972.

Craighead, John J., Jay S. Sumner, and John A. Mitchell. *The Grizzly Bears of Yellowstone: Their Ecology in the Yellowstone Ecosystem, 1959–1992.* Washington, DC: Island Press, 1995.

Craighead, John J., Jay S. Sumner, and G. B. Scaggs. *A Definitive System for Analysis of Grizzly Bear Habitat and Other Wilderness Resources.* Pittsburgh, PA: The Richard King Mellon Foundation, 1982.

———. *A Definitive System for Analysis of Grizzly Bear Habitat and Other Wilderness Resources, Utilizing LANDSAT Multispectral Imagery and Computer Technology.* Wildlife-Wildlands Institute Monograph No. 1. Missoula, MT: U of M Foundation / University of Montana, 1982.

Cramond, Mike. *Killer Bears.* New York: Outdoor Life Books / Scribner's, 1981.

———. *Of Bears and Man.* Norman: University of Oklahoma Press, 1986.

Debruyn, Terry D. *Walking with Bears.* New York: Lyons Press, 1999.

Devlin, Sherry. "Tales of the Grizzly," *Missoulian,* Missoula, Montana, August 21, 2014.

Devlin, Vince. "Surprised Grizzly Shakes Hiker," *Missoulian,* Missoula, Montana, October 1, 2015.

East, Ben. *Bears: A Veteran Outdoorsman's Account of the Most Fascinating and Dangerous Animals in North America.* New York: Outdoor Life / Crown, 1977.

———. *Outdoor Life, Narrow Escapes and Wilderness Adventures.* Outdoor Life / E. P. Dutton & Co., 1960.

———. *Survival: 23 True Sportsmen's Adventures.* New York: Outdoor Life Book / E. P. Dutton & Co., 1967.

"Encounter Bear at Trout Lake," *Hungry Horse News,* Kalispell, Montana, August 4, 1967.

Etling, Kathy. *Bear Attacks: Classic Tales of Dangerous North American Bears.* 2 vols. Long Beach, CA: Safari Press, Inc., 1997.

"51 Grizzly Mortalities," Montana Public Radio, www.mtpr.org/post/51-grizzly -mortalities-deadliest-year-record-montana-bears.

Fish, Chet, ed. *The Outdoor Life Bear Book.* New York: Outdoor Life Books / Times Mirror Magazines, Inc., 1983.

Fletcher, David. *Hunted: A True Story of Survival*. New York: Carroll & Graf / Avalon Publishing Group, Inc., 2003.

Ford, Barbara. *Black Bear: Spirit of the Wilderness*. Boston: Houghton Mifflin Co., 1981.

Frauson, Bob, and David Casteel, as told to Sherry Devlin. "Montana Life," *Missoulian*, Missoula, Montana, September 16, 1990.

French, Dr. Steven P. "Bear Attacks," in "Wild and Domestic Animal Attacks," *The Management of Wilderness and Environmental Emergencies*, 3rd ed. St. Louis, MO: The C. V. Mosby Company, 1994.

Gallagher, Susan. "Survivor of '59 Glacier Grizzly Attack to Reunite with His Rescuer," Associated Press, June 16, 2009.

Garfield, Brad. *Bear vs. Man: Recent Attacks and How to Avoid the Increasing Danger*. Minocqua, WI: Willow Creek Press, 2001.

Germann, Denise. "Grizzly Mauls Hiker," *HuffPost Green*, 2012.

Gilchrist, Duncan. *All About Bears*. Hamilton, MT: Outdoor Expeditions and Books, 1989.

Godlovitch, Stanley, Rosalind Godlovitch, and John Harris, eds. *Animals, Men and Morals: An Enquiry into the Maltreatment of Non-Humans*. New York: Grove Press, 1971.

Grandin, Temple, and Catherine Johnson. *Animals in Translation*. New York: Harcourt, Inc., 2005.

"A Grizzly Ate My Brother" (posted by Joe Williams's sister, as Kiwiheart), Kos Media, DailyKos.com, www.dailykos.com/stories/2009/06/20/745033/-A-Grizzly-Ate -My-Brother-Perseverance-in-Tough-Times, June 20, 2009.

"Grizzly Bears Approaching People," Associated Press, quoted in the *Flathead Beacon*, Kalispell, Montana, June 23, 2017.

"Grizzly Mauls Hiker," *Missoulian*, Missoula, Montana, August 8, 2011.

Gullet, Nicky. "51 Grizzly Mortalities: Deadliest Year on Record for Montana Bears," Montana Public Radio, report quoted in the *Missoulian*, February 24, 2019.

Gunther, Kerry A. "Bears and Menstruating Women," Yell 707, Information Paper BMO-7, Yellowstone National Park, Wyoming, May 2002.

Hart, Donna, and Robert W. Sussman. *Man the Hunted: Primates, Predators, and Human Evolution*. New York: Westview Press, 2005.

Haynes, Bessie Doak, and Edgar Haynes, eds. *The Grizzly Bear: Portraits from Life*. Norman: University of Oklahoma Press, 1966.

Herrero, Stephen. *Bear Attacks: Their Causes and Avoidance*. Piscataway, NJ: Nick Lyons Books / Winchester Press, an imprint of New Century Publishers, Inc., 1985.

———. *Bear Attacks: Their Causes and Avoidance*. 2nd rev. ed. Guilford, CT: Lyons Press, 2002.

Herrero, Stephen, Andrew Higgins, James E. Cardoza, Laura I. Hajduk, and Tom S. Smith. "Fatal Attacks by American Black Bear on People: 1900–2009," *Journal of Wildlife Management* 75(3): 596–603; 2011; DOI: 10.1002/jwmg.72.

Hoshino, Michio. *Grizzly*. San Francisco: Chronicle Books, 1987.

———. Karen Colligan-Taylor, trans. *The Grizzly Bear Family Book*. London: Picture Book Studio Ltd., 1993.

Houston, Pam, ed. *Women on Hunting*. New York: Ecco Press / Penguin Putnam, 1995.

"Ike Issues Urgent Appeal to Restore Aid Fund Cuts," *Daily Inter Lake*, Kalispell, Montana, June 12, 1956.

The Inside Trail: Voice of the Glacier Park Foundation, Winter 1998.

Jenkins, Ken L. *Grizzly Reflections*. Reflections of the Wilderness Series. Merrillville, IN: ICS Books, Inc., 1995.

Jonkel, Charles. *How to Live in Bear Country*. Missoula, MT: Ursid Research Center, n. d.

Kerasote, Ted. *Bloodties: Nature, Culture, and the Hunt*. New York: Random House, 1995.

Knibb, David G. *Grizzly Wars: The Public Fight over the Great Bear*. Cheney: Eastern Washington University Press, 2008.

Lapinski, Mike. *Self Defense for Nature Lovers: Handling Dangerous Situations with Wild Critters*. Stevensville, MT: Stoneydale Press Publishing Co., 1998.

———. *True Stories of Bear Attacks: Who Survived and Why*. Portland, OR: Westwinds Press / Graphic Arts Center Publishing Co., 2004.

Laycock, George. *Wilderness Legend: Grizzly*. Minocqua, WI: NorthWord Press, Inc., 1997.

Long, Ben. *Great Montana Bear Stories*. Helena, MT: Riverbend Publishing, 2002.

Long, John, ed. *Attacked! By Beasts of Prey and other Deadly Creatures: True Stories of Survivors*. Camden, ME: Ragged Mountain Press / McGraw-Hill Companies, 1998.

Lordan, Frances, as told to Brian Kennedy. "Horrible to Watch Animal Eat You Alive: California Couple Recalls Moments of Grizzly Terror," *Hungry Horse News*, Kalispell, Montana, September 13, 1984.

McMillion, Scott. *Mark of the Grizzly*. Helena, MT: Falcon Publishing, 1998.

McNamee, Thomas. *The Grizzly Bear*. New York, Knopf, 1984.

Mills, Enos A. *The Grizzly: Our Greatest Wild Animal*. New York: Ballantine Books, Inc., 1919, 1973.

"Missing Without a Trace," *Daily Inter Lake*, Montana, dailyinterlake.com/archive/ article, May 3, 2010.

Murphy, Bob. *Bears I Have Known: A Park Ranger's True Tales from Yellowstone and Glacier National Parks*. Helena, MT: Riverbend Publishing, 2006.

Neal, Chuck. *Grizzlies in the Mist*. Moose, WY: Homestead Publishing, 2003.

Nelson, Alan. "In Glacier—Naturalist Tells of Bear Attack," United Press International, reproduced in *Daily Inter Lake*, July 20, 1960.

Nelson, Jim. *Bear Encounters: Tales from the Wild*. Auburn, WA: Lone Pine Publishing, 2005.

Nerison, Tom, as told to Jim Mann. "I Hit Grizzly in the Face," *Daily Inter Lake*, Kalispell, Montana, June 10, 2009.

Olsen, Lance. *Great Bear Foundation Field Guide to the Grizzly Bear*. Seattle, WA: Sasquatch Books, 1992.

Ormond, Clyde. *Bear! Black, Grizzly, Brown, Polar*. Harrisburg, PA: The Stackpole Company, 1961.

Ostrom, G. George. "Where the Girl Died," *Hungry Horse News*, Kalispell, Montana, September 29, 1976.

Patent, Dorothy Hinshaw. *The Way of the Grizzly*. New York: Clarion Books, 1986.

Peacock, Doug. *Grizzly Years: In Search of the American Wilderness*. New York: Henry Holt & Co., 1990.

Peacock, Doug, and Andrea Peacock. *The Essential Grizzly: The Mingled Fates of Men and Bears*. Guilford, CT: Lyons Press, 2006.

Preston-Mafham, Ken. *Practical Wildlife Photography*. New York: Focal Press, an imprint of the Butterworth Group, 1982.

Prodgers, Jeanette. *The Only Good Bear Is a Dead Bear: A Collection of the West's Best Bear Stories*. Helena, MT: Jeanette Prodgers / Falcon Press Publishing, 1986.

Rezendes, Paul. *The Wild Within: Adventures in Nature and Animal Teachings*. New York: Jeremy P. Tarcher / Putnam / Penguin Putnam, 1998.

Ricciuti, Edward R. *Killer Animals*. New York: Walker and Co., 1976.

Robbins, Jim. "Bears versus Bikes," *New York Times*, October 8, 2019.

Robbins, Michael. "Death in the Wild," *Rocky Mountain* magazine (January–February 1981).

Robinson, Michael H., and Lionel Tiger, eds. *Man and Beast Revisited*. Washington, DC: Smithsonian Institution Press, 1991.

Rockwell, David. *Giving Voice to Bear: North American Indian Myths, Rituals, and Images of the Bear*. Niwot, CO: Roberts Rinehart Publishers, 1991.

Rubbert, Tim. *Hiking with Grizzlies: Lessons Learned*. Helena, MT: Riverbend Publishing, 2006.

Ruffin, Albert. "Attacked by a Grizzly Bear: The Ordeal of a Boy All But Eaten Alive," *Life* magazine, August 27, 1965.

Russell, Andy, intro. *Great Bear Adventures: True Tales from the Wild*. Stillwater, MN: Voyageur Press, Inc., n. d.

Samson, Jack. *The Bear Book*. Clinton, NJ: Amwell Press, 1979.

———. *The Grizzly Book*. Clinton, NJ: Amwell Press, 1981.

Savage, Candace. *Grizzly Bears*. San Francisco: Sierra Club, 1990.

Schemnitz, Sanford D. *Wildlife Management Techniques Manual*. Washington, DC: The Wildlife Society, Inc., 1980.

Schneider, Bill. *Bear Aware: Hiking and Camping in Bear Country*. Helena, MT: Falcon Press, 1996.

———. *Where the Grizzly Walks*. Missoula, MT: Mountain Press Publishing Co., 1977.

Schullery, Paul. *The Bear Hunter's Century: Profiles from the Golden Age of Bear Hunting*. Silver City, NM: High-Lonesome Books, 1988, 1998.

———. *Lewis and Clark among the Grizzlies: Legend and Legacy in the American West*. Guilford, CT: Falcon Press / Globe Pequot Press, 2002.

———, ed. *Mark of the Bear: Legend and Lore of an American Icon*. San Francisco: Sierra Club Books, 1996.

———. *Mountain Time*. New York: Nick Lyons Books / Schocken Books, 1984.

Schultz, James Willard. *William Jackson, Indian Scout*, reprinted in 1976 by William K. Cavanagh, First National Bank Building, Springfield, Illinois 62701.

Scott, Tristan. "Bones, Clothing May Belong to Missing Glacier Park Hiker," *Missoulian*, August 2, 2011.

———. "Lost, Never Found," *Flathead Beacon*, Kalispell, Montana, August 6, 2014.

"Search Crews Comb Glacier Park for Missing Michigan Man," Associated Press, July 1, 2003.

Shelton, James Gary. *Bear Attacks: The Deadly Truth*. Hagensborg, British Columbia, Canada: Pallister Publishing, 1998.

———. *Bear Attacks II: Myth and Reality*. Hagensborg, British Columbia, Canada: Pallister Publishing, 2001.

———. *Bear Encounter Survival Guide*. Hagensborg, British Columbia, Canada: self-published, 1994 (Box 95, Hagensborg, BC, V0T 1H0 Canada).

Shepard, Paul, and Barry Sanders. *The Sacred Paw: The Bear in Nature, Myth, and Literature*. New York: Viking Penguin, Inc., 1985.

Smith, Dave. *The Backcountry Bear Basics: The Definitive Guide to Avoiding Unpleasant Encounters*. Seattle, WA: The Mountaineers, 1997.

Smith, Richard P. *The Book of the Black Bear*. Piscataway, NJ: Winchester Press / New Century Publishers, 1985.

Snow, Kathleen. *Taken by Bear in Yellowstone*. Guilford, CT: Lyons Press, 2016.

Thomson, David. *In the Shining Mountains: A Would-be Mountain Man in Search of the Wilderness*. New York: Alfred A. Knopf, 1979.

"Trail Still Cold in Search for Missing Man in Glacier National Park," Associated Press, July 16, 2019.

"Two Attacked by Griz a Year Ago," *Hungry Horse News*, October 15, 1992, Columbia Falls, Montana.

Volz, Matt. "Bear Researcher Attacked by Grizzly to Stay on Career Path," Associated Press, quoted in the *Spokesman Review*, Spokane, Washington, June 21, 2018.

INDEX

ABOUT THE AUTHOR

Kathleen Snow has specialized in recent years in writing about our national parks. She is a member of the Montana Writers Guild. In 2016 Lyons Press published her nonfiction *Taken by Bear in Yellowstone: More than a Century of Harrowing Encounters between Grizzlies and Humans.*

Also in 2016 the University of Montana Press published her *Searching for Bear Eyes: A Yellowstone Park Mystery.* Her nonfiction has appeared in *Harper's Magazine, Women in Natural Resources,* and other periodicals.